TWENTY-EIGHTH HANFORD SYMPOSIUM
ON HEALTH AND THE ENVIRONMENT

Environmental Monitoring, Restoration and Assessment: *What Have We Learned?*

Robert H. Gray, Editor

Sponsored by the
United States Department of Energy
and Battelle, Pacific Northwest Laboratories

1990

Pacific Northwest Laboratory
Richland, Washington 99352

DISCLAIMER

This report was prepared as an account of work sponsored by an agency of the United States Government. Neither the United States Government nor any agency thereof, nor Battelle Memorial Institute, nor any of their employees, makes **any warranty, expressed or implied, or assumes any legal liability or responsibility for the accuracy, completeness, or usefulness of any information, apparatus, product, or process disclosed, or represents that its use would not infringe privately owned rights.** Reference herein to any specific commercial product, process, or service by trade name, trademark, manufacturer, or otherwise does not necessarily constitute or imply its endorsement, recommendation, or favoring by the United States Government or any agency thereof, or Battelle Memorial Institute. The views and opinions of authors expressed herein do not necessarily state or reflect those of the United States Government or any agency thereof.

PACIFIC NORTHWEST LABORATORY
operated by
BATTELLE MEMORIAL INSTITUTE
for the
UNITED STATES DEPARTMENT OF ENERGY
under Contract DE-AC06-76RLO 1830

Library of Congress Cataloging-in-Publication Data

Hanford Symposium on Health and the Environment (28th: 1989: Richland, Wash.)
Environmental monitoring, restoration, and assessment: What have we learned? / Twenty-eighth Hanford Symposium on Health and the Environment, October 16-19, 1989, Richland, Washington, U.S.A.: edited by Robert H. Gray: sponsored by the United States Department of Energy and Battelle, Pacific Northwest Laboratories.
p. cm.
ISBN 0-935470-56-5: $57.50
1. Environmental monitoring — United States. I. Gray, Robert H. II. United States Dept. of Energy. III. Pacific Northwest Laboratory. IV. Title.
QH541.15. M64H37   1989   90-328
363.7'00973 — dc 20   CIP

Additional copies may be ordered through Battelle Press, 505 King Avenue, Columbus, Ohio 43201-2693. 614/424-6393. Toll free 1-800-451-3543.

CONTENTS

MODELING AND DOSE ASSESSMENT

UNCERTAINTY, DESIGN, DATA ANALYSIS

DATA MANAGEMENT AND QUALITY ASSURANCE

POSTERS

PREFACE

The Twenty-Eighth Hanford Symposium on Health and the Environment was held in Richland, Washington, October 16-19, 1989. The symposium was sponsored by the U.S. Department of Energy and the Pacific Northwest Laboratory, operated by Battelle Memorial Institute.

The symposium, entitled "Environmental Monitoring, Restoration and Assessment: What Have We Learned?" was organized to review and evaluate some of the monitoring and assessment programs that have been conducted or are currently in place. Potential health and environmental effects of energy-related and other industrial activities have been monitored and assessed at various government and private facilities for over three decades. Most monitoring is required under government regulations; some monitoring is implemented because facility operators consider it prudent practice. As a result of these activities, there is now a substantial radiological, physical, and chemical data base for various environmental components, both in the United States and abroad.

Symposium participants, both platform and poster presenters, were asked to consider, among other topics, the following: Has the expenditure of millions of dollars for radiological monitoring and assessment activities been worth the effort? How do we decide when enough monitoring is enough? Can we adequately assess the impacts of nonradiological components—both inorganic and organic—of wastes? Are current regulatory requirements too restrictive or too lenient? Can monitoring and assessment be made more cost effective?

Papers were solicited in the areas of environmental monitoring; environmental regulations; remediation, restoration, and decommissioning; modeling and dose assessment; uncertainty, design, and data analysis; and data management and quality assurance.

The sessions on environmental monitoring covered a range of topics, including monitoring at Department of Energy and other facilities; organochlorine and elemental contaminants in fish; ^{131}I in animal thyroids; ^{90}Sr in Canada goose eggshells; uranium mill tailings remedial action activities; radionuclides in wildlife and farm products; contaminants in ground waters; air quality at toxic waste sites; and geophysical surveys for assessing hazardous waste sites. A special panel discussion focused on legal and policy issues relative to federal facilities. A session on environmental regulations considered requirements for

ix

ground-water monitoring at hazardous waste sites; applicable or relevant requirements (ARAR) for radioactive mixed waste; the Comprehensive Environmental Response Compensation and Liability Act (CERCLA); and closure criteria for inactive waste sites. Sessions on remediation, restoration, and decommissioning dealt with interim remedial actions at radioactive waste facilities; strip-mine reclamation; decommissioning nuclear facilities; remediating ground water; and development of protective barriers. Sessions on modeling and dose assessment reviewed the relationships among ground-water modeling, risk assessment and postclosure alternatives; the history of surveillance and assessment by various organizations at the Nevada Test and Hanford Nuclear Sites; assessment of radiological and chemical risks at mixed-waste sites; and the use of computer models to assess impacts. Other sessions discussed monitoring network design and data analysis; complying with cleanliness standards; and assessment of subsampling and measurement error. The final session considered data management and quality assurance, including data processing, reporting, and computer systems.

I am grateful to the authors, session chairpersons, and other participants who contributed to a successful symposium. R. E. Gephart and W. L. Templeton participated as members of the program committee. H. Babad, R. O. Gilbert, W. E. Kennedy, M. R. Siegel, R. M. Smith, and R. D. Stenner served on the Technical Steering Committee. Special thanks are due T. A. Zinn and A. S. Jones, the symposium secretaries, who dealt with numerous details associated with planning, correspondence, and registration. V. G. Horstman and the local arrangements committee did an excellent job of providing for the physical comforts of participants and the smooth operation of the meeting. F. M. Rogers ensured that visual aids appeared when needed and without error. P. J. Cowley, D. R. Dahl, R. E. Gephart, R. O. Gilbert, B. A. Napier, and W. L. Templeton helped review several of the manuscripts. I am especially grateful to D. L. Felton for her assistance in editing and proofreading the numerous drafts of the papers contained in this volume. Finally, I thank Marianna Cross, who helped process the text.

Robert H. Gray, Editor

H. M. Parker
Lecture

H. M. Parker Lecturer, 1989

Dade W. Moeller

INTRODUCTION

The H. M. Parker Public Lecture is presented each year on the occasion of the Hanford Symposium on Health and the Environment. These lectures are sponsored by the Department of Energy; the Pacific Northwest Laboratory; and the Herbert M. Parker Foundation for Education in the Radiological Sciences. *

The objectives of the H. M. Parker lecture series are:

1. to memorialize H. M. Parker and his outstanding contributions to radiological sciences and radiation protection;

2. to honor contemporary scientists who evoke H. M. Parker's high technical standards and concern for protection of the health of workers and the public; and

3. to enhance the public's understanding of radiological health issues.

We are pleased to have Dr. Dade Moeller of the Harvard School of Public Health as our fourth H. M. Parker Lecturer. Dr. Moeller is particularly suited to give this lecture because he has been actively involved in ensuring the protection of the health of radiation workers and the public for more than 40 years. As an educator of considerable renown, he has worked diligently at enhancing the public's understanding of radiological health concerns. His work on radiation protection associated with the development and use of nuclear power as well as his research on natural radiation have made him singularly well qualified to put important radiation health issues into perspective for the public.

Dr. Moeller began his career at Georgia Institute of Technology, where he received a Bachelor of Science in Civil Engineering in 1948 and a Master of Science in Sanitary Engineering in 1948. He received his Doctor of Philosophy degree in Nuclear Engineering from North Carolina State University in 1957. Dr. Moeller has been involved in the area of public health since the end of World War II. From 1948 to 1966 he was a commissioned officer in the U.S. Public Health Service. During that period Dr. Moeller was assigned to Atomic Energy Commission installations at Oak Ridge and Los Alamos. His duties

---

* The Herbert M. Parker Foundation is incorporated in the State of Washington. As a nonprofit corporation, it can receive public donations to perpetuate the lecture series and support other educational activities.

there were related to health problems associated with reactor cooling-water systems, management of radioactive wastes, and environmental radiation surveillance. He has been at Harvard since 1966 and is currently Professor of Engineering in Environmental Health. He is also Associate Dean for Continuing Education in the School of Public Health. As director of a training program for many years, Dr. Moeller has contributed to the continuing education of practicing radiation protection personnel throughout the world. His skills as a teacher were recognized in 1983 when he received the Harvard Faculty-Student Teaching Award. Dr. Moeller's educational activities represent a significant contribution to the fields of radiation protection and general environmental health.

Dr. Moeller was a member of the Advisory Committee on Reactor Safeguards for the U.S. Nuclear Regulatory Commission (NRC) from 1973 to 1988. He served as chairman in 1976. During this time Dr. Moeller was a spokesman for health and environmental issues regarding reactor safety. He recruited numerous health and environmental experts as consultants to help address reactor siting and operational problems. He is currently chairman of the NRC's Advisory Committee on Nuclear Waste. His work for the NRC was recognized in 1978 when he received the Nuclear Regulatory Commission's Special Achievement Certificate, and again in 1988 when he received its Meritorious Achievement Award.

Dr. Moeller has been a member of the National Council on Radiation Protection and Measurements since 1967. He was a member of its Board of Directors from 1978 to 1985 and has served on several of its Scientific Committees. Since 1973 he has chaired Scientific Committee 28 on Radiation Exposure from Consumer Products and Miscellaneous Sources. He is also chairman of Scientific Committee 82 on Control of Radon Inside Residences and is a member of Committee 62 on Priorities for Dose Reduction Efforts.

From 1978 to 1985 he served on the International Commission on Radiological Protection's Committee 4, Application of the Commission's Recommendations.

He has served the National Institute of Environmental Health Sciences as a member of the Committee on Professional and Scientific Manpower Training. From 1977 to 1980 he was a member of the National Academy of Sciences Committee on Biological Effects of Ionizing Radiation, which resulted in the BEIR-III report. He has also served as Chairman of the American Board of Health Physics (1967-1970), which certifies professionals in radiation protection.

Dr. Moeller is a Diplomate of the American Academy of Environmental Engineers, and he is certified by the American Board of Health Physics. From 1965 to 1980 he was a consultant on radiological health to the World Health Organization.

He has received many awards and honors over the course of his professional career:

- He was elected a Member of the National Academy of Engineering in 1978;
- He served as President of the Health Physics Society in 1971-1972; and
- He received the Distinguished Achievement Award of the Health Physics Society in 1982.

Dr. Moeller is a Fellow of the American Nuclear Society, the American Public Health Association, and the Health Physics Society. He was selected as a Sigma Xi Lecturer for 1989, representing the Health Physics Society.

Dr. Moeller is the author of more than 150 publications. With several others, he holds the patent for a method and apparatus for reduction of exposures to radon decay products. His research contributions have extended over a broad spectrum of radiation protection. He has directed considerable effort to achieving public understanding of natural and man-made radiation sources.

I am pleased and privileged to present Dr. Dade Moeller as our fourth H. M. Parker Lecturer, speaking on the topic "Natural Radiation In the Environment."

W. J. Bair

NATURAL RADIATION IN THE ENVIRONMENT

D. W. Moeller

Office of Continuing Education, Harvard School of Public Health, Boston, Massachusetts

PRELIMINARY COMMENTS

It is an honor to take part in this, the Twenty-Eighth Hanford Symposium on Health and the Environment and, especially, to have been invited to present the 1989 Herbert M. Parker Lecture. I had the privilege of interacting with Herb in a variety of professional activities and serving with him on several subcommittees of the Advisory Committee on Reactor Safeguards. I have many fond memories of his intellect, his ability to get immediately to the heart of a matter, his uncanny ability to provide a clear and concise way in which to word a complicated statement and, above all, his humor, for example, his Lauriston S. Taylor lecture, which he titled "The Squares of the Natural Numbers in Radiation Protection."

I was also impressed by his love of his wife and family, having enjoyed visits to his home here in Richland and dinners with him and his daughter in Washington, DC, and with his clever ways of resolving issues among his children. Some were definitely biblical in origin. A good example is how he would have one of his twins divide a piece of candy into two portions and give the other the opportunity to make the first selection. You can rest assured that the one doing the dividing was careful not to show partiality to either side.

I was also impressed with Herb's total commitment to nuclear safety, and the absolute honesty, accuracy, and integrity with which he approached every issue. He was a "giant among giants," and we miss him!

INTRODUCTION

My topic is "Natural Radiation in the Environment." If you do not already know it, you will soon realize that we live in a "sea of radiation." Understanding the components of this "sea" is important for a variety of reasons. First, radiation has been with us since the beginning of the universe. Scientists tell us that the warmth provided by relatively large concentrations of naturally occurring radioactive materials, during the first few billions of years, helped life evolve. Second, the fact that we live in the presence of the dose rates associated with these original sources provides us with knowledge relative to what can be considered acceptable levels of exposure.

However, it is important to note that the dose rates received by each person from natural sources are not the same. Rather, they are heavily dependent on our living habits. Discussed below are the various components of natural background radiation and the key factors that influence the dose rates that such sources contribute to the public.

COMPONENTS OF NATURAL RADIATION

There are two basic types of natural radiation; namely, sources that contribute exposure from outside the body and those that contribute exposure from inside. For each type, there are two other contributing sources.

External Sources

The two primary sources of external exposure are cosmic radiation (from outer space) and terrestrial (from naturally occurring radioactive materials in soil).

Cosmic Radiation. Dose rates from cosmic radiation vary with altitude (Figure 1) (NCRP, 1987a) because the atmosphere serves as a shield from radiations coming from outer space. The higher we go, the thinner the protective atmosphere and the greater the dose rate received. The dose rate from cosmic radiation at sea level (as in Boston) is about 30 mrem (0.3 mSv)/year; at an altitude of 1 mile (as in Denver), the dose rate is about 50 mrem (0.5 mSv)/year; in Mexico City (at an altitude of over 8,000 ft), the dose rate is 80 mrem (0.8 mSv)/year; and in La Paz, Bolivia (at an altitude of almost 12,000 ft), the dose rate is 150 mrem (1.5 mSv)/year (Mark, 1988).

Those of us who do not live at high altitudes may still experience increased doses from cosmic radiation. In a cross-country flight on a jet, passengers receive 2 to 3 mrem extra from cosmic radiation. People going on long flights over the polar regions may receive up to 10 mrem (0.1 mSv) per trip. For approximately 100,000 people who serve as commercial airline pilots and flight crews, annual dose rates in excess of 500 mrem (5 mSv) are common. Dose estimates for astronauts who travel in outer space range from 160 to 1100 mrem (1.6 to 11 mSv) for those involved in lunar flights, 1600 to 7700 mrem

(16 to 77 mSv) for those taking part in experiments in Skylab, and 20 to 500 mrem (0.2 to 5 mSv) for those flying on the shuttle (Benton, 1984).

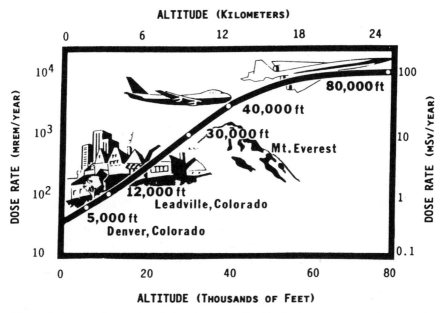

Figure 1. Increase in cosmic radiation dose rate with altitude.

Terrestrial Radiation. Location plays a significant role in the dose rates from terrestrial radiation. Dose rates over freshwater lakes with a minimum of dissolved and suspended minerals are essentially zero because water serves as an excellent shield. Dose rates over the open ocean are about 20 mrem (0.2 mSv)/year because salt water contains a multitude of naturally occurring radioactive materials. Dose rates above sandy soils such as those in Florida and on Long Island may be as low as 5 to 15 mrem (0.05 to 0.15 mSv)/year. Above sedimentary rock they may range from 30 to 55 mrem (0.3 to 0.55 mSv)/year, while over granitic rock such as that in Vermont and New Hampshire, and over soils containing high concentrations of uranium, like that in the Colorado Plateau, they may reach 160 mrem (1.6 mSv)/year. Thus, dose rates to members of the population from terrestrial sources vary widely with location. However, dose rates for the contiguous 48 states can generally be divided into the three principal regions shown in Figure 2 (Oakley, 1972).

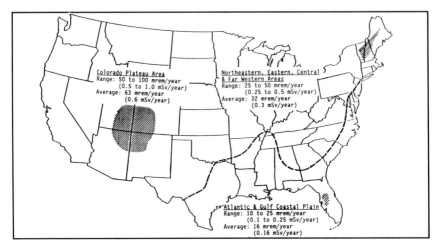

Figure 2. Dose rates from natural terrestrial sources in the United States.

Because people spend a major portion of their time indoors, the dose rates they receive from naturally occurring radionuclides can be heavily influenced by the nature of the materials used in constructing the building they are in. For example, dose rates inside houses built of concrete and/or brick, which frequently contain relatively large quantities of naturally occurring radioactive materials, generally exceed terrestrial dose rates outdoors. In contrast, dose rates inside houses constructed of wood are generally lower than terrestrial dose rates outdoors (Figure 3). Wood contains essentially no naturally occurring radioactive materials that lead to external doses and, furthermore, wood serves as a good shield against radiation from the ground beneath or outside a house.

Because dose rates from cosmic and terrestrial sources vary widely, there are major differences in those received by various segments of the U.S. population. Figure 4 shows estimates of the distribution of dose rates to the U.S. population from terrestrial and cosmic sources. This graph is based on data originally published by Oakley (1972) and has been modified to take into account newer information.

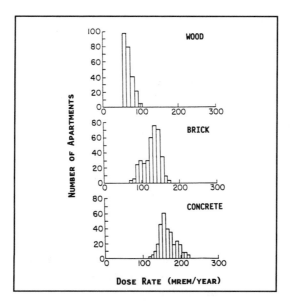

Figure 3. Influence of construction materials on dose rates inside apartments.

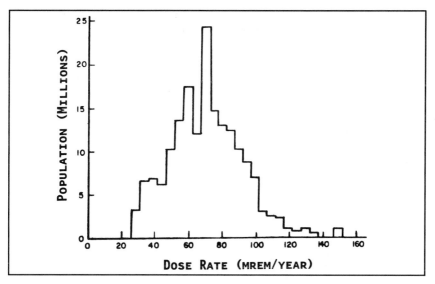

Figure 4. U.S. population distribution versus dose rate from terrestrial and cosmic radiation.

Internal Sources

Internal sources of natural radiation can also be divided into two categories: those that arise through ingestion and those that arise through inhalation of radioactive materials.

Ingestion. The principal naturally occurring radioactive materials that contribute to internal exposure through ingestion are potassium and radium. A common source of potassium is the banana. This radionuclide, common to muscular tissue, contributes an annual dose of about 15 mrem (0.15 mSv) to women and about 19 mrem (0.19 mSv) to men. Because some radiations emitted by potassium are highly penetrating, the potassium in our bodies also exposes people nearby; associated dose rates are estimated to range from 1 to 2 mrem (0.01 to 0.02 mSv)/year. Although we might be inclined to avoid foods containing potassium to reduce these doses, it is important to recognize that potassium in the body is under homeostatic control in the body. Any dietary intake above a minimum will maintain the normal balance. Maintaining such a balance is essential to health. Commercial products, such as Gatorade,® which contains relatively large quantities of potassium, are specifically designed to restore the potassium balance for athletes who have exercised and perspired heavily.

In contrast, radium is not essential to the body, and the amounts ingested can be significantly affected by what, and how much, we eat and drink. For the average adult, dose rates from this source to bone are about 17 mrem (0.17 mSv)/year (NCRP, 1987a). For selected populations, dose rates can be much higher. Well waters in certain areas of the country such as Illinois contain relatively high concentrations of radium. People drinking these waters receive higher dose rates.

One of the most significant sources of radium is the Brazil nut, which is produced exclusively in the Amazon Valley. One of the chemical elements that is essential to the vitality of the Brazil nut tree is barium. In meeting its demand for this element, the tree "mistakenly" takes up radium as a substitute. The entire tree, its bark, trunk, and roots, as well as the nuts it produces, all contain high concentrations of radium. Average concentrations of radium in Brazil nuts range from 1 to 2 pCi/g, with some samples containing up to 4 pCi/g (Penna-Franca et al., 1968). A person eating one-quarter to half a pound of Brazil nuts, not a large amount, in a single day will exceed the radium intake limit for radiation workers.

Inhalation. The major source of radiation exposure from inhalation of naturally occurring radioactive materials is radon and its airborne decay products. Because radon is produced through decay of radium and uranium, it is commonly found in areas where these two radionuclides are present. All decay products of uranium, prior to radon, are solid elements and remain in soil. However, radon is a gas and, once formed, tends to emerge from the soil and enter the air. If radon is released outdoors, it is highly diluted in the atmosphere and does not represent a problem. If radon is released in a house, where dilution is limited, relatively high concentrations can accumulate.

Although there are potential sources of radon inside buildings other than soil, in general the only one that is significant is the water supply. Sources such as building materials, and natural gas used in unvented kitchen stoves, generally do not represent a problem. Thus, the potential for high radon concentrations inside a home is primarily a function of the geology of the area (Figure 5).

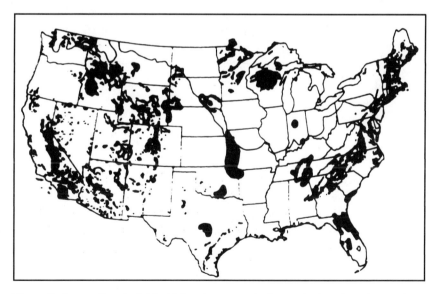

Figure 5. Areas with potential for high radon concentrations; selections based on geology.

Several factors influence the concentrations of radon in homes and in a particular place in the home; for example, where you are within the home and how well it is sealed, that is, the degree to which indoor air is diluted with air from outside. A poorly maintained, drafty house will have radon concentrations 70% to 80% of those for a "normal" house. In contrast, a tightly sealed house will have radon concentrations ranging from 1.1 to 1.3 times those for the "normal" house. For houses in which the ground beneath the basement is the primary source of radon, concentrations in the basement are generally almost twice those on the first floor; those on the second floor may be 90% of those on the first floor; and those on the third floor may be 50% of those on the first floor (Cohen, 1989).

For homes in which the water supply contains high radon concentrations, the concentrations in the air can be significantly affected by the ways the water is used. Simply flushing the toilet can lead to releases. Operation of dishwashers and clothes washers and, most especially, use of a shower, can cause significant short-term increases in the airborne radon concentrations in a home (Figure 6) (Hess, personal communication*). Overall, an estimated 50% of the radon in water used in a home becomes airborne and is available for breathing. A concentration of 10,000 pCi/L of radon in water will generally produce an airborne radon concentration of about 1 pCi/L in a home.

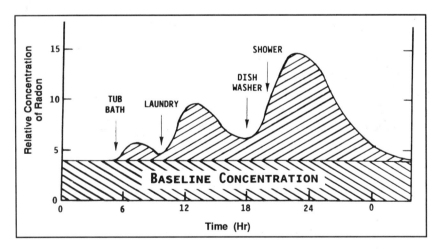

Figure 6. Influence of water use on indoor radon concentrations.

---

* Hess, C. T., University of Maine, Orono, Maine. Personal communication, 1987.

The U.S. Environmental Protection Agency (EPA) and state and local public health departments are currently encouraging people to monitor their homes for radon. Estimates by the National Council on Radiation Protection and Measurements (NCRP, 1987b) indicate that this source contributes an average dose rate of about 2400 mrem (24 mSv)/year to the lungs of the U.S. public. This is an effective dose equivalent rate of about 200 mrem (2 mSv)/year and represents the single most important source of general radiation exposure to the U.S. public today. The estimated distribution of radon concentrations in U.S. houses is shown in Figure 7 (Nero et al., 1986).

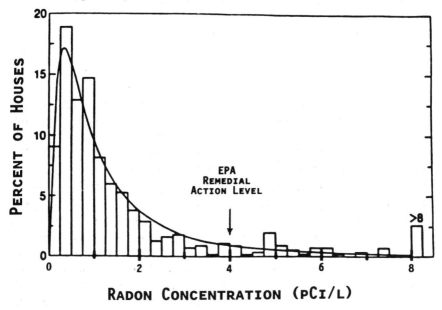

Figure 7. Frequency distribution of radon concentrations in U.S. homes.

OTHER EXPOSURES FROM NATURAL SOURCES

The naturally occurring radiation sources summarized above are those to which members of the public, in general, are exposed. Many additional exposures occur as a result of using various consumer products. Examples are given below.

Luminous Compounds and Glazes

Although radium is no longer routinely incorporated into luminous dial clocks and watches, millions of these items are still in use in the

United States. Associated dose rates to the whole body range from about 0.5 to 3 mrem (5 to 30 mSv)/year (Moeller et al., 1988). Localized dose rates to portions of the body in contact with such items can range up to 300 mrem (3 mSv)/year. Today, artificially produced tritium has largely replaced the use of radium in such products. However, it will be some time before the radium sources cease to be in use.

Other related products that can be sources of exposure include eyeglasses tinted with uranium or thorium, which can produce dose rates of 4,000 mrem (40 mSv)/year to the cornea; bathroom tile; false teeth glazed with uranium, leading to dose rates of ~700 mrem (7 mSv)/year to the basal mucosa of the gums of some 45 million denture wearers; and "Fiesta-ware" china, which produces dose rates of 10 to 20 mrem (0.1 to 0.2 mSv)/*hour* to diners (Moeller et al., 1988).

Cigarette Smokers

Two naturally occurring radioactive materials, lead and polonium, are commonly present in tobacco. Their presence results primarily from deposition on tobacco leaves of airborne radioactive materials resulting from the radon decay. These are longer-lived decay products of the radon gas that is currently a problem inside houses.

Because tobacco leaves are large and sticky, they readily retain these materials once deposited. When tobacco is incorporated into cigarettes, and the smoker lights up, radon decay products are volatilized and enter the lungs. The resulting dose to small segments of the bronchial epithelium of approximately 55 million U.S. smokers is about 16,000 mrem (160 mSv)/year (NCRP, 1987c). This is the greatest dose received by the population from any consumer product and probably represents the single greatest source of radiation exposure to this segment of the U.S. population. The whole-body dose equivalent of this dose to the lungs of a two-pack-a-day smoker is about 1,300 mrem (13 mSv)/year. This is more than 10 times the long-term dose rate limit for members of the public.

SUMMARY AND COMMENTARY

Table 1 shows typical dose rates from selected artificial radiation sources in our everyday lives. In spite of these sources, natural radiation remains the major source of exposure to the U.S. population. Radon and its airborne decay products account for over half (55%) of the total dose received by the average member of the public (Figure 8).

When dose rates from cosmic and terrestrial sources, and other radionuclides in the body, are considered, natural sources contribute 82% of the total dose to the average nonsmoking member of the U.S. public (NCRP, 1987b). Thus, it would be sound public health practice to direct more attention both to the control of natural radiation sources and to evaluations of their potential health effects.

Table 1. Dose rates from artificial radiation sources.

Source	Dose Rate
Chest X-Ray Examination	10 to 15 mrem
Television Set	< 0.5 mrem/year
Smoke Detector	0.01 mrem/year
Nuclear Power Plant	< 5 mrem/year

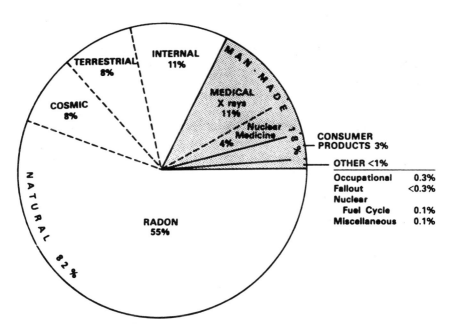

Figure 8. Contributions of various radiation sources to U.S. population dose (nonsmokers).

Studies of the behavior of naturally occurring radioactive materials in our environment are proving useful for other reasons. Scientists seeking to develop methods for the disposal of high-level radioactive wastes in a deep underground geologic repository have found it beneficial to study the long-term behavior of naturally occurring radionuclides. Naturally occurring radioactive materials may provide analogs for predicting the behavior of artificial wastes that have been placed in a repository. Underground behavior of other naturally occurring radionuclides, such as radon, are also being evaluated as a possible means to predict natural events such as earthquakes.

In terms of the control of radiation exposures, experience has shown that in many cases reductions in population doses from natural sources can be accomplished far more effectively and at lower cost than for artificial sources. Thus, control of natural sources should be given more attention. However, there are limitations on what can be done with certain natural sources. For example, it is almost impossible to reduce the dose rates from cosmic radiation. In contrast, buildings can be constructed to minimize dose rates from terrestrial sources and building materials, and low-cost techniques are readily available to control radon in houses.

There are limits on how much data can be obtained for assessing health effects of radiation exposures through studies of natural sources. Although comparisons have been made of the health of populations living in areas such as Denver, with high cosmic and terrestrial dose rates, and in Boston or New York, where dose rates are lower, many factors make it difficult to draw definitive conclusions. One factor is air pollution and, most particularly, any differences in the percentages of cigarette smokers in each place. Another is the ethnic background of the populations in the two areas. Other factors include their social and economic statuses. Finally, at the low dose rates involved, the number of people who must be studied (even where all factors are known and carefully controlled) to provide data that are statistically significant is extremely large. Assuming that the difference in dose rates between two populations was 150 mrem (1.5 mSv)/year, the population size required to produce useful data relative to detecting an increase in the incidence of leukemia, even if the two groups were carefully followed for a lengthy period of time, would be over half a million (Table 2) (Eisenbud, 1973).

Table 2. Population sizes required to detect increase in leukemia (10 years observation).

Dose from Birth To Age 34 (mrem)	Annual Dose (mrem)	Required Population
5,000	150	600,000
10,000	300	160,000
20,000	600	50,000
100,000	3,000	1,000

It is interesting to examine overall trends with time in the doses received by peoples of the world from naturally occurring radiation sources. Although biased, the data in Figure 9 indicate that people, through changes in living habits, have in many cases added to their dose rates. In the early days, people lived in caves that were undoubtedly of natural origin. In all probability, these caves were located in limestone areas carved out of the ground by flowing underground streams. Because limestone is almost devoid of naturally occurring radioactive materials, dose rates to cave-dwellers were minimal. Because such caves were often located in the side or at the foot of a mountain, this provided considerable shielding against cosmic radiation.

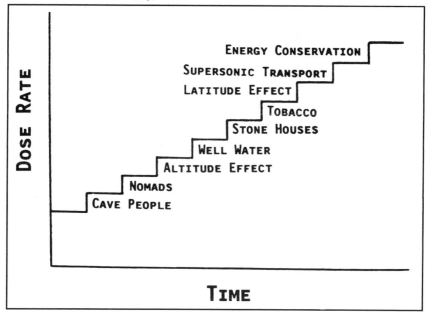

Figure 9. Changes over time in dose rates from natural background.

Later, people moved outdoors and became nomads and hunters. They slept on the ground, where they breathed concentrated radon and its decay products as they emanated from soil. Initially, such peoples lived along the shore of a lake or the bank of a stream and used the water for drinking. Later, they moved into the hills, thus increasing their dose rates from cosmic radiation and, becoming tired of the daily journey down to the lake or stream for water, they dug wells and began to consume radium. After leaving the caves, these people first lived in thatched-roof huts; later, they learned to build log cabins; both represented minimal sources of radiation exposure. Still later, they learned to make concrete and brick and to build houses of stone, all of which increased their dose rates. In the latter part of the 15th century, explorers traveled to the New World, where the Indians introduced them to tobacco and exposed their lungs to large doses of radiation. With subsequent population increases, people moved from the tropics toward the North and South Poles. This, coupled with the advent of jet airplanes, which carried people to higher altitudes, increased dose rates from cosmic radiation. More recently, energy shortages have caused many people to insulate and "tighten" their homes, thus increasing their dose rates from radon. Although the accompanying increases in dose rates from natural sources due to these changes cannot be quantified, they are undoubtedly larger than the contributions from many artificial sources that are subject to strict regulatory controls.

REFERENCES

Benton, E. V. 1984. Summary of current radiation dosimetry results on manned spacecraft. *Adv. Space Res.* 4:153-160.

Cohen, B. L. 1989. Measured radon levels in U.S. homes, pp. 170-180. In: Proceedings of the Twenty-Fourth Annual Meeting of the National Council on Radiation Protection and Measurements. National Council on Radiation Protection and Measurements, Bethesda, MD.

Eisenbud, M. 1973. *Environmental Radioactivity*, 2nd ed. Academic Press, New York.

Mark, C. 1988. Variability of Natural Background Radiation, Special Report. U.S. Nuclear Regulatory Commission, Washington, DC.

Moeller, D. W., J. W. Hickey, and G. D. Schmidt. 1988. Radiation from consumer products. *Consumers' Res.* 71:25-29.

NCRP. 1987a. Exposure of the Population in the United States and Canada from Natural Background Radiation, Report No. 94. National Council on Radiation Protection and Measurements, Bethesda, MD.

NCRP. 1987b. Ionizing Radiation Exposure of the Population of the United States, Report No. 93. National Council on Radiation Protection and Measurements, Bethesda, MD.

NCRP. 1987c. Radiation Exposure of the U.S. Population from Consumer Products and Miscellaneous Sources, Report No. 95. National Council on Radiation Protection and Measurements, Bethesda, MD.

Nero, A. V., M. B. Schwehr, W. W. Nazaroff, and K. L. Revzan. 1986. Distribution of airborne radon-222 concentrations in U.S. homes. *Science 234*:992-997.

Oakley, D. T. 1972. Natural Radiation Exposure in the United States, Report ORP/SID 72-1. U.S. Environmental Protection Agency, Washington, DC.

Penna-Franca, E., M. Fiszman, N. Lobao, C. Costa-Ribeiro, H. Trindade, P. L. Dos Santos, and D. Batista. 1968. Radioactivity in Brazil nuts. *Health Phys. 14*:95-99.

ENVIRONMENTAL MONITORING AT U.S. DEPARTMENT OF ENERGY FACILITIES

R. A. Geiger[1] and K. A. Higley[2]

[1]U.S. Department of Energy, Washington, DC*

[2]Pacific Northwest Laboratory, Richland, Washington

Key Words: *Environmental monitoring, approach, DOE, EPA*

ABSTRACT

The U.S. Department of Energy (DOE) requires that environmental monitoring programs be conducted at each of its facilities. The emphasis on environmental monitoring can be attributed partly to increased public awareness and understanding of DOE operations and partly to concerns resulting from possible contamination of the environment as a result of the Three Mile Island and Chernobyl incidents. Advances in computer modeling and technology have contributed to monitoring procedures that are designed to provide greater protection to the public and the environment. We will briefly discuss the regulatory history for environmental monitoring and concentrate on integrating DOE environmental monitoring requirements with Environmental Protection Agency (EPA) regulations. Cost-effectiveness, size, and complexity of an environmental monitoring program will be considered. A specific example will compare and contrast DOE and EPA approaches and requirements.

INTRODUCTION

Effluent releases from Department of Energy (DOE) facilities may affect the public and the environment. Thus, because of the public's awareness and concern about potential risks, DOE has increased its environmental monitoring effort at and in the vicinity of its facilities. DOE requires development of a facility-specific environmental monitoring program (EMP) to evaluate control technologies in use and to assess impacts of releases from operations. An effective EMP will minimize risk to the public and the environment by ensuring compliance with applicable federal, state, and local regulations, and by using accepted techniques and methods to more accurately assess public doses from contaminants released from DOE operations.

---

*Current address: U.S. Department of Energy, Richland Operations Office, Richland, Washington.

1

HISTORY OF ENVIRONMENTAL MONITORING IN DOE

The Atomic Energy Commission (AEC), one of DOE's predecessor agencies, required EMP beginning in the late 1940s. In the early 1950s, AEC required baseline, preoperational EMP to control risks to the public and the environment. AEC Manual Chapter 0513 (AEC, 1973) required development of EMP at AEC installations. AEC and the Energy Research and Development Administration's (ERDA) Manual Chapters were replaced by DOE's system of Orders in 1976. Early EMP requirements were not specific; consequently, programs varied in magnitude and complexity among facilities. Because DOE was most concerned with radiation effects, the principal EMP focus was originally on radioactive emissions from operations. In the 1970s and 1980s, DOE broadened its environmental monitoring activities to demonstrate compliance with all environmental regulations.

CURRENT APPROACHES AND REQUIREMENTS

EMP requirements at DOE facilities are currently more prescriptive than in the past. However, DOE Orders have sufficient flexibility so that field operations can accommodate their unique activities while complying with the requirements.

Environmental monitoring is composed of two principal activities:

- Effluent monitoring involves the collection and analysis of liquid or airborne effluents to characterize and quantify contaminants. Data are used to assess exposure of and risk to the public and to demonstrate compliance with applicable regulations.

- Environmental surveillance involves the collection and analysis of soil, foodstuffs, biota, and other media from DOE sites and environs, and the measurement of external radiation. Data are used to assess potential exposure to the public, evaluate impacts on the environment, and demonstrate compliance with applicable standards.

Technological advances have improved our ability to more accurately measure contaminants in the environment. Similarly, recent improvements in computer modeling have enabled us to better assess potential risks from exposures to contaminants in the environment. By encouraging communication among environmental monitoring personnel, DOE continues to support methods development and refinement of computer codes and models. The scope and magnitude of EMP requirements reflect diverse activities at different sites and the variety of contaminants that are discharged as a result of DOE operations.

INTEGRATION OF DOE ORDERS AND EPA REGULATIONS

DOE and its contractors are required to comply with EPA regulations. For nonradiological contaminants, DOE generally references EPA regulations; DOE Orders identify Department-specific procedural requirements (e.g., management and administrative responsibilities). Each year more EMP funds are spent on environmental monitoring for nonradioactive pollutants because of increasing regulatory emphasis on these materials. Except where environmental monitoring requirements for radionuclides are specified in an EPA regulation, DOE Orders specify EMP requirements and guidance for facilities owned by or operated for DOE.

On June 27, 1989, DOE indicated that negotiations on comprehensive environmental compliance oversight agreements would begin with states where DOE facilities were located. An agreement signed on June 28, 1989, provided the State of Colorado a more active role in verifying environmental monitoring data at the Rocky Flats Plant. In a statement made on August 21, 1989, the Secretary of Energy offered the governors of eleven states (California, Ohio, Florida, Idaho, Missouri, New York, New Mexico, South Carolina, Tennessee, Texas, and Washington) an opportunity to enter into agreements with provisions similar to the one with Colorado to independently validate DOE's environmental monitoring data.

DOE currently participates with states and EPA in sample exchange programs to assure comparability of analytical results. An example is the Agreement in Principal signed on February 27, 1989, between Washington's Department of Health and DOE's Richland Operations. A more active and cooperative oversight role by the states provides for verification of site-specific data and adds credibility to DOE's environmental monitoring programs.

An example of DOE/EPA interaction was the development of the National Emission Standards for Hazardous Air Pollutants for Radionuclides (EPA, 1985). When EPA began work on this rule in 1983, DOE provided considerable input because of its experience in monitoring radioactive emissions. EPA tested and validated its computer model (AIRDOS-EPA) in 1983 for estimating radiation doses from routine releases at DOE's Savannah River Site. EPA published the final rule on February 5, 1985 (EPA, 1985). Although the information collection and reporting requirements were never promulgated, DOE committed to providing annual radioactive release information and dose estimates to EPA. Recognizing that 40 CFR Part 61, Subpart H was to be revised, DOE and EPA met regularly before publication of the proposed rule on March 7, 1989 (EPA, 1989). DOE provided EPA with its revised (draft) monitoring procedures for airborne radionuclides for consideration in the new rule (DOE, 1989). EPA promulgated the final revised rule for National Emissions Standards for Hazardous Air Pollutants on December 15, 1989. The final rule included increased effluent monitoring requirements for radionuclides released to the air. EPA's new rule, like the draft DOE Order, provides for some flexibility in monitoring radioactive airborne effluents based on the magnitude of source terms.

CONCLUSION

DOE and/or its contractors have conducted environmental monitoring at DOE facilities for several decades. The Department's requirements for environmental monitoring are more prescriptive than in the past, but are generally not incompatible with those in effect or proposed by EPA.

ACKNOWLEDGMENT

Work supported by the U.S. DOE under Contract DE-AC06-76RLO 1830.

REFERENCES

AEC. 1973. Effluent and environmental monitoring and reporting, AEC Manual Chapter 0513. Atomic Energy Commission, Washington, DC.

DOE. 1989. Radiological effluent monitoring and environmental surveillance, DOE Order 5400.XY (draft). Department of Energy, Washington, DC.

EPA. 1985. National emission standards for hazardous air pollutants, Code of Federal Regulations, Title 40, Part 61, Subpart H. Environmental Protection Agency, Washington, DC.

EPA. 1989. National emission standards for hazardous air pollutants; Regulation of radionuclides - proposed rule and notice of public hearing. *Fed Reg.* 54:9612-9668.

PERSISTENT ORGANOCHLORINE AND ELEMENTAL CONTAMINANTS IN FRESHWATER FISH OF THE UNITED STATES: THE NATIONAL CONTAMINANT BIOMONITORING PROGRAM

C. J. Schmitt

U.S. Fish and Wildlife Service, National Fisheries Contaminant Research Center, Columbia, Missouri

Key Words: *Monitoring, organochlorines, elements, fish*

ABSTRACT

The National Contaminant Biomonitoring Program (NCBP) is maintained by the U.S. Fish and Wildlife Service (FWS) to document temporal and geographic trends in concentrations of persistent environmental contaminants that may threaten fish and wildlife. The NCBP also provides information on the success of regulatory actions in reducing environmental concentrations of toxic materials. Since 1967, the FWS has periodically determined concentrations of potentially toxic elements and selected organochlorine chemicals in composite samples of whole fish collected from a nationwide network which now comprises 114 stations in major rivers and the Great Lakes. The NCBP has documented the pervasive and persistent nature of organochlorine chemical contamination. It has also shown that concentrations of some organochlorines and elements in fish are generally lower now than previously. Thus, regulatory actions and modified agricultural practices can reduce concentrations of persistent, accumulable, hazardous materials in the environment. As elemental and organochlorine concentrations decline, new monitoring strategies will be required to effectively manage substances that either do not bioaccumulate or are difficult to analyze.

INTRODUCTION

The National Contaminant Biomonitoring Program (NCBP) was established to document trends in the occurrence of persistent toxic chemicals that may threaten fish and wildlife resources. Initiated in 1967 as part of the National Pesticide Monitoring Program (NPMP), the NCBP was expanded from an initial focus on organochlorine insecticides to include industrial chemicals, herbicides, and potentially toxic elemental contaminants that accumulate in fish. Basic program objectives are to provide continuing measurements of contaminant concentrations in fishes from the nation's major freshwater habitats; to interpret geographic and temporal trends in contaminant concentrations and assess the effectiveness of regulatory efforts and changing agricultural, industrial, and mining practices; to maintain an archive for fish samples and a data base to document present and future contaminant-related fishery resource problems; and to search for new and previously unrecognized environmental contaminants, and develop methods for their analysis.

METHODS OF STUDY

Although the basic NCBP framework is similar to that of the original NPMP, monitoring contaminants in freshwater fish has undergone a series of changes since collections began in 1967. Initially, fish were collected from 50 sampling stations in the Great Lakes and major rivers throughout the United States (Stations 1-50; Figure 1). Three predominant species were collected at each station in spring and fall in 1967 and 1968. From 1969 to 1974, annual collections were made in fall. In 1970, the number of stations was increased to 100 with the addition of Stations 51-100 (Figure 1). In 1976, 17 stations were added, and 5 existing stations were deleted; in 1984, collections were re-initiated at one inactive station, bringing the total to 113. From 1976 to 1981, about half the stations were sampled in the fall of even-numbered years and half during odd-numbered years. From 1984 to 1988, all active stations were sampled in the fall of even-numbered years.

Since 1970, collaborators have been requested to collect three samples from each station, two of a representative bottom-feeding species and one of a representative predatory species, from a list of preferred species. Each sample comprises five whole, adult specimens of the same species, which are shipped to the laboratory frozen. In the laboratory, fish are sawed into small pieces and ground thoroughly. Separate aliquots are prepared for organic and inorganic analyses, and an archive sample is prepared and stored in the freezer. The organic aliquot is solvent-extracted, cleaned up by gel permeation chromatography, and fractionated by Florisil® and silica gel chromatography. Each fraction is analyzed for residues of organochlorine contaminants by gas chromatography. Lipid and moisture content are also determined. Additional analyses by gas chromatography/mass spectrometry are performed to confirm initial findings and identify new or previously undetected environmental contaminants. The inorganic aliquot is acid-digested and analyzed for arsenic, cadmium, copper, mercury, lead, selenium, and zinc by atomic adsorption spectrophotometry. The last collection for which data have been reported is that of 1984. Station locations, collection details, analytical and statistical procedures, and results have been published for each completed collection (Henderson et al., 1969, 1971, 1972; Walsh et al., 1977; Ludke and Schmitt, 1980; May and McKinney, 1981; Ribick et al., 1981; Schmitt, 1981; Lowe et al., 1985; Schmitt and Brumbaugh, in press; Schmitt et al., 1981, 1983, 1985, in press; Baumann and May, 1984).

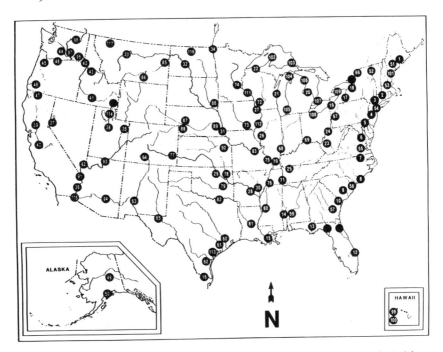

Figure 1. National Contaminant Biomonitoring Program stations; fish were collected from 1967 through 1984 (see text). Numbered circles, active; solid circles, inactive.

KEY FINDINGS

Reductions in the use of persistent toxic substances that accumulate in biota have resulted in lower concentrations in fish. The most significant regulatory success over the 20-yr history of NCBP has been with DDT, the insecticide for which the NCBP (as the NPMP) was conceived. Although DDT residues remain almost ubiquitous, concentrations in fish peaked before 1970; thereafter, mean concentrations declined, from about 1 μg/g (total DDT) in 1970 to about 0.25 μg/g in 1984 (Figure 2A). During the same period, average percent DDE (the most persistent metabolite of DDT) increased from

48% in 1970 to 73% in 1984 (Figure 2A). Collectively, these data indicate that there has been little recent influx of unweathered DDT to the aquatic environment. Concentrations greater than background now occur only at stations affected by point-sources (former sites of DDT manufacture or formulation) or those in watersheds where DDT was used to control cotton pests. At most stations, little parent insecticide (p, p'-DDT) was present in 1984.

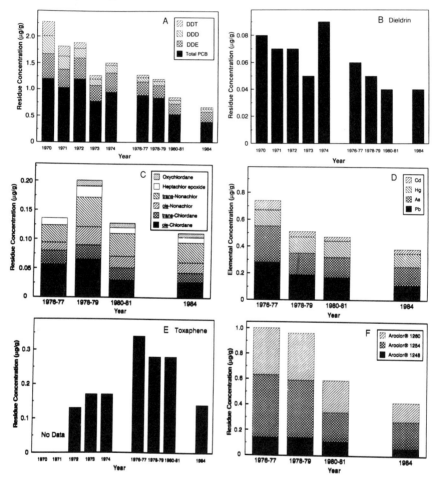

Figure 2A-F. Geometric mean concentrations (μg/g, wet weight) of organochlorine residues and elemental contaminants in composite samples of whole fish, determined by the National Contaminant Biomonitoring Program from 1967 through 1984. A, p, p'-DDT homologs and total polychlorinated biphenyls (PCB); B, dieldrin; C, chlordane components; D, elemental contaminants; E, toxaphene; and F, PCB (as Aroclor® mixtures).

Cyclodiene insecticide concentrations have also declined. Aldrin, dieldrin, heptachlor, and chlordane, which were used to control soil-dwelling insects, have been removed from the market. Consequently, no unmetabolized aldrin or heptachlor (which are rapidly metabolized to dieldrin and heptachlor epoxide, respectively) have been detected since the late 1970s, even where concentrations of the more persistent metabolites remain comparatively high. Dieldrin concentrations peaked in the mid-1970s, and levels in 1984 were only 50% of those measured between 1970 and 1974 (Figure 2B). Chlordane concentrations peaked in about 1978; residues of most chlordane components (including heptachlor epoxide, a minor constituent) declined significantly from 1978 to 1984, while the percent *trans*-nonachlor (the most persistent component) increased (Figure 2C), indicating reduced flux to the aquatic environment. In 1984, chlordane and dieldrin concentrations were highest in the Midwest, where these insecticides were used to control corn rootworms and termites (Schnoor, 1981; Arruda et al., 1987), and in Hawaii, where they were used to control subterranean and dry-wood termites (Bevenue et al., 1972; Tanita et al., 1976).

Nationally, mercury concentrations declined more than 25% between the late 1960s and 1974. Since then, there has been no discernible change (Figure 2D). Among NCBP sites, elevated mercury concentrations now occur only at locations historically influenced by point-sources (open-cell chloralkali plants, paper mills, and gold and silver mines). At these sites, mercury concentrations in fish have generally declined about 50% since 1970.

Lead concentrations declined steadily from 1976 to 1984 (Figure 2D), a finding consistent with trends reported for U.S. river water (Smith et al., 1987), riverine sediments (Trefry et al., 1985), and the atmosphere (Eisenreich et al., 1986). These declines have been attributed primarily to reductions in the lead content of motor fuels. Lead concentrations in fish also declined at stations influenced by mining and industrial discharges, suggesting that controls at these sources have also reduced quantities of lead in the aquatic environment.

Mean arsenic and cadmium concentrations also declined from 1976 to 1984 (Figure 2D); however, the changes were not uniform in magnitude, either geographically or temporally. Environmental concentrations of these elements and of selenium are intimately tied to point sources and to combustion of fossil fuels (especially coal). Environmental concentrations of selenium are also tied to irrigation practices in the arid, seleniferous regions of the west, where levels in

NCBP samples have historically been highest. Arsenic concentrations are also related to the continuing use of arsenical herbicides and defoliants. Declining arsenic and cadmium concentrations in fish contradict the general trend of increasing concentrations in water from 1974 to 1981, which Smith et al. (1987) attributed to recent increases in coal combustion.

SOME PROBLEMS THAT APPEARED TO GO AWAY DID NOT

Toxaphene replaced DDT as the insecticide of choice for controlling insects in cotton and, for many years, was the most heavily used pesticide in the United States (Eichers et al., 1978). Cotton pests eventually became resistant to toxaphene, as they had to DDT. Human health concerns and the occurrence of residues in fish far from known sources prompted cancellation of toxaphene registration for most uses in 1982 (EPA, 1982). Toxaphene concentrations in NCBP samples peaked about 1980 and have since declined more than 50% (Figure 2E), especially in areas of formerly heavy use (primarily in the Cotton Belt) and in the Great Lakes, where residues presumably derive from atmospheric transport (Ribick et al., 1982). However, a study of toxaphene in Great Lakes fish (Gooch and Matsamura, 1987) showed that concentrations of the most toxic constituents of this multicomponent insecticidal mixture have not changed, despite declining overall concentrations. Moreover, most analytical procedures, including the high-resolution method used for NCBP samples (Ribick et al., 1982), do not discriminate among the most toxic components, which are present at low concentrations in most environmental samples. Consequently, hazards posed by toxaphene residues in the environment remain to be evaluated.

Toxicity of remaining polychlorinated biphenyl (PCB) residues is also unknown. The NCBP has documented declining concentrations and increasing percentages of mixtures containing weathered components of these ubiquitous environmental pollutants since the mid-1970s (Figure 2F). However, like toxaphene, PCB comprise an entire class of compounds (Hutzinger et al., 1974), of which relatively few are toxic (Safe, 1987). Most analytical procedures, including the capillary-column method used through 1984 for NCBP analyses, cannot discriminate between toxic congeners, which usually constitute <1% of the total PCB present, and nontoxic congeners. Furthermore, toxic congeners tend to accumulate preferentially in fish (Huckins et al., 1988). Fortunately, in contrast to toxaphene, both analytical (e.g., Mullin et al., 1984) and bioassay (e.g., Safe, 1987) methods can be used to estimate concentrations of toxic PCB congeners in fish.

CONCLUSIONS AND RECOMMENDATIONS

The NCBP has succeeded in its primary objective of documenting temporal and geographic trends in the occurrence and concentration of persistent substances that bioaccumulate and which may constitute a hazard to piscivorous fish and wildlife. In general, concentrations of some organochlorine and elemental contaminants in fish are lower now than previously. Nevertheless, continued monitoring will be required to gauge the toxicological significance of remaining residues of persistent contaminants and of those transported in the atmosphere. As concentrations of these substances decline, new strategies that incorporate bioassessment methods will be required to monitor and evaluate emerging problems posed by ephemeral substances and those that do not bioaccumulate. Techniques under consideration for use by the NCBP include measuring macromolecular adducts of organic chemicals (Stalling et al., in press); induction of detoxification enzymes (Fabacher, 1982); and direct bioassays of water (Finger and Bulak, 1988) and extracts of fish and sediments for toxic and genotoxic activity (Safe, 1987; Fabacher et al., 1988).

REFERENCES

Arruda, J. A., M. S. Cringan, D. Gilliland, S. G. Haslouer, J. E. Fry, R. Broxterman, and K. L. Brunson. 1987. Correspondence between urban areas and the concentrations of chlordane in fish from the Kansas River. *Bull. Environ. Contam. Toxicol.* *39*:563-570.

Baumann, P. C. and T. W. May. 1984. Selenium residues in fish from inland waters of the United States, pp. 7-1-7-16. In: Workshop proceedings: The effects of trace elements on aquatic organisms. Prepared by the Carolina Power and Light Co. for the Electric Power Research Institute, Palo Alto, CA.

Bevenue, A., J. W. Hylin, Y. Kawano, and T. W. Kelley. 1972. Organochlorine pesticide residues in water, sediment, algae, and fish, Hawaii—1974. *Pestic. Monit. J.* *6*:56-64.

Eichers, T. R., P. A. Andrilenas, and T .W. Anderson. 1978. Farmers' use of pesticides in 1976, Agricultural Economic Report No. 418. U.S. Department of Agriculture, Economics, Statistics, and Cooperative Service, Washington, DC.

Eisenreich, S. J., N. A. Metzer, N. R. Urban, and J. A. Robbins. 1986. Response of atmospheric lead to decreased use of lead in gasoline. *Environ. Sci. Technol.* *20*:171-174.

EPA. 1982. Toxaphene, intent to cancel or restrict registration of pesticide products containing toxaphene; denial of applications for registration of pesticides containing toxaphene; determination concluding the rebuttable presumption against registrations; availability of decision document. *Fed. Reg.* *47*:53784-53793.

Fabacher, D. L., C. J. Schmitt, J. E. Besser, and M. J. Mac. 1988. Chemical characterization and mutagenic properties of polycyclic aromatic compounds in sediment from tributaries of the Great Lakes. *Environ. Toxicol. Chem.* *7*:529-543.

Fabacher, D. L. 1982. Hepatic microsomes from freshwater fish-I. In vitro cytochrome P-450 chemical interactions. *Comp. Biochem. Physiol.* *73C*:277-283.

Finger, S. E. and J. S. Bulak. 1988. Toxicity of water from three South Carolina rivers to larval striped bass. *Trans. Am. Fish. Soc.* *117*:521-528.

Gooch, J. W. and F. Matsamura. 1987. Toxicity of chlorinated bornane (toxaphene) residues isolated from Great Lakes lake trout *(Salvelinus namaycush). Arch. Environ. Contam. Toxicol.* *16*:349-355.

Henderson, C., A. Inglis, and W. L. Johnson. 1971. Organochlorine insecticide residues in fish, fall 1969. *Pestic. Monit. J.* *5*:1-11.

Henderson, C., A. Inglis, and W. L. Johnson. 1972. Mercury residues in fish, 1969-1970. *Pestic. Monit. J.* *6*:144-159.

Henderson, C., W. L. Johnson, and A. Inglis. 1969. Organochlorine insecticide residues in fish. *Pestic. Monit. J.* *3*:145-171.

Huckins, J. N, T. R. Schwartz, J. D. Petty, and L. M. Smith. 1988. Determination, fate, and potential significance of PCBs in fish and sediment samples with emphasis on selected AHH-inducing congeners. *Chemosphere* *17*:1995-2016.

Hutzinger, O., S. Safe, and V. Zitko. 1974. *The Chemistry of PCBs.* CRC Press, Cleveland, OH.

Lowe, T. P., T. W. May, W. G. Brumbaugh, and D. A. Kane. 1985. National Contaminant Biomonitoring Program: Concentrations of seven elements in freshwater fish, 1978-1981. *Arch. Environ. Contam. Toxicol.* *14*:363-388.

Ludke, J. L. and C. J. Schmitt. 1980. Monitoring contaminant residues in freshwater fishes in the United States: The National Pesticide Monitoring Program, pp. 97-110. In: Proceedings, 3rd USA-USSR Symposium on the Effects of Pollutants upon Aquatic Ecosystems, EPA-6009-80-034, W. R. Swain and V. R. Shannon (eds.). U.S. Environmental Protection Agency, Duluth, MN.

May, T. W. and G. L. McKinney. 1981. Cadmium, mercury, arsenic, and selenium concentrations in freshwater fish, 1976-1977-National Pesticide Monitoring Program. *Pestic. Monit. J.* *15*:14-38.

Mullin, M. D., C. M. Pochini, S. McCrindle, M. Romkes, S. H. Safe, and L. M. Safe. 1984. High-resolution PCB analysis: Synthesis and chromatographic properties of all 209 PCB congeners. *Environ. Sci. Technol.* *18*:468-476.

Ribick, M. A., L .M. Smith, G. R. Dubay, and D. L. Stalling. 1981. Applications and results of analytical methods used in monitoring environmental contaminants, pp. 249-269. In: Aquatic Toxicology and Hazard Assessment: 4th conference, D. L. Branson and K. Dixon (eds.). Chicago, IL, STP 737. American Society for Testing and Materials, Philadelphia, PA.

Ribick, M. A., G. R. Dubay, J. D. Petty, D. L. Stalling, and C. J. Schmitt. 1982. Toxaphene residues in fish: Identification, quantification and confirmation at part-per-billion levels. *Environ. Sci. Technol.* *16*:310-318.

Safe, S. 1987. Determination of 2,3,7,8-TCDD toxic equivalency factors (TEFS): Support for the use of the *in vitro* AHH induction assay. *Chemosphere* *16*:791-802.

Schmitt, C. J. 1981. Analysis of variance as a method for examining contaminant residues in fish: National Pesticide Monitoring Program, pp. 270-298. In: Aquatic Toxicology and Hazard Assessment: 4th conference, STP 737, Branson, D. R. and K. L. Dixon (eds.). American Society for Testing and Materials, Philadelphia, PA.

Schmitt, C. J. and W. G. Brumbaugh. 1990. National Contaminant Biomonitoring Program: Concentrations of arsenic, cadmium, copper, lead, mercury, selenium, and zinc in U.S. freshwater fish, 1984. *Arch. Environ. Contam. Toxicol.* *19*:731-747.

Schmitt, C. J., J. L. Ludke, and D. Walsh. 1981. Organochlorine residues in fish, 1970-1974: National Pesticide Monitoring Program. *Pestic. Monit. J.* *14*:136-206.

Schmitt, C. J., M. A. Ribick, J. L. Ludke, and T. W. May. 1983. Organochlorine residues in freshwater fish, 1976-1979: National Pesticide Monitoring Program, Resource Publicaton No. 152. U.S. Fish and Wildlife Service, Washington, DC.

Schmitt, C. J., J. L. Zajicek, and P. H. Peterman. 1990. National Contaminant Biomonitoring Program: Residues of organochlorine chemicals in U.S. freshwater fish, 1984. *Arch. Environ. Contam. Toxicol.* *19*:748-782.

Schmitt, C. J., J. L. Zajicek, and M. A. Ribick. 1985. National Pesticide Monitoring Program: Residues of organochlorine chemicals in freshwater fish, 1980-81. *Arch. Environ. Contam. Toxicol.* *14*:225-260.

Schnoor, J. L. 1981. Fate and transport of dieldrin in Coralville Reservoir: Residues in fish and water following a pesticide ban. *Science 211*:840-842.

Smith, R. A., R. B. Alexander, and M. G. Wolman. 1987. Water quality trends in the Nation's rivers. *Science 235*:1607-1615.

Stalling, D. L. C. J. Schmitt, J. E. McEntire, and D. C. England. Adducted deoxynucleosides in DNA from blood and liver of brown bullheads *(Ictalurus nebulosus)* from Lake Erie at Cleveland, Ohio. *Environ. Sci. Technol.* (in press).

Tanita, R., J. M. Johnson, M. Chun, and J. Maciolek. 1976. Organochlorine pesticides in the Hawaii Kai Marina, 1970-74. *Pestic. Monit. J. 10*:24-29.

Trefry, J. H. S., S. Metz, R.P. Trocine, and T.A. Nelsen. 1985. A decline in lead transport by the Mississippi River. *Science 230*:439-441.

Walsh, D., B. Berger, and J. Bean. 1977. Heavy metal residues in fish, 1971-1973. *Pestic. Monit. J. 11*:5-34.

ENVIRONMENTAL RADIOIODINE IN THYROIDS OF GRAZING ANIMALS

L. Van Middlesworth

Department of Physiology and Biophysics, University of Tennessee, Memphis, Tennessee

Key Words: *Radioiodine, worldwide monitoring, animal thyroids, fallout*

ABSTRACT

Animal thyroids are excellent indicators of environmental contamination from radioiodine, a fact largely unappreciated before 1954. From continuous monitoring of excised thyroids in NaI well-detectors, we know that high-altitude releases of mixed fission products caused increases of 10^3 to 10^5 times the minimal detectable level of ^{131}I (3.7 mBq/g) in sheep thyroids from the United States, Europe, Asia, Australia, and New Zealand. Within 6 weeks after high-altitude releases, sheep thyroids from different continents of the same hemisphere contained comparable concentrations of ^{131}I: more than 10^4 times greater concentrations than cow's milk and 5×10^3 times greater concentrations than human thyroids from similar areas. In contrast, during the low-altitude Chernobyl release, average ^{131}I concentrations in animal thyroids, at distances greater than 1200 km from Chernobyl, were distributed as the inverse square of the distance from the source.

^{129}I concentrations measured since 1984 with a germanium well-detector in thyroids of sheep slaughtered in Birmingham, England, ranged from 3 to 50 mBq/g organ weight. Similar quantities of ^{125}I were present intermittently in thyroids of sheep slaughtered in Birminingham since 1986. The source of the ^{125}I, which is not a fission product, is not clear. For comparison, deer thyroids from the Savannah River Reservation, USA, contained 10 to 7×10^5 mBq ^{129}I/g. Although this isotope is not a biological hazard, it is a long-lived tracer of fission products.

INTRODUCTION

I will review what has been learned from monitoring iodine fallout over the past 35 yr. Before June 1954, 43 nuclear weapons tests had been conducted (Carter and Moghissi, 1977). However, it was not realized that thyroids of grazing animals had probably been labeled with ^{131}I by each test. After a test series at Bikini in 1954, a fortuitous observation in Memphis, Tennessee, revealed that cattle thyroids contained up to 150 Bq ^{131}I/g (Van Middlesworth, 1954). One week later, cattle slaughtered in San Francisco, California, contained up to 22 Bq ^{131}I/g (Van Middlesworth, 1954). Five months later, after a nuclear test in the Soviet Union, the amount of ^{131}I in cattle thyroids increased from 1.0 to 10 Bq ^{131}I/g (Figure 1). After a test series in Nevada in 1955, thyroids showed a maximum of more than 740 Bq ^{131}I/g in cattle and up to 1.9 Bq ^{131}I/g in thyroids of people in Memphis (Van Middlesworth, 1956; Comar et al., 1957). Animal thyroids obtained regularly from volunteer veterinarians and scientists in Europe, Asia, and North America showed changes in ^{131}I levels that correlated with nuclear tests (Van Middlesworth, 1956).

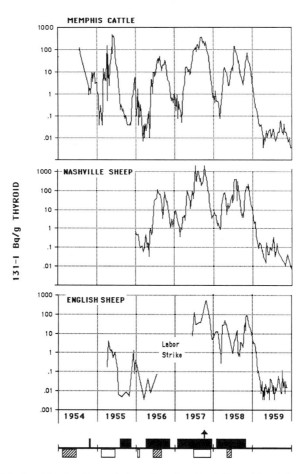

Figure 1. ^{131}I in thyroids of cattle and sheep from London, UK, and from Tennessee, USA, during 1954-1959, associated with repeated series of nuclear weapons tests in the atmosphere and a nuclear reactor accident at Windscale, UK. Solid boxes, tests in USSR; hatched boxes, tests by USA on islands in Pacific Ocean; open boxes, tests in Nevada. Arrow marks accident at Windscale. Curves connect mean values of 6-8 thyroids collected on sampling date.

MAXIMUM FALLOUT AND REACTOR ACCIDENT

In 1957 and 1958 at least 129 nuclear tests were conducted by the United States, the United Kingdom, and the USSR (Carter and Moghissi, 1977), and the first nuclear reactor accident was reported from England (Atomic Energy Office, 1957). Repeated test series accompanied prolonged contamination with [131]I (Figure 2) in animals of the northern hemisphere, even though the isotope's physical half-life was only 8 days. In 1957 and 1958, the integrated dose of ^{131}I in sheep thyroids from Nashville, Tennessee, averaged 0.35 Sv (Van Middlesworth, 1960a). Figure 1 shows that in 1957 the generalized contamination of thyroids in the northern hemisphere made it difficult to separate the effects of the Windscale (UK) release, except in areas close to the accident (Van Middlesworth, 1958, 1960a).

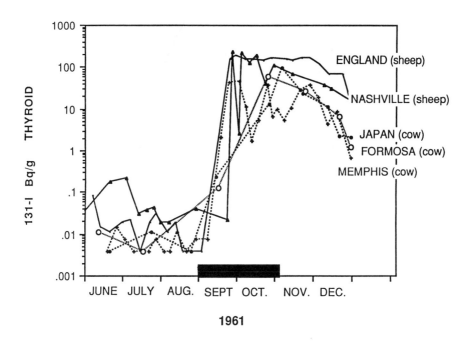

Figure 2. Relatively uniform distribution of ^{131}I in animal thyroids from northern hemisphere after high-altitude nuclear weapons tests in USSR. Solid bars show series of 30 atmospheric nuclear tests in USSR from September 1 through November 4, 1961. A series of deep-underground nuclear tests were conducted by USA from September 15 through April the following year. Concentrations, although from different continents, are similar within species.

TEST BAN TREATY AND RESUMPTION OF TESTS, 1961

The ban on nuclear tests, signed in 1958 by the United States and the USSR, reduced worldwide contamination from ^{131}I within 2 months. Monitoring thyroids has become more sensitive as background radioactivity has declined. In 1960, abrupt increases of ^{131}I were reported in animal thyroids from the northern hemisphere and in selected areas of the southern hemisphere. The increases correlated with a series of atmospheric nuclear tests conducted in Africa by the French government (Van Middlesworth, 1960b). In May and June 1961, during a gradual release of 153 Ci ^{131}I from the Savannah River Plant (Marter, 1963), radioactive milk was found in the Savannah River area and more than 0.2 Bq [131]I /g thyroid was measured in Nashville sheep (Figure 2).

The test-ban treaty restricted nuclear testing in the atmosphere by the United States and USSR until 1961, when a series of tests were conducted by both countries, and ^{131}I in animal thyroids promptly returned to levels observed in 1958-1959 (Figure 2). The 1961 data for sheep thyroids from the United Kingdom and Nashville suggest almost uniform distribution of ^{131}I fission products in sheep slaughtered in widely different parts of the hemisphere (Van Middlesworth, 1963). After 1963, the United States and the USSR are believed to have discontinued further nuclear tests in the atmosphere.

HANFORD SYMPOSIUM

The Hanford Symposium of 1962 (Bustad, 1963a) summarized monitoring observations and experiments showing that the major source of radioiodine in animal thyroids was fallout on vegetation. [131]I was found in milk that was ingested by people. Straub and Fooks (1963) showed that ^{131}I levels in milk were reduced two orders of magnitude by sheltering the cattle and feeding them uncontaminated food. Bustad (1963b) simulated a single contaminating event by adding ^{131}I label, on a one-time basis, to feed for experimental cows. This resulted in a continuous increase of ^{131}I in their milk for 10 days. Although the milk had a lower concentration of radioiodine than the diet, the thyroids contained 2×10^4 higher concentration of ^{131}I than the milk. Soldat (1963) reported that an accidental fallout resulted in bovine thyroids containing 3.8×10^3 more ^{131}I than did milk; these results were compared to those from earlier monitoring in England after the Windscale accident. Fallout data on ^{131}I in humans were reported by six different groups (Van Middlesworth, 1963; Beirwaltes et al., 1963; Pendleton et al., 1963; Cohn and Gusameno, 1963; Visalli and Goldin, 1963; Eisenbud et al., 1963). Eisenbud et al. (1963) reported that children in New York had a thyroid burden of ^{131}I/g equal to the concentration of ^{131}I/L of ingested milk. In the same symposium, Langeman (1963) reviewed the literature which showed that prophylactic ingestion of potassium iodide can greatly reduce the thyroid uptake of ^{131}I.

After 1963, ^{131}I contamination became progressively less in the northern hemisphere, even though weapons tests were conducted by the People's Republic of China from 1964 through 1980 (Carter, 1979). The ^{131}I levels in animal thyroids were small compared to those of the previous decade. Testing also continued in the southern hemisphere, and we measured ^{131}I in sheep from Australia (Melick and Van Middlesworth, 1974). In late 1974, a maximum concentration of ^{131}I originating in the southern hemisphere was detected in the northern hemisphere, 2 months after its release (Van Middlesworth, 1975). From October 1976 to December 1977, the thyroids of sheep and cattle in England and North America averaged between 7 and 18 Bq ^{131}I/g, after atmospheric nuclear tests in China (Carter, 1979). One-tenth of those levels were found in the spring of 1978 and the fall of 1980. From October to December 1981, animal thyroids from these same areas averaged 0.25 to 0.5 Bq ^{131}I /g, but these have not been fully evaluated.

NATURAL RADIUM IN THYROIDS

During 1975 and 1976, ^{131}I levels were low. Continuous monitoring of thyroids showed that approximately 20% of cattle thyroids from Cali, Colombia, had low-level radioactivity that, unlike radioiodine, had a long half-life. The radionuclides were ^{226}Ra, ^{228}Ra, and their daughters. About 90% of cattle thyroids from Nigeria, West Africa (the percentage was less from other areas), contained 30 to 1000 mBq ^{226}Ra and ^{228}Ra/g (Wogman et al., 1977). Autoradiographs showed that radium was concentrated in colloid "nodules" (Van Middlesworth, 1972). The radiation dose from this natural radium in bovine thyroids from Africa averaged 0.4 Sv per year to the thyroid. No concentrated radium deposits were found in human thyroids.

REACTOR ACCIDENT AT CHERNOBYL, 1986

The concept of worldwide contamination from radioiodine released at ground level was not widely accepted in 1980. Iodine-131 was too low to measure until May 6, 1986. After the Chernobyl reactor accident on April 26, 1986, ^{131}I was found in the thyroids of cattle and sheep in Europe, Asia, and North America (Van Middlesworth, 1989; Figure 3). However, 4 days after the accident, there was no ^{131}I in animals at Birmingham, UK, or Ulm, West Germany. We first found radioiodine in thyroids from Germany and England 10 days after the accident; maximum levels occurred on the 25th day, and measurable levels persisted for 100 days. Barely measurable quantities (0.015 Bq/g) were found in sheep thyroids from Australia 40 days after the accident.

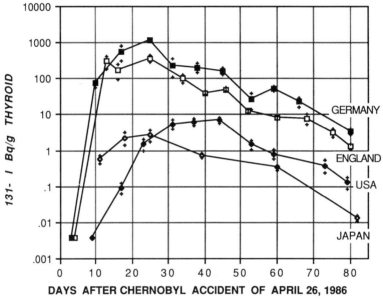

Figure 3. [131]I in cattle and sheep thyroids from different parts of northern hemisphere after nuclear accident at Chernobyl, USSR. Curves connect average values of 8-10 thyroids; ±1 SD shown by +. Samples from Ulm, West Germany; Tokyo, Japan; and Memphis, Tennessee, USA, were collected from cattle. Samples from Birmingham, UK, were collected from sheep (from Van Middlesworth, 1989).

In locations that we studied, maximum concentrations of ^{131}I from Chernobyl were usually less than those from nuclear weapons testing. Our most radioactive samples originated 1200 km from Chernobyl (at Bad Hall, Austria). To estimate possible ^{131}I exposure at various distances from Chernobyl, our maximum values for ^{131}I/g thyroid were plotted versus the inverse square of the distance between the slaughter points and Chernobyl. A straight-line, least-squares linear regression model was fitted to the data. This revealed a correlation coefficient of 0.69 (Figure 4).

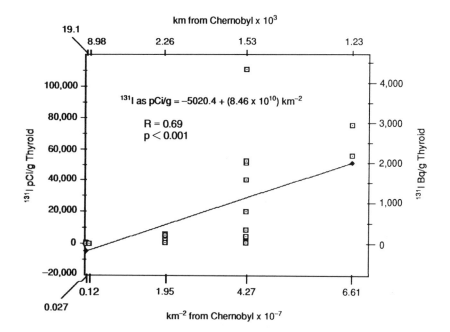

Figure 4. Maximum ^{131}I values in combined samples of cattle and sheep thyroids from Bad Hall, Austria; Ulm, West Germany; Birmingham, UK; Tokyo, Japan; and Memphis, Tennessee, USA, plotted versus the inverse square of the distance from Chernobyl.

Health officers in countries near the accident requested or required that dairy animals be removed from exposed pastures; the intake of fresh milk was discontinued and, in some areas, nonradioactive therapeutic iodine was dispensed.

[137]Cs, [129]I, AND ^{125}I IN ANIMAL THYROIDS

After ^{131}I from Chernobyl decayed, the same specimens were analyzed for [137]Cs. As an example, the maximum concentration of ^{137}Cs in thyroids from Ulm, West Germany, was 0.1 to 0.2 Bq/g 30 to 60 days after the accident (Van Middlesworth and Loos, 1988). The ^{137}Cs concentrations fell during the succeeding 7 months to 0.004 Bq/g and then, surprisingly, increased again, 10 months after the accident, to 0.07 Bq/g. Four to five additional months were necessary before ^{137}Cs became less than 0.001 Bq/g. The second increase of ^{137}Cs was not associated with additional ^{131}I and probably came from the original accident.

We have detected no ^{131}I in sheep thyroids since 1986 and, without interference from ^{131}I, low-energy K conversion and K capture x rays have been measured in sheep from the UK. The [129]I has averaged 0.3 to 10 mBq/g (Van Middlesworth, 1984), and ^{125}I has been present intermittently in similar quantities. By way of comparison, thyroids of deer killed on the Savannah River reservation in the United States contained about 50 times more [129]I than that in the English sheep. Howe and coworkers (Howe and Hunt, 1985; Howe et al., 1984; Bowalt and Howe, 1985; Howe and Lloyd, 1986) concluded that ^{125}I, used for medical purposes, was being discharged into rivers in the United Kingdom. Bowlt and Tiplady have recently reported [129]I in human thyroids obtained from the Stellafield, UK, area.

Up to 1973 the distribution of [129]I in the United States was carefully recorded by Brauer et al. (1974), and a monograph published by the National Council on Radiation Protection (NCRP, 1983) concluded that [129]I will probably never be a significant radiation hazard because of its long half-life.

Conclusions based on our environmental monitoring of radioiodine are: (1) Worldwide distribution of ^{131}I declined, after atmospheric nuclear tests were discontinued, until the major release from Chernobyl. (2) Radioactive iodine released at high altitudes mixed uniformly into the biosphere within a few weeks; ground-level releases resulted in concentration differences that were highly dependent on distance. (3) Nonhazardous levels of radioiodine were readily detected at very low thresholds by monitoring animal thyroids. (4) Thyroid concentrations of ^{131}I, ^{137}Cs, [134]Cs, and [129]I measured in cattle may provide useful information regarding the sources and ages of fission product mixtures.

ACKNOWLEDGMENT

The author expresses his appreciation to James G. Karas, Systems Analyst, University of Tennessee, for his statistical assistance.

REFERENCES

Atomic Energy Office. 1957. Accident at Windscale No.1 Pile on 10th October, 1957. HM Stationery Office, London.

Beierwaltes, W. H., M. T. J. Hilger, and A. Wegst. 1963. Radioiodine concentration in fetal human thyroid from fallout. *Health Phys.* 9:1263-1266.

Bowlt, C. and J. R. Howe, 1985. Radioactive iodine-125 and iodine-129 derived from environmental pollution in members of the public. *Lancet 2*:1420.

Bowlt, C. and P. Tiplady. 1989. Radioiodine in human thyroid glands and incidence of thyroid cancer in Cumbria. *Br. Med. J. 299*:301-302.

Brauer, F. P., J. K. Soldat, H. Tenny, and R. S. Strebin, Jr. 1974. Natural iodine and iodine-129 in mammalian thyroids and environment samples taken from locations in the United States, pp. 43-66. In: Environmental Surveillance Around Nuclear Installations II, IAEA Publication No. STI/PUB/353. International Atomic Energy Agency, Vienna, Austria.

Bustad, L. K. (ed.). 1963a. Biology of radioiodine. *Health Phys. 9*:(12) (entire issue).

Bustad, L. K., D. H. Wood, E. E. Elefson, H. A. Ragan, and R. O. McClellan. 1963b. ^{131}I in milk and thyroid of dairy cattle following a single contamination event and prolonged daily administration. *Health Phys. 9*:1231-1234.

Carter, M. W. 1979. Nuclear testing 1975-78. *Health Phys. 36*:432-437.

Carter, M. W. and A. A. Moghissi. 1977. Three decades of testing. *Health Phys. 33*:55-71.

Cohn, S. H., and E. A. Gusmano. 1963. Uptake and transfer of fallout ^{131}I in pregnant women. *Health Phys. 9*:1267-1269.

Comar, C. L., B. F. Trum, V. S. G. Kuhn, R. H. Wasserman, M. M. Nold, and J. C. Schooley. 1957. Thyroid radioactivity after nuclear weapons tests. *Science 126*:16-18.

Eisenbud, M., B. Pasternack, G. Laurer, Y. Mochizuki, M. E. Wrenn, L. Block, and R. Mowafy. 1963. Estimation of the thyroid doses in a population exposed to ^{131}I from weapons tests. *Health Phys. 9*:1281-1289.

Howe, J. R. and A. E. Hunt. 1984. Swan thyroid glands and river algae as indicators of iodine-125 and iodine-131 in the river Trent and its tributaries. *Sci. Tot. Environ. 35*:387-401.

Howe, J.R. and M. K. Lloyd 1986. Radio-iodine in thyroid glands of swans, farm animals and humans, also in algae and river water from the Thames valley, England. *Sci. Tot. Environ. 48*:13-31.

Howe, J.R., M. K. Lloyd, A. E. Hunt, and F. G. Clegg. 1984. The origin of ^{125}I in animal thyroids. *Health Phys. 46*:244-245.

Lengemann, F. W. and J. C. Thompson, Jr. 1963. Prophylactic and therapeutic measures for radioiodine contamination. *Health Phys. 9*:1391-1397.

Marter, W. L. 1963. Radioiodine release incident at the Savannah River Plant. *Health Phys. 9*:1105-1109.

Melick, R. and L. Van Middlesworth. 1974. Radioiodine in animal thyroid glands from 1966-72. *Med. J Australia 1*:298-301.

NCRP. 1983. Iodine-129 Evaluation of Releases from Nuclear Power Generation, NCRP Report No. 75. National Council for Radiation Protection and Measurement, Bethesda, MD.

Pendleton, R. C., C. W. Mays, R. D. Lloyd, and A. L. Brooks. 1963. Differential accumulation of ^{131}I from local fallout in people and milk. *Health Phys.* 9:1253-1262.

Soldat, J. K. 1965. Environmental evaluation of an acute release of ^{131}I to the atmosphere. *Health Phys. 11*:1009-1015.

Straub, C. P., and J. H. Fooks. 1963. Cooperative field studies on environmental factors influencing ^{131}I levels in milk. *Health Phys. 9*:1187-1195.

Van Middlesworth, L. 1954. Radioactivity in animal thyroids from various areas. *Nucleonics 12*: 56-57.

Van Middlesworth, L. 1956. Radioactivity in thyroid glands following nuclear weapons tests. *Science 123*:982-983.

Van Middlesworth, L. 1960a. Re-evaluation of certain aspects of iodine metabolism. *Recent Prog. Horm. Res. 16*:405-438.

Van Middlesworth, L. 1960b. World-wide distribution of iodine-131 in animal thyroids following announcements of isolated nuclear weapons tests in North Africa. *Nature 188*:748-749.

Van Middlesworth, L. 1963. Factors influencing the thyroid uptake of iodine isotopes from nuclear fission—A review. *Health Phys. 9*:1197-1211.

Van Middlesworth, L. 1972. Concentrated sources of alpha particles within thyroid glands. *Endocrinology 91*:1534-1536.

Van Middlesworth, L. 1975. Radioiodine in animal thyroids during nuclear tests in both hemispheres. *Health Phys. 29*:861-863.

Van Middlesworth, L. 1984. Iodine-129 in ovine thyroids from England. *Health Phys. 47*:488-490.

Van Middlesworth, L. 1989. Effects of radiation on the thyroid gland. *Adv. Int. Med. 34*:265-284.

Van Middlesworth, L. and U. Loos. 1988. Cesium-137 and ^{131}I in thyroids of cattle and sheep after nuclear accidents and weapons tests. *Health Phys. 55*:809-811.

Visalli, F. I., and A. S. Goldin. 1963. Fallout ^{131}I in children—in vivo measurement. *Health Phys. 9*:1271-1277.

Wogman, N. A., R. L. Brodzinski, and L. Van Middlesworth. 1977. Radium accumulation in animal thyroid glands: A possible method for uranium and thorium prospecting. *J. Radioanal. Chem. 41*:115-125.

STRONTIUM-90 IN CANADA GOOSE EGGSHELLS: NONFATAL MONITORING FOR CONTAMINATION IN WILDLIFE

W. H. Rickard and L. E. Eberhardt

Pacific Northwest Laboratory, Richland, Washington

Key Words: *Canada goose, eggshells, ^{90}Sr, Columbia River*

ABSTRACT

We measured ^{90}Sr in eggshells from Canada geese *(Branta canadensis moffitti)* that nested on Columbia River islands up- and downstream from deactivated plutonium production reactors on the U.S. Department of Energy's Hanford Site in southeastern Washington. We also measured ^{90}Sr in wing bones of goose carcasses. Background levels of ^{90}Sr were based on eggshells collected on an island upstream of the reactors. A few eggshells collected from nests on a single island downstream of the reactors had slightly higher than background levels of ^{90}Sr. This may have resulted from geese eating shoreline plants or crops irrigated with Columbia River water that contained ^{90}Sr released into the river through ground-water seepage.

INTRODUCTION

For the last 45 yr, ^{90}Sr, a moderately long-lived (half-life = 29.1 yr) radionuclide produced during the nuclear fission process, has been ubiquitously deposited over the earth's surface mixed with particulate debris originating from atmospheric testing of nuclear weapons (Bowen, 1979; Eisenbud, 1987). Strontium-90 is also present in irradiated fuel. In the 1960s, up to eight once-through-cooled reactors and a secondary cooling reactor (N Reactor) operated on the Hanford Site upstream from the city of Richland, Washington (Figure 1). By 1971, only N Reactor was operating. When it was shut down in 1987, four decades of reactor operations at Hanford ended. During the years of N Reactor operations, ^{90}Sr seeped into the ground from aqueous waste streams and has moved with ground-water flows, entering the Columbia River (Rokkan, 1986). However, elevated strontium levels are currently not detectable in drinking-water samples collected downstream at Richland, the nearest population center (Jaquish and Bryce, 1989).

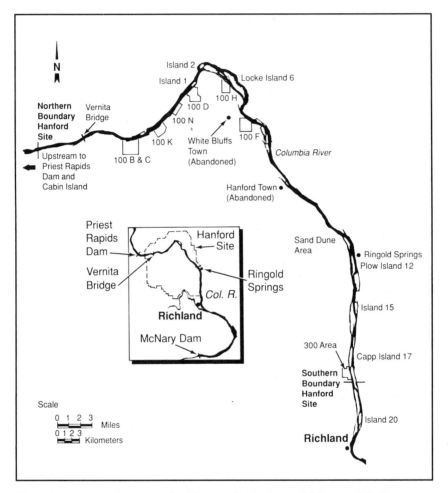

Figure 1. Locations of goose nesting islands at Hanford and of N-Reactor (100 N).

Strontium-90, like calcium, is expected to concentrate in the bones and eggshells of birds (Till and Meyer, 1983). The purpose of our survey was to determine if eggshells from Canada geese that nest on four Columbia River islands (Figure 2), downstream from N reactor, contained elevated ^{90}Sr levels compared with eggshells from geese nesting on an upriver island. We also measured ^{90}Sr in wing bones of goose carcasses.

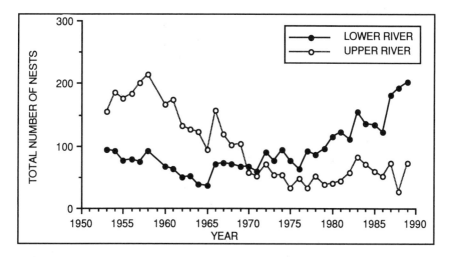

Figure 2. Canada goose nest counts on Columbia River islands upriver and downriver from Ringold Springs (1953-1989).

LIFE HISTORY OF NESTING CANADA GEESE ON THE HANFORD SITE

Canada geese usually begin to nest on Columbia River islands in March, and eggs hatch in April and May. During brood rearing, which lasts through summer, parent geese closely attend their young, which cannot fly (Eberhardt, 1987). Almost all forage plants ingested by parent and juvenile geese are those that grow along the wetted shoreline of the Columbia River or on one of the few irrigated fields close to the shore. One field is located east of Island 12 near Ringold (Figure 1). When the young birds are able to fly, they often forage at long distances from the river. In autumn, a large influx of migrant Canada geese intermingles with resident geese.

METHODS EMPLOYED

Immediately after hatching, eggshells were collected from 52 nests (in spring, 1988) on Islands 2, 12 (Plow Island), 15, and 17 (Capp Island), all downstream from N Reactor (Figure 1), and from Cabin Island, in the lower portion of Priest Rapids Dam reservoir, upstream from N Reactor (Figure 1). Wing bones were also collected from eight goose carcasses found on the islands. Death was probably caused by gunshot wounds incurred during the 1987-1988 fall-winter hunting season.

Eggshells were washed under running tap water, gently scrubbed to remove attached blood, feces, and mucus, and inner membranes were removed. Wing bones were scraped clean of attached flesh. All samples were air-dried and analyzed for [90]Sr (chemical separation and beta-counting; Jaquish and Bryce, 1989) by U.S. Testing Company, Richland, Washington.

RESULTS AND DISCUSSION

Because ^{90}Sr did not appear to be normally distributed, we performed a natural log transformation before conducting parametric statistical analyses. The ^{90}Sr concentrations in eggshells from the five islands were significantly different (one-way ANOVA; $P = 0.001$; $F = 10.9$; df $= 4, 47$). Concentrations of ^{90}Sr in eggshells from Island 12 (near Ringold Springs) were significantly higher ($P < 0\ 0.05$, Scheffé F test) than those from the other four islands (Table 1). Average ^{90}Sr concentration in eggshells from Island 12 was 1.475 pCi/g dry weight, compared to 0.8405, 0.6015, 0.5339, and 0.538 pCi/g dry weight for those from Cabin Island and Islands 2, 15, and 17, respectively. Using as background the average ^{90}Sr concentration (0.8405 pCi/g eggshell) measured at Cabin Island, upstream of N reactor, only Island 12 had above-background ^{90}Sr levels.

TABLE 1. Concentrations of [90]Sr (pCi per g dry weight) in goose eggshells collected from islands in the Columbia River upstream and downstream from Hanford reactors.

Collection Location	N	Mean	Median	Range Minimum	Range Maximum
Upstream Island					
Cabin Island	12	0.840	0.718	0.414	1.490
Downstream Islands					
Island 2	8	0.601	0.600	0.533	0.891
Island 12	12	1.475	1.355	0.658	2.450
Island 15	8	0.534	0.530	0.278	0.767
Island 17	12	0.536	0.460	0.306	1.290

Average ^{90}Sr concentration in wing bones was 0.517 pCi/g dry weight (range, 0.199 - 0.805), a value similar to concentrations in eggshells. These migrant geese were probably not raised along the Hanford Reach; thus, ^{90}Sr concentrations in wing bones are indicative of background levels. In addition, ^{90}Sr concentrations in eggshells are indicative of those in bones of parent birds.

About 38% of the goose eggshell weight is calcium (Rickard and Price, 1990). The shell from a single goose egg weighs about 17 g, and the average clutch size is five eggs; thus, the eggshell weight of a clutch is about 85 g. Using the maximum ^{90}Sr value, in eggshells from Island 12, an average clutch contained 208 pCi ^{90}Sr and 32 g of calcium.

For eggshells to contain higher-than-background concentrations of ^{90}Sr, geese must ingest plants with higher-than-background levels of [90]Sr. The only shoreline plants with elevated ^{90}Sr levels are those close to N Reactor (Rickard and Price, 1990). However, the number of plants analyzed was small; more detailed sampling might show elevated ^{90}Sr levels farther downstream. Alfalfa *(Medicago sativa)* irrigated with Columbia River water, on which the geese may have fed, may have enhanced levels of [90]Sr. Although alfalfa routinely collected from fields irrigated with Columbia River water downstream from the Hanford reactors do not show elevated ^{90}Sr levels (Jaquish and Bryce, 1989), geese may have foraged in fields that were not sampled.

Nesting performance of Canada geese on Hanford Reach islands has been monitored since 1950 (Hanson and Eberhardt, 1971; Fitzner and Rickard, 1983). Although the number of nests has varied from year to year, the population appears stable. Most posthatching mortality is caused by predators or hunters. Initially, upstream islands (above Ringold Springs, Figure 1) were favored by nesting geese (Figure 2). In recent years, the downstream islands have been favored. The shift is attributed to more frequent intrusions by coyotes *(Canis latrans)* on upriver islands and fewer intrusions on downriver islands (Fitzner and Rickard, 1983).

CONCLUSIONS

Strontium-90 is ubiquitous in the foraging environment of Canada geese that nest on the Hanford Reach of the Columbia River; ^{90}Sr will likely persist in the biosphere for decades because of its long half-life and because of recycling between soil and plants. Most ^{90}Sr in goose eggshells and bone detected in this survey probably originated from worldwide fallout. However, eggshells of a few geese that nested on Island 12, downstream from N reactor, had slightly elevated ^{90}Sr levels. The ^{90}Sr in these eggshells may be from ground-water seepage into the Columbia River from N reactor and subsequent uptake by shoreline plants that were eaten by geese. By sampling eggshells we can obtain biological samples that are representative of ^{90}Sr concentrations in bones without killing the geese. None of the ^{90}Sr concentrations in eggshells and bones were at levels expected to affect the health or reproductive success of the goose population.

Sampling goose eggshells is useful in long-term environmental monitoring programs to document historical changes in eggshell chemistry. This nondestructive sampling method is important because the Canada goose population is a valuable esthetic and recreational resource. The method may also be useful for other egg-laying species.

ACKNOWLEDGMENT

Work supported by the U.S. Department of Energy under Contract DE-AC06-76RLO 1830.

REFERENCES

Bowen, H. J. M. 1979. *Environmental Chemistry of the Elements.* Academic Press, London.

Eberhardt, L. E. 1987. Ecology of Great Basin Canada goose broods in southcentral Washington, Doctoral Dissertation. Oregon State University, Corvallis, OR, 93 pp.

Eisenbud, M. 1987. *Environmental Radioactivity from Natural, Industrial, and Military Sources*, 3rd edition. Academic Press, Orlando, FL.

Fitzner, R. E. and W. H. Rickard. 1983. Canada goose nesting performance along the Hanford reach of the Columbia River, 1971-1981. *Northwest Sci.* 57:267-272.

Hanson, W. C. and L. L. Eberhardt. 1971. A Columbia River Canada goose population. *Wildl. Monogr. 28*:1-61.

Jaquish, R. E. and R. W. Bryce (eds.). 1989. Hanford Site Environmental Report for Calendar Year 1988, PNL-6825. Pacific Northwest Laboratory, Richland, WA.

Rickard, W. H. and K. R. Price. 1990. Strontium-90 in Canada goose eggshells and reed canary grass from the Columbia River, Washington. *Environ. Monit. Assess. 14*:71-76.

Rokkan. D. K. 1986. UNC Nuclear Industries Reactor and Fuels Production Facilities 1985 Effluent Release Report, UNI 3880. UNC Nuclear Industries, Richland, WA.

Till, J. E. and H. R. Meyer (eds.). 1983. Radiological Assessment - A Textbook on Environmental Dose Analysis, NUREG/CR-3332 (0RNL-5968). Nuclear Regulatory Commission, Washington, DC.

ENVIRONMENTAL MONITORING: THE URANIUM MILL TAILINGS REMEDIAL ACTION PROJECT

H. R. Meyer,[1] J. B. Turner,[1] M. F. Petelka,[1] M. C. Daily,[1] and D. E. Mann[2]

[1]Chem-Nuclear Systems, Inc., Albuquerque, New Mexico

[2]U.S. Department of Energy, Albuquerque, New Mexico

Key Words: *environmental, monitoring, tailings, radon, radium, thorium*

ABSTRACT

The Uranium Mill Tailings Remedial Action Project is the country's most successful remediation program; 5 of 24 large mill-tailings sites are finished, and 7 are underway. From the beginning, Chem-Nuclear Systems, Inc. has been responsible for all radiation protection, cleanup standards verification (EPA, 1983), and environmental monitoring on the project. The data base developed over the last 6 yr is standardized and quality-controlled. Multiple-location and background measurements at each site have quantified radon, ^{226}Ra, and ^{230}Th concentrations, and gamma dose rate. Summaries of preconstruction environmental data and data recorded during and after remedial action are presented. The type and effectiveness of remedial actions performed on each tailings pile are discussed.

INTRODUCTION

The Uranium Mill Tailings Remedial Action Project (UMTRAP) was authorized by Congress to remediate the hazards associated with 24 uranium processing sites, located mostly in the western United States. (Figure 1). Large quantities of uranium mill tailings, finely powdered residues from ore grinding and uranium extraction, remain at each site. Typical amounts range from 500,000 to 5 million tons, originally placed, as a slurry, in large piles on the ground. Many sites also contain mill structures in disrepair. The tailings release radioactive radon gas and, during windy weather, dusts containing ^{226}Ra and ^{230}Th. The purpose of the UMTRA Project is to mitigate potential inhalation hazards to nearby residents and to minimize potential ground-water impacts. Typically, remedial action consists of isolating all tailings, including recovered windblown material, in a single pile, which is covered with clay diffusion barriers and rock armor to prevent release of radon and particulates for 200 to 1000 yr. At certain sites, some tailings were used in the construction of offsite buildings. About 6000 of these properties containing excessive levels of radon gas are also

being remediated. MK-Ferguson Co. (MK-F) is the contractor managing
the majority of the work. Chem-Nuclear Systems, Inc. (CNSI) is a
subcontractor providing radiological services, including environmental
monitoring. The U.S. Department of Energy (DOE), Albuquerque, New
Mexico, manages the UMTRA Project. We will summarize key
environmental monitoring data for certain sites and evaluate the
success of remedial action where it has been completed.

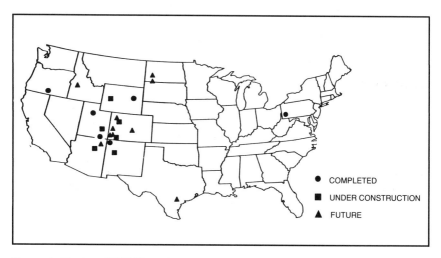

Figure 1. Uranium Mill Tailings Remedial Action Project (UMTRAP) sites. ●, completed;
■, under construction; ▲, future.

All data are subject to written, approved quality controls and routine
onsite auditing. Appropriate standards and calibration techniques
ensure accuracy (Meyer, 1987a). Because the Project involves up to
eight simultaneously managed sites in various parts of the country,
we developed a graphics quality-control monitoring system to quickly
determine if concentrations of selected radionuclides exceed allowable
limits. All sites are linked to Albuquerque using personal computers
and a modem-based intermittent network. Data are analyzed in
Albuquerque using the Paradox 386 database management system
(Borland, Scotts Valley, California) and various peripheral programs.
Graphs of all monitoring data, including running averages and allowable
limits, are routinely reviewed by site, CNSI, and MK-F managers.

MONITORING RADON

When the Project began in 1983, real-time monitoring of radon gas
concentrations in the environment was required because: (1) radon

in the environment had to be maintained below the DOE allowable limit of 3 pCi/L, annual average, and (2) residents at the site perimeter (particularly at the first remediated site in Canonsburg, Pennsylvania), who were concerned about radon levels, needed real-time information to assure their cooperation (Meyer, 1987b). The Eberline RGM-2 (Eberline, Santa Fe, New Mexico) was selected to monitor environmental radon. The instrument is constructed in a large steel box to protect it from the environment. Thirty-seven such instruments are currently in use, at eight sites. The instruments are routinely calibrated at DOE's Technical Measurements Center, Grand Junction, Colorado, and are checked for changes in background count rates at field locations. Electronic and other checks are also performed routinely in CNSI's Albuquerque laboratory. CNSI continuously monitors radon in air at each site, beginning 30 days prior to remedial action and concluding 30 days after the final radon barrier is placed. Remedial action at a site typically takes 2 yr; the RGM-2 integrates radon concentration in air over a 1-hr period. Thus, each monitoring station provides about 20,000 data points during operations. A typical site has four to six RGM at the tailings pile perimeter and in the local community (Figure 2). The 2 to 3 million quality-controlled radon data points to be recorded over the life of the Project represent a considerable resource (Meyer, 1984).

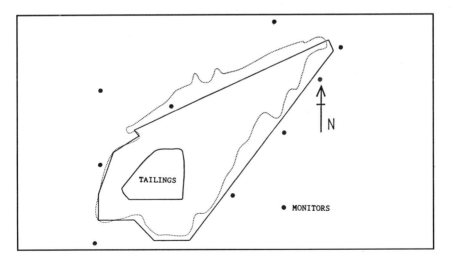

Figure 2. Typical layout of environmental monitors at a Uranium Mill Tailings Remedial Action Project (UMTRAP) Site (Tuba City, Arizona). Dotted line, area of windblown contamination; solid line, official site boundary.

Figure 3 shows radon monitoring data for two of the sites completed to date (Shiprock, New Mexico, and Tuba City, Arizona). Because ^{222}Ra is naturally present from decay of natural uranium-chain isotopes, background levels in air in the United States range from 0.1 to 1.0 pCi/L. Placement of a clay barrier over the Shiprock tailings pile in early 1986 reduced radon concentrations in air to near-background levels. Radon levels in Tuba City were low throughout operations, and were not noticeably affected by barrier placement.

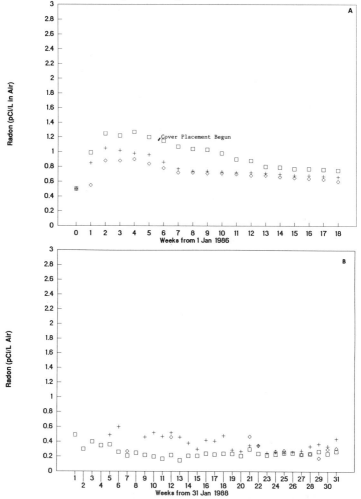

Figure 3. Radon monitoring data. A, Shiprock, New Mexico (concentrations averaged annually); B, Tuba City, Arizona (averaged weekly). Symbols represent three monitoring locations at each site; 3 pCi/L = allowable annual radon concentration.

MONITORING AIR PARTICULATES

When remedial action began, developing a full chemistry laboratory to analyze ^{226}Ra and ^{230}Th was not cost-effective, particularly at remote sites. Instead, we developed a method to monitor the radioactivity of airborne particulates off site under field conditions. Alpha-particle detectors monitor gross alpha activity on glass-fiber filters taken from six to eight continuously operated air samplers, located around a typical site and in any nearby community (Figure 2). The samplers are flow-calibrated routinely and flow-checked twice per week. The alpha-counting systems, either gas-flow proportional counters (both bench-type and fully automated) or zinc sulfide scintillators, are calibrated daily using standard sources. Air concentrations are evaluated twice weekly, and quarterly composites of all filters are shipped to an independent laboratory for chemical dissolution and isotopic analyses by alpha spectrometry. The site-specific relationship between the twice-weekly gross alpha air-concentration measurements and the quarterly isotopic analyses establishes a concentration limit for each site. This approach has passed numerous Project, state, and federal reviews and audits (Skinner, 1985).

Figure 4 shows air-concentration data for two completed Project sites, based on twice-weekly analyses of continuous air samples at six to eight locations on each site. Approximately 100 integrated measurements are made each year at each site and monitoring location. About 40,000 quality-controlled air particulate measurements will thus be available when the Project is completed. Figure 4 shows the effect of remedial action (excavation, relocation into a single pile, and covered with clay, soil, and rock barriers) on radioactive air particulate concentration.

MONITORING ENVIRONMENTAL GAMMA RADIATION LEVELS

Integrated gamma dose is monitored by thermoluminescent dosimeters (TLD). A TLD network is located around each site (Figure 2). Because gamma levels are not expected to vary greatly with time, they are integrated and measured quarterly by Eberline Instrument Corporation's NAVLAP-certified dosimetry program in Albuquerque, New Mexico. Quality control is performed by Eberline's in-house program and checked independently by CNSI's Columbia, South Carolina, laboratory. Comparisons are made of Albuquerque and site-based dose rates (using calibrated pressurized ion chambers to establish gamma fields at each site). Environmental gamma dose has generally remained at near-background levels throughout operations.

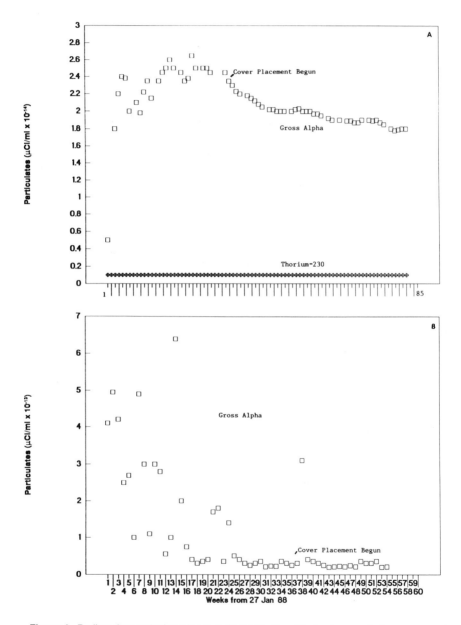

Figure 4. Radioactive particulates in air. A, Shiprock, New Mexico (concentrations averaged annually); B, Tuba City, Arizona (unaveraged). Symbols represent three monitoring locations.

DATA AVAILABILITY

The UMTRA Project provides an opportunity to monitor environmental radioactivity at 24 locations, principally in the western United States. Data are being collected in accordance with standardized, quality controlled procedures, using equipment of suitable accuracy and sensitivity. Individuals interested in access to the detailed data base should contact the authors to determine suitability for their specific purpose. Other data, including worker gamma and air particulate exposure, a worker subset of quarterly urinalyses, and soil cleanup verification results (Gilbert, 1987), including radium in soil and automated gamma scan information, may also be available to researchers on request.

ACKNOWLEDGMENT

Work supported by U.S. Department of Energy under contract DA-AC04843AL18796.

REFERENCES

EPA. 1983. Standards for remedial actions at inactive uranium processing sites; Final role, 40 CFR 192. *Fed. Reg. 48*:590-604.

Gilbert, R. O., M. L. Miller, and H. R. Meyer. 1987. On the design of a sampling plan to verify compliance with EPA standards for radium-226 in soil at uranium mill tailings remedial action sites, p. 77. In: USEPA Conferences on Interpretation of Environmental Data. IV: Compliance Sampling, EPA-230-03-047, October 5-6, 1987. U.S. Environmental Protection Agency, Office of Policy Planning and Evaluation, Washington, DC.

Meyer, H. R. and C. Daily. 1987a. QA verification procedures in uranium mill tailings processing fire remedial actions, p. 12. In: Proceedings, American Society for Quality Control Annual Meeting, Las Vegas, NV, February 9-11, 1987. Convention Records, San Diego, CA.

Meyer, H. R. 1987b. Hazardous and radioactive wastes: Public health issues and concerns. In: Proceedings, American Institute of Chemical Engineers Meeting, Houston, TX, March 1987. American Institute of Chemical Engineers, New York, NY.

Meyer, H. R., D. J. Skinner, J. H. Coffman, and W. J. Arthur. 1984. Environmental protection in the UMTRA Project, p. 216. In: Proceedings of the USDOE Environmental Protection Information Meeting, November, 1984. CONF-841187V2, NTIS, Springfield, VA.

Skinner, D. J. and H. R. Meyer. 1985. Demonstration of 10 CFR 20 air particulate compliance requirements on the UMTRA Project, p. 160. In: Proceedings, Health Physics Society Symposium, Environmental Radiation, January, 1985. Health Physics Society Executive Secretary, Laramie, WY.

TRENDS IN RADIONUCLIDE CONCENTRATIONS FOR WILDLIFE AND FOOD PRODUCTS NEAR HANFORD FOR THE PERIOD 1971-1988

L. L. Cadwell, L. E. Eberhardt, K. R. Price, and D. W. Carlile*

Pacific Northwest Laboratory, Richland, Washington

Key Words: *Radionuclide trends, wildlife, food products, Hanford Site*

ABSTRACT

We evaluated the Hanford environmental data base for trends in radionuclide concentrations in wildlife and food products sampled from 1971 through 1988 on or near the U.S. Department of Energy's Hanford Site in southeastern Washington. Although statistical analyses showed short-term changes, no upward trends in radionuclide concentrations were detected. Many samples showed a significant decline in some radionuclides, particularly for ^{137}Cs. Concentrations of ^{65}Zn also showed a downward trend in many samples.

Cessation of atmospheric testing by the United States and the USSR in 1971 contributed to the decline in radionuclide levels in some samples. Contaminants discharged to the Columbia River at Hanford were reduced after shutdown of the last once-through cooling-water reactor in 1971. A decline in concentrations of ^{65}Zn in oysters from Willapa Bay and ^{60}Co and ^{65}Zn in mountain whitefish from the Hanford Reach of the Columbia River are attributable to reactor closure. There was also an apparent reduction in availability of radiological contamination to Hanford wildlife after decommissioning of waste-water disposal ponds and remediation of contaminated terrestrial sites.

INTRODUCTION

Radiological monitoring has been conducted to document the presence or absence of contaminants on and near the U.S. Department of Energy's Hanford Site and to evaluate radiological impacts from Hanford operations. Environmental monitoring includes annual sampling of wildlife near the 100 and 200 Area nuclear facilities (Figure 1). Food products are collected from nearby and distant farms and from grocery stores. Fish are collected from the Columbia River, which flows through the site. In the past, oysters were also collected downstream at Willapa

---

*Current address: Alaska Department of Fish and Game, Juneau, Alaska.

Bay, near the mouth of the Columbia River. Sampling methods, analytical procedures, and interpretation of results for wildlife, food products, and other sample media are reported annually. (See Jaquish and Bryce, 1989, for the most recent annual report.) We reviewed the last 18 yr (1971 through 1988) of wildlife and food product monitoring data for long-term trends.

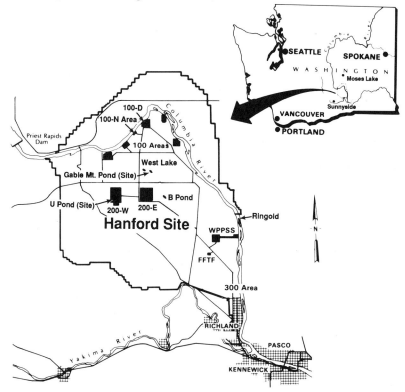

Figure 1. The Hanford Site, southeastern Washington, including 100 and 200 Areas, ponds, and Columbia River.

METHODS

Six wildlife and six food product categories were identified for trend analyses. Wildlife tissue samples include mule deer *(Odocoileus hemionus);* rabbits and hares (collectively referred to as rabbits); upland game birds, including ring-necked pheasants *(Phasianus colchicus)*, California quail *(Callipepla californica)*, and gray partridge *(Perdix perdix);* waterfowl; mice; and mountain whitefish *(Prosopium williamsoni)*. Food products include leafy vegetables, milk, beef, chickens, eggs, and oysters.

Radionuclides evaluated for trends (Table 1) included those of known Hanford origin or of general interest because of their potential for biological transport through food chains. Annual median concentrations (pCi/g wet weight) were used to evaluate the data for wildlife and food products. The median concentration is less sensitive than the mean to extreme values (e.g., unusually high or low values) and is more representative of a central tendency for log-normally distributed radionuclide concentration data.

Table 1. Trends in median radionuclide concentrations in wildlife and food products collected from 1971 through 1988 at or near Hanford.

Radionuclide	Trends		
	Decrease[a]	Undetectable[b]	Unknown[c]
^{137}Cs	Rabbits Mule deer Upland game birds Local milk Beef Oysters	Waterfowl Local eggs	Mice Distant milk Distant eggs Distant leafy vegetables Local leafy vegetables
^{90}Sr	Local milk	Rabbits Mule deer Local leafy vegetables Distant leafy vegetables Beef Local chickens Distant chickens Local eggs	Distant milk Distant eggs
^{65}Zn	Mountain whitefish Local milk Distant milk Oysters	Distant chickens Local chickens	Local leafy vegetables Distant leafy vegetables Local eggs Distant eggs
^{54}Mn			Mice
^{131}I	Local milk Distant milk		
^{60}Co	Mountain whitefish		Mice
$^{239-240}$Pu		Mule deer	

a Significant (P = 0.05) regression analyses and significant (P < 0.05) *t* test for slope.
b Nonsignificant regression analyses.
c Trend direction is unknown because of autocorrelation, small sample sizes, and/or large number of samples below detection limits.

Simple linear regressions were performed on annual median radionuclide concentrations to evaluate trends (increases or decreases through time), rather than to define statistical relationships between concentration and time. If a regression fit was significant, the slope of the regression line was tested (*t* test) to determine if the slope was significantly different from zero. In some cases, median values were log-normally transformed before regression to satisfy assumptions necessary for trend analysis (Gilbert, 1987). Assumptions included normality and independence of errors.

RESULTS AND DISCUSSION

No long-term increases were observed in wildlife or food-product radionuclide concentrations. Some wildlife and food products showed decreasing trends; for others, tests for trends were not statistically significant, and they are listed as "undetectable" (Table 1). Samples that could not be analyzed for trends because they failed to meet test assumptions are listed in Table 1 as having "unknown" trends.

Median annual concentrations of two activation products, ^{60}Co and [65]Zn, declined significantly in mountain whitefish muscle, as did [65]Zn in oysters (Table 1). A rapid decline in ^{60}Co in mountain whitefish was observed from 1971 through 1976 (Figure 2). Median concentrations of [65]Zn in mountain whitefish and oysters decreased from 58.5 and 165 mBq/g (1.58 and 4.46 pCi/g), respectively, in 1971 to 4.1 and 21.5 mBq/g (0.11 and 0.58 pCi/g) in 1973. The declines were attributed to the shutdown in 1971 of the last reactor that discharged primary cooling water to the river. Cushing et al. (1981) documented similar declines in other Columbia River biota following reactor closure.

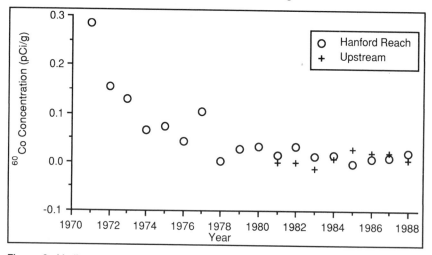

Figure 2. Median concentrations (pCi/g) of ^{60}Co in whitefish muscle collected upstream from Hanford and in Hanford Reach of the Columbia River. To convert to SI units, multiply by 0.037.

From 1981 through 1988, median concentrations of ^{60}Co in mountain whitefish collected upstream of the Hanford Site were similar to those in mountain whitefish in the Hanford Reach (Figure 2). Upstream samples were not collected before 1981.

Median annual concentrations of ^{65}Zn and ^{131}I in milk from local and distant dairies declined significantly, as did ^{137}Cs and ^{90}Sr in local milk from 1971 through 1988 (Table 1). Median annual concentration of ^{65}Zn and ^{131}I in milk from local and distant dairies declined significantly, as did ^{137}Cs and ^{90}Sr in local milk from 1971 through 1988 (Table 1). The decline occurred most rapidly from 1971 through 1976. The pattern was also representative of ^{65}Zn and ^{131}I concentrations in milk. Although autocorrelations in the data prevented trend analysis for ^{137}Cs and ^{90}Sr on milk from distant dairies, the nearly identical patterns for ^{137}Cs in milk at distant and local dairies (Figure 3) suggest that the trend for declining ^{137}Cs observed at local dairies also occurred at distant dairies.

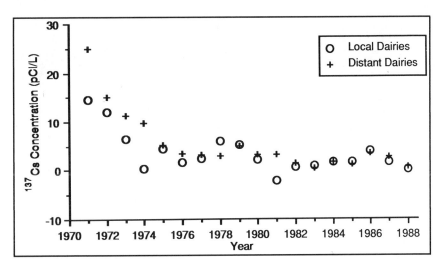

Figure 3. Median concentrations (pCi/L) of ^{60}Co in milk obtained from dairies near the Hanford Site (local) and from distant dairies, from 1971 through 1988. To convert to SI units, multiply by 0.037.

Decreases in radionuclide concentrations in milk are consistent with declining atmospheric fallout subsequent to the 1971 treaty, signed by the United States and the Soviet Union, to limit atmospheric testing of nuclear weapons. Gross beta analyses of atmospheric particulates from eastern Washington from 1971 through 1975 also showed decreasing radioactivity in air (Speer et al., 1976).

Local beef and Willapa Bay oysters showed significant declines in median annual ^{137}Cs concentrations (Table 1). The declines, similar to those in milk, may also reflect decreased fallout subsequent to the 1971 limitations on atmospheric testing of nuclear weapons. Because there were no data, comparisons could not be made with distant or control samples. However, maximum ^{137}Cs concentrations for these foods were low compared with ^{137}Cs concentrations in many types of Hanford wildlife (Table 2), suggesting that the source term was fallout.

Table 2. Maximum radionuclide concentration (pCi/g wet weight)[a] in selected wildlife and food products collected at or near Hanford from 1971 through 1988.

Sample Type	Radionuclide	N	Maximum
Wildlife			
Mule deer	^{137}Cs	91	1.08
Rabbits	^{137}Cs	141	1.94
Upland game birds	^{137}Cs	238	0.09
Mountain whitefish (Hanford)	^{65}Zn	225	1.59
Mountain whitefish (Hanford)	^{60}Co	203	0.28
Waterfowl (Hanford)	^{137}Cs	358	52.3
Food products			
Local milk[b]	^{90}Sr	344	2.35
Local milk[b]	^{65}Zn	1866	19.1
Local milk[a]	^{131}I	1929	0.93
Local milk[a]	^{137}Cs	1868	14.45
Distant milk[a]	^{65}Zn	460	18.1
Distant milk[a]	^{131}I	478	0.81
Local beef	^{137}Cs	107	0.04
Oysters	^{65}Zn	42	4.47
Oysters	^{137}Cs	40	0.04

[a] To convert to SI units (Bq), multiply by 0.037.
[b] pCi/L.

Rabbits, mule deer, and upland game birds on the Hanford Site showed significant declines in ^{137}Cs concentrations in muscle (Table 1). Most animals were collected near the 100 and 200 Areas (Figure 1), which contain nuclear facilities. Maximum cesium values (Table 2) were several orders of magnitude above median values, indicating that some individuals had been contaminated by local sources. However, no control samples were obtained, and it is unclear what fraction of the total ^{137}Cs in these animals resulted from fallout and what fraction may have been of Hanford origin. Declining concentrations of ^{137}Cs in mule deer, rabbits, and upland game birds may reflect a combination of decreased atmospheric fallout since the 1971 Test Ban Treaty and cleanup of surface contamination near Hanford facilities. Since 1980 contaminated ponds and ditches have been drained, and terrestrial sites have been covered with clean soil and stabilized with vegetation (A. R. Johnson, Westinghouse Hanford Company, personal communication).

Concentrations of ^{137}Cs in waterfowl, ^{90}Sr and [239-240]Pu in mule deer, and ^{90}Sr in rabbits from Hanford showed no detectable long-term trends (Table 1). Eberhardt et al. (1989) summarized median and maximum radionuclide concentrations for these animals and noted that samples probably included radioactivity of Hanford origin. Annual median ^{137}Cs concentrations in Hanford waterfowl peaked in the late 1970s and early 1980s and declined thereafter (Figure 4). Data in Eberhardt et al. (1989) also suggest that ^{90}Sr in mule deer bone and [239-240]Pu in deer liver declined after peaking in the late 1970s and early 1980s. Despite the lack of long-term trends, a pattern of decreasing radionuclide concentrations is apparent in some Hanford wildlife from 1978 through 1988. The pattern is consistent with the earlier observation that remediation of environmental surface contaminants may have decreased the availability of radionuclides to some Hanford wildlife.

No detectable trends (Table 1) were apparent in concentrations of ^{137}Cs in local eggs; ^{90}Sr in local and distant leafy vegetables, beef, local and distant chickens, and local eggs; and [65]Zn in distant and local chickens. Annual median radionuclide concentrations in these food products appeared to vary randomly among years (Eberhardt et al., 1989).

The "unknown" trend category (Table 1) resulted from peculiarities of the data that precluded long-term trend analyses. For example, mice could not be analyzed for long-term trends because sampling was conducted for only a few years. Furthermore, samples were from different locations, and sample sizes were generally small. Other examples of samples with unknown trends include ^{137}Cs concentrations in leafy vegetables and distant milk. Many of the median values for leafy vegetables were negative; the analysis for trend was not conducted. The test for autocorrelation for ^{137}Cs in distant milk samples was significant, thus an assumption required to conduct the test for trend was not met, and no test was conducted.

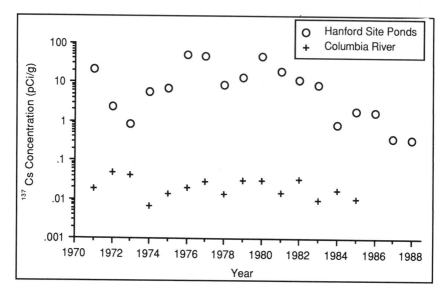

Figure 4. Median concentrations (pCi/g) of ^{60}Co in waterfowl from Hanford ponds and from the Columbia River, from 1971 through 1988. To convert to SI units, multiply by 0.037.

CONCLUSIONS

Radiological data for selected wildlife and food products collected on and near the Hanford Site from 1971 through 1988 were summarized, and annual median values were analyzed for long-term trends. Several wildlife species showed significantly decreasing radionuclide concentrations (Table 1). Milk, beef, and oysters also showed significant declines in several radionuclides. Although declines in radiological concentrations in tissues of biota may result from radioactive decay and biological elimination, long-term declines indicate a decreasing availability of radionuclides in the environment. Three factors probably contributed to the declines: (1) reduced radionuclide input to the Columbia River following the 1971 shutdown of the last once-through cooling reactor at Hanford, which was responsible for declining radionuclide concentrations in fish and oysters; (2) reduced fallout following limitations on atmospheric testing of nuclear weapons, which was responsible for decreased radionuclide concentrations in some food products; and (3) waste-management activities that have apparently reduced the availability of radioactive materials to Hanford wildlife since the late 1970s.

ACKNOWLEDGMENT

Work supported by the U.S. Department of Energy under Contract DE-AC06-76RLO 1830.

REFERENCES

Cushing, C. E., D. G. Watson, A. J. Scott, and J. M. Gurtinsen. 1981. Decrease of radionuclides in Columbia River biota following closure of Hanford reactors. *Health Phys.* *41*:59-67.

Eberhardt, L. E., L. L. Cadwell, K. R. Price, and D. W. Carlisle. 1989. Trends in Radionuclide Concentrations for Selected Wildlife and Food Products Near the Hanford Site from 1971 Through 1988, PNL-6992. NTIS, Springfield, VA.

Gilbert, R. O. 1987. *Statistical Methods for Environmental Pollution Monitoring.* Van Nostrand Reinhold Company, New York.

Jaquish, R. E. and R. H. Bryce. 1989. Environmental Monitoring at Hanford for 1988, PNL-6464. NTIS, Springfield, VA.

Speer, D. R., J. J. Fix, and P. J. Blumer. 1976. Environmental Surveillance at Hanford for CY-1975, BNWL-1979. Pacific Northwest Laboratory, Richland, WA.

IDENTIFICATION OF CONTAMINANTS OF CONCERN IN HANFORD GROUND WATERS

D. R. Sherwood,* J. C. Evans, and R. W. Bryce

Pacific Northwest Laboratory, Richland, Washington

Key Words: *Ground water, Hanford, contaminants*

ABSTRACT

More than 1500 waste-disposal sites have been identified at the U.S. Department of Energy Hanford Site. At the request of the U.S. Environmental Protection Agency, these sites were aggregated into four administrative areas for listing on the National Priority List. Within the four aggregate areas, 646 inactive sites were selected for further evaluation using the Hazard Ranking System (HRS). Evaluation of inactive waste sites by HRS provided valuable insight to design a focused radiological- and hazardous-substance monitoring network. Hanford Site-wide ground-water monitoring was expanded to address not only radioactive constituents but also hazardous chemicals. The HRS scoring process considers the likelihood of ground-water contamination from past disposal practices at inactive waste sites. The network designed to monitor ground water at those facilities identified ^{129}I, ^{99}Tc, ^{90}Sr, uranium, chromium, carbon tetrachloride, and cyanide.

INTRODUCTION

In 1985, the U.S. Department of Energy (DOE) published DOE Order 5480.14 (DOE, 1985) to organize an inactive-waste-site evaluation program paralleling the Comprehensive Environmental Response, Compensation, and Liability Act (CERCLA) of 1980. The Act was used by the U.S. Environmental Protection Agency (EPA) to regulate nongovernment inactive waste sites. Both programs used EPA Hazard Ranking System (HRS) (EPA, 1984) to evaluate relative hazards from inactive hazardous waste sites along five exposure routes: ground water, surface water, air, direct contact, and fire and explosion.

Primary pathways of concern from inactive waste sites at Hanford are through ground and surface waters. The dominant contaminant transport pathway is from inactive waste sites through unsaturated

---

*Current address: U.S. Environmental Protection Agency, Richland, Washington.

sediments to ground water, and through ground water directly to potentially exposed populations or from ground water via surface water to potentially exposed populations.

To identify contaminants, we focused on characteristics of the HRS ground-water route that applied to ground-water monitoring network design. Results will aid future characterization, assessment, and remediation of inactive Hanford waste sites.

HRS GROUND-WATER ROUTE

Evaluation of relative hazard from the ground-water pathway includes five components: observed release, route characteristics, containment, waste characteristics, and target populations. Only four components are considered in a ground-water route evaluation; either observed release or route characteristics are used with the other four components.

Observed release is known or circumstantial evidence for contaminant release into ground water. If no release is observed, route characteristics, including depth to aquifer, net precipitation, unsaturated permeability, and physical state of the waste are used to evaluate potential release to ground water. Containment is defined as a liner or barrier that impedes migration of contaminants from the waste site. Waste characteristics refer to quantity, toxicity, and persistence of each hazardous waste. The final component is the distance to potentially exposed target populations and their ground-water uses. After values are assigned for each property, a ground-water route score is calculated.

APPLICATION TO NETWORK DESIGN

Information on observed releases and waste characteristics was used to select additional monitoring locations and analytes. The observed constituent was used to identify inactive waste sites likely to have contaminated ground water. Direct evidence of observed release at the 646 inactive Hanford waste sites was not available because monitoring wells did not exist near all facilities and ground-water plumes emanating from operating areas overlap, inhibiting source identification. Consequently, to identify suspected releases of contaminated water to the aquifer, observed release was based on volume of liquid disposed at each site, physical size of the facility, and depth to ground water.

Disposal facility area, multiplied by the distance to ground water, provided a total soil-column volume between the waste site bottom and water table. If liquid volume disposed was greater than 10% of total soil-column volume, observed release was assumed. Sites with observed releases were obvious locations for ground-water contamination, and adjacent wells were added to the network. Waste data were reviewed to identify radioactive and chemical substances present in each inactive waste site with an observed release.

A broad spectrum of radioactive and chemical substances potentially present in ground water were identified from inactive-waste-site inventories and knowledge of contaminant mobility. Radionuclide inventories (Stenner et al., 1988) and radionuclide mobility (DOE, 1987) were used to augment the list of radioactive constituents.

Tritium, gross alpha, gross beta, and gamma scans were historically used to monitor radionuclide contamination in Hanford ground waters. Strontium-90 and ^{129}I were also analyzed but only to assess their offsite migration, not to identify their sources. Thus, radionuclide-specific analyses for ^{14}C, ^{63}Ni, and ^{99}Tc were added, and ^{90}Sr and ^{129}I analyses were expanded near observed release sites. If ^{14}C, ^{90}Sr, ^{99}Tc, and ^{129}I were present in liquid waste streams, their high mobility (DOE, 1987) would result in their release to Hanford ground waters.

A slightly different approach was undertaken for hazardous chemicals. Nitrate ion was the contaminant most often investigated in past ground-water monitoring efforts. Some chromium analyses were also performed in the 100 and 300 Areas, but few other chemicals were routinely analyzed. Expansion of hazardous chemical monitoring included establishing background or naturally occurring concentrations of certain constituents and identifying anthropogenic substances from past liquid discharges. Since January 1, 1987, 226 of 484 wells previously monitored for radiological constituents have been analyzed for a broad spectrum of radioactive, inorganic, and organic constituents, including select radionuclides, cations, anions, trace metals, volatile organics, and cyanide (Evans et al., 1988, 1989).

RESULTS

The expanded monitoring network has identified several new contaminants, including ^{99}Tc, carbon tetrachloride, and cyanide, thus establishing a link between past disposal practices and existing contaminant plumes. A more direct link has been established between disposal activities and the presence of ^{129}I, ^{90}Sr, uranium, and chromium in Hanford ground waters.

Technetium-99 was found in wells across the site (Figure 1).
Concentrations greater than the maximum concentration limit (MCL)
of 900 pCi/L (EPA, 1976) were found in the 100-H, 200-East, 200-
West, and 600 Areas. Maximum ^{99}Tc concentration, 29,100 pCi/L, was
detected north of 200-East Area.

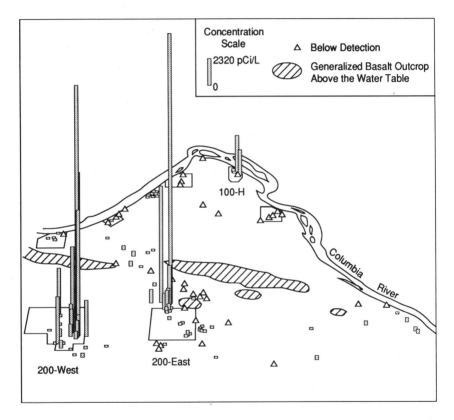

Figure 1. Maximum ^{99}Tc concentrations in ground-water monitoring wells at Hanford,
January 1, 1987 to June 30, 1988 (Evans et al., 1989). Diamonds indicate quantities below
detection limits.

Carbon tetrachloride has been detected beneath much of the 200-
West Area (Figure 2); concentrations exceeded the 5-ppb MCL in 48
wells; maximum concentration, 5550 ppb, was near the Plutonium
Finishing Plant (PFP). An estimated 260,000 kg carbon tetrachloride
was disposed to inactive waste sites servicing the PFP (Stenner et
al., 1988).

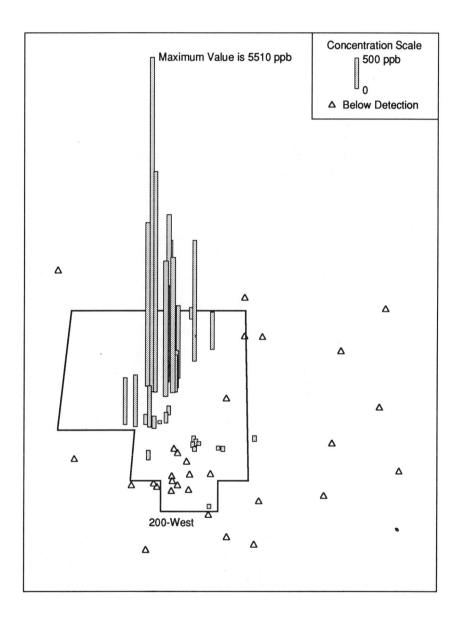

Figure 2. Maximum carbon tetrachloride concentrations in 200-West Area ground-water monitoring wells at Hanford, January 1, 1987 to June 30, 1988 (Evans et al., 1989). Diamonds indicate quantities below detection limits.

Cyanide has been found in isolated locations within the 200-East and 200-West Areas, and north of the 200-East Area (Figure 3), where the maximum concentration was 1120 ppb. There is no cyanide MCL for ground water.

Concentrations of ^{129}I exceeded the 1-pCi/L MCL (EPA, 1976) in a widely dispersed area between the 200-West and 200-East Areas and the Columbia River. Figure 4 shows the relationship between the tritium plume and ^{129}I in Hanford ground waters. Maximum ^{129}I concentration, 87.8 ppb, was detected near the 200-West Area.

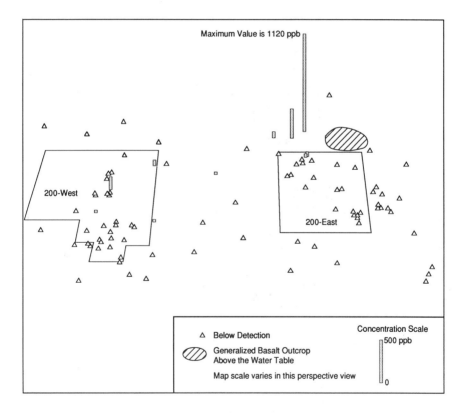

Figure 3. Maximum cyanide concentrations in 200-West Area ground-water monitoring wells at Hanford, January 1, 1987 to June 30, 1988 (Evans et al., 1988). ▨, generalized basalt outcrop above water table. Diamonds indicate quantities below detection limits.

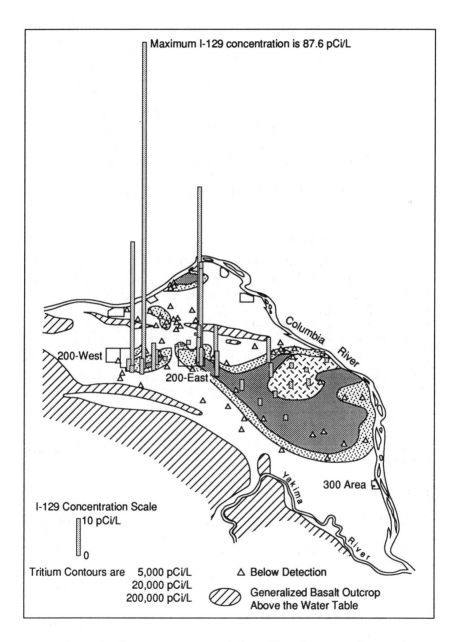

Figure 4. Maximum [129]I concentrations, overlaid on tritium plume map, for ground-water monitoring wells at Hanford, January 1, 1987 to June 30, 1988.

Concentrations of ^{90}Sr greater than the 8-pCi/L MCL (EPA, 1976) were detected throughout the site; most values were only slightly above the MCL. Peak ^{90}Sr concentrations that far exceeded the MCL occurred in the 100-N Area and in isolated locations within the 200-East Area; maximum concentrations were 10,400 and 6270 pCi/L, respectively.

Uranium concentrations in ground water have been monitored for many years throughout the site. Because uranium is a primary product of Hanford operations, its presence is expected. Maximum uranium concentrations, 11,500 pCi/L, were found in the 200-West Area near the uranium purification plant. Elevated concentrations were also found near uranium fuel fabrication waste sites in the 100-H and 300 Areas.

FUTURE APPLICATIONS

The expanded ground-water monitoring program has identified contaminants in Hanford ground waters on a site-wide basis. In many cases, the data link existing ground-water contamination with known sources. Each known source will be the subject of a Remedial Investigation/Feasibility Study under CERCLA or a Facility Investigation/Corrective Measures Study under the Resource Conservation and Recovery Act. Information obtained through the expanded ground-water monitoring program will provide the technical basis to design focused waste-site investigations for inactive waste sites at Hanford.

ACKNOWLEDGMENT

Work supported by the U.S. Department of Energy under Contract DE-AC06-76RLO 1830.

REFERENCES

DOE. 1985. Comprehensive Environmental Response, Compensation and Liability Act, U.S. Department of Energy Order 5480, Chapter 14. U.S. Department of Energy, Washington, DC.

DOE. 1987. Final Environmental Statement: Disposal of Hanford Defense, High-Level, Transuranic and Tank Wastes, DOE/EIS-0113. U.S. Department of Energy, Washington, DC.

EPA. 1976. National Interim Primary Drinking Water Regulations, EPA-570/9-76-003. U.S. Environmental Protection Agency, Office of Water Supply, Washington, DC.

EPA. 1988. Uncontrolled Hazardous Waste Site Ranking System; A Users Manual, HW-10, 40 CFR Part 300, 300.86, Appendix A, pp. 55-84. U.S. Environmental Protection Agency, Washington, DC.

Evans, J. C., D. I. Dennison, R. W. Bryce, P. J. Mitchell, D. R. Sherwood, K. M. Krupka, N. W. Hinman, E. A. Jacobson, and M. D. Freshley. 1988. Hanford Site Ground Water Monitoring for July through December 1987, PNL-6315-2. NTIS, Springfield, VA.

Evans, J. C., R. W. Bryce, and D. R. Sherwood. 1989. Hanford Site Ground Water Monitoring for January through June 1989, PNL-6886-1. NTIS, Springfield, VA.

Stenner, R. D., K. H. Cramer, K. A. Higley, S. J. Jette, D. A. Lamar, T. J. McLaughlin, D. R. Sherwood, and N. C. Van Houten. 1988. Hazard Ranking System Evaluation of CERCLA Inactive Waste Sites at Hanford, PNL-6456. NTIS, Springfield, VA.

AIR-QUALITY MONITORING AT TOXIC WASTE SITES: A HANFORD PERSPECTIVE

G. L. Laws and C. S. Glantz

Pacific Northwest Laboratory, Richland, Washington

Key Words: *Air-quality monitoring, air sampling, remedial investigation, waste sites*

ABSTRACT

Air-quality monitoring is part of remedial investigation (RI) activities at waste sites in the 1100-EM-1 Operable Unit on the U.S. Department of Energy's Hanford Site. Sampling is being conducted for volatile organic compounds, semivolatile organic compounds (including pesticides and polychlorinated biphenyls), metals, and asbestos. Monitoring will be conducted in three phases: before, during, and after intrusive RI activities. Battery-powered monitoring equipment is positioned at one location upwind of each site (to measure background) and, typically, at two locations downwind. Control samples identify contamination that may occur during handling or analysis. All samples are analyzed by approved U.S. Environmental Protection Agency methods. Results from the first monitoring have been assessed and are being used to upgrade sampling and laboratory analysis procedures.

INTRODUCTION

At the U.S. Department of Energy's Hanford Site in Washington State, there are over 1500 waste-disposal sites containing chemical and/or radiological materials. These areas will undergo remedial investigation (RI) under the Comprehensive Environmental Response, Compensation and Liability Act to determine the nature and extent of threat posed to the environment and local population. One pathway by which waste materials affect the environment is through atmospheric transport. Buried liquids can evaporate and release hazardous vapors; particles and fibers can be lifted off the surface and become suspended in the atmosphere. Because of the potential for the atmospheric transport of pollutants, air-quality monitoring is an important RI activity.

Previously, only limited information was available on the operational procedures for conducting air-quality monitoring at waste sites. We will discuss the air-quality monitoring program (sampling equipment, procedures, and analytical techniques) currently being conducted at the first Hanford unit to undergo RI, the 1100-EM-1 Operable Unit.

AIR-QUALITY MONITORING IN THE 1100-EM-1 OPERABLE UNIT

Waste sites in the 1100 Area were grouped into three areas for air-quality monitoring: the Horn Rapids landfill (HRL), the 1100-2 and 1100-3 disposal pits (DSP), and the battery acid pit (BAP). The HRL encompasses about 80,000 m² and contains office and construction wastes, including paint cans, solvents, oils, and asbestos. Wastes are buried to depths of 12 m. The DSP includes two nearly adjacent waste sites covering a combined area of about 5,000 m². These sites were used to dispose of solvents, paints, thinners, antifreeze, degreasers, and construction wastes. The BAP is a small, unlined pit (covering about 30 m²) that was used to dispose of about 15,000 gal of battery acid and other liquid materials.

Because of the variety of wastes at these sites, a wide range of pollutants may be emitted to the atmosphere. Therefore, the air-quality monitoring program at the 1100-EM-1 RI samples for a wide range of volatile organic compounds (VOC), semivolatile organic compounds (SVOC) (including pesticides and polychlorinated biphenyls [PCB]), metals, and asbestos.

Samples are typically collected at three locations near each waste site. Sampling is conducted at only one waste site at a time. One monitoring location is upwind of the site to characterize ambient conditions. Two monitoring locations are typically downwind of the waste site to detect pollutants that may be emitted.

The high costs of field sampling and laboratory analysis severely limit the number of air samples taken. Sampling is therefore conducted only once during each of three monitoring phases: before, during, and after intrusive RI activities are conducted. The first sampling phase was completed at the 1100-EM-1 Operable Unit in the spring of 1989. The second phase is scheduled for fall, 1989. Although one sampling does not allow us to quantify the range of air quality from waste-site emissions, it provides an indication of the magnitude of the impact from RI activities on local air quality and identifies situations where more detailed monitoring may be required.

SAMPLING EQUIPMENT

For air monitoring, four different types of sampling media are used. Air is drawn through each medium using one of two types of sampling devices. Because two waste sites (HRL and DSP) are remote, battery-powered sampling equipment is used.

General Metal Works (Village of Cleves, Ohio) Model PS-1 high-volume samplers are used to collect airborne particulates and SVOC. The battery-driven pump draws air through a 4-in. Teflon® filter (capturing particulates), then through a 3-in.-long, cylindrical glass cartridge containing a polyurethane foam (PUF) plug that adsorbs SVOC, including pesticides and PCB. The pump allows sampling at rates up to 155 L/min. Power is provided by two 12-V rechargeable batteries, connected in series to provide a 24-V power source. The instrument can operate at full power for over 4 hr.

Spectrex (Redwood City, California) Model PAS-3000 personal air samplers are used to sample VOC and asbestos fibers. Asbestos fibers are collected on a 25-mm-dia. filter made from mixed cellulose esters, with an effective pore size of 0.8 μm. The VOC are collected with carbon molecular sieve (CMS) cartridges (Carbotrap model 300, Supelco, Inc., Bellefonte, Pennsylvania). Each stainless-steel cartridge is filled with three specialized adsorbents: Carbotrap C, Carbotrap, and Carbosieve S-III. Glass wool plugs to separate adsorbent materials are packed in the ends of the cartridge. The CMS cartridge is designed to adsorb and desorb all hydrocarbons listed in U.S. Environmental Protection Agency (EPA) Methods TO-1, TO-2, and TO-3 (EPA, 1983), whether present individually or in complex mixtures. Although maximum flow rate through the cartridges exceeds 300 ml/min, rates are adjusted downward (less than 100 ml/min) for most field operations. The sampler can run for 100 hr using a single 12-V battery.

Several alternatives are available for sampling VOC. Two that are common use SUMMA® polished canisters (DBA Molectrics Inc., Inglewood, California) (EPA, 1988) and Tenax® (Enka N.V., The Netherlands) gas chromatography (GC) adsorbent cartridges (EPA, 1984). The SUMMA process modifies the interior of a stainless-steel canister so that it is free of active adsorption sites. To sample, a stainless-steel tube (similar to the cartridge used in the CMS) is filled with the Tenax material, and air is drawn through the tube.

EXPERIMENTAL PROCEDURE AND ANALYSIS

The clean-handling procedures outlined in EPA Methods TO-2 (EPA, 1983) and TO-4 (EPA, 1984, 1986) are used for all sampling equipment. Sampling modules are brought to the field and installed in housings just before a sampling event. Additional modules are taken into the field but are not exposed to outside air to identify potential contamination that may occur during sample handling and analysis.

Calibration checks on sample flow rates are conducted at the beginning and near the end of each sampling event. Events last from 1 to 8 hr, the exact duration depending on meteorological conditions, instrument performance, and anticipated pollutant concentrations. Meteorological conditions are monitored throughout the sampling period using a portable tower equipped with a wind vane, anemometer, and temperature sensor. A datalogger processes information from the meteorological instruments into 5-min averages, stored on cassette tape for later analysis. Samples are placed in clean containers, sealed from contact with outside air, and returned to the laboratory for temporary storage before being transported to other laboratories for analysis.

During analyses, SVOC, PCB, and pesticides are removed from the PUF material via Soxhlet extraction and analyzed using GC and mass spectroscopy (GC/MS) following procedures in EPA Method T0-4 (EPA, 1984, 1986). The Teflon filters are analyzed for particulates and metals by nondestructive X-ray fluorescence. The CMS samples are analyzed using procedures (thermal desorption GC, electron capture, and flame ionization detectors) described in EPA Method T0-2 (EPA, 1983). Asbestos filters are analyzed using phase contrast microscopy.

RESULTS AND DISCUSSION

Data from the first phase of air-quality monitoring in each 1100-EM-1 waste area showed concentrations of several VOC and SVOC that were slightly higher than ambient levels at monitoring locations downwind of the waste sites. Pesticides, PCB, heavy metals, and asbestos fibers were not detected at any sites.

Four improvements are being made in sample handling and analysis for VOC, based on lessons learned during the first phase of monitoring. First, there were impurities in the initial CMS samples, either from incomplete cleaning of the cartridges or too long a delay between cartridge cleaning and use. This problem was corrected through development of more stringent cleaning procedures. Second, several VOC for which calibration standards were not prepared were detected in the CMS samples. Additional calibration will be conducted to correct this problem. Third, to prevent the CMS cartridges from being overloaded with certain compounds, shorter exposure times (about 1 hr) will be used in the second monitoring phase, and the performance of a multiple-segment CMS cartridge will be evaluated. Fourth, a measurable amount of VOC may be adhering to airborne particulates and is therefore not being collected in the CMS cartridge. To address this concern, we will analyze a portion of our Teflon filter samples for VOC.

Two improvements are being made in the sampling and analysis procedures for SVOC. First, PUF sampling needs to be conducted for longer periods of time. Sampling periods of only 1 to 3 hr were typical during the first monitoring phase. Second, to improve detection of PCB, we will conduct tests in which a sorbent material (such as Tenax) is sandwiched between layers of PUF material (Lewis and Jackson, 1982).

Slightly higher concentrations of some compounds were commonly detected at several upwind monitoring locations than at corresponding downwind locations. This may reflect local automotive emissions or nearby industrial sources. Upwind monitors are closer to these sources than those downwind. This situation will be considered in future analyses.

ACKNOWLEDGMENTS

The authors are indebted to Roy Gephart, Chuck Veverka, and Richard Lee, of PNL; Loren Thompson of U.S. Testing; and Maureen Hamilton of NHS Inc. for assistance during the course of our work. Work supported by the U.S. Department of Energy (DOE) under contract DE-AC-06-76RLO 1830.

REFERENCES

EPA. 1983. Quality Assurance Handbook for Air Pollution Measurement Systems, Volume II of Ambient Specific Methods, EPA/600/4-77-027a, Section 2. U.S. Environmental Protection Agency, Washington, DC.

EPA. 1984. Compendium of Methods for the Determination of Toxic Organic Compounds in Ambient Air, EPA/600/4-84-041. U.S. Environmental Protection Agency, Washington, DC.

EPA. 1986. Supplement to EPA/600/4-84-041: Compendium of Methods for the Determination of Toxic Organic Compounds in Ambient Air, EPA/600/4-87-006. U.S. Environmental Protection Agency, Washington, DC.

EPA. 1988. Compendium Method T0-14, The Determination of Volatile Organic Compounds (VOCs) in Ambient Air Using SUMMA Passivated Canister Sampling and Gas Chromatographic Analysis. U.S. Environmental Protection Agency, Research Triangle Park, NC.

Lewis, R. G. and M. D. Jackson. 1982. Modification and evaluation of a high-volume air sampler for pesticides and semivolatile industrial organic chemicals. *Anal. Chem.* 4:592-594.

AUTOMATION OF GEOPHYSICAL SURVEYS USED IN ASSESSMENT OF HAZARDOUS WASTE

B. A. Berven, J. E. Nyquist, M. S. Blair, C. A. Little, and R. B. Gammage

Oak Ridge National Laboratory, Oak Ridge, Tennessee

Key Words: *Instrumentation, survey, geophysics, computer applications*

ABSTRACT

We recently merged two technologies to automate the geophysical survey process. We used the terrain conductivity meter (Geonics EM-31) to measure subsurface conductivity and detect anomalies such as water-filled trenches or buried water or gas lines. An ultrasonic ranging and data system was developed to locate a surveyor in a specified area, using triangulation with ultrasonic time-lapse positioning. The surveyor's position was transmitted once per second to a microcomputer in the field. Simultaneously, the instantaneous measurement taken by the surveyor's portable instrument was transmitted to the microcomputer, using a radiofrequency link. Up to 3600 paired measurements and locations can be stored in the microcomputer for hourly analysis. This is a significant advance over conventional techniques because more data can be stored with fewer errors. Furthermore, the data can be analyzed in the field. Output from the analysis includes report-ready tables, two-dimensional contour plots, and three-dimensional mesh plots. These plots show areas of subsurface conductivity while investigators are in the field; additional data can be obtained (if necessary) quickly and cost-effectively.

INTRODUCTION

The Ultra Sonic Ranging and Data System (USRADS) was originally developed to automate the radiological surveys and facilitate collection of radiological data cost-effectively and accurately. More recently, the USRADS technology has been merged with commercially available geophysical devices to automate geophysical surveys at hazardous-waste sites. In this paper we describe each technology and results of combining them.

USRADS SYSTEM DEVELOPMENT

Methodology

The distance between two points can be ascertained by measuring the speed of sound in air (approximately 340 m/sec). The position on a grid from which an ultrasonic signal is transmitted may be determined by measuring the delay in reception at microphones (stationary receivers) at known locations within the grid.

USRADS uses an ultrasonic signal emitted from a backpack carried by a surveyor in the field (Figure 1). A portable computer (PC) in the field interfaces with the master receiver, which is tuned to 17 specific radiofrequency (rf) bands. As the ultrasonic signal is received by the 15 stationary receivers, each a unique rf signal to the master receiver, the position of the stationary receiver is determined by the software program in the PC. The PC computes the position of the surveyors, using the time delay in signal reception from the stationary receivers. The 16th rf channel transmits the measurement from the portable instrument carried by the surveyor. A 17th rf channel provides information from the PC to the surveyor about the system status (e.g.: Is the PC interacting with the master receiver? Are at least three stationary receivers "hearing" the ultrasonic signal?). The position is computed, and instrument measurement is recorded each second.

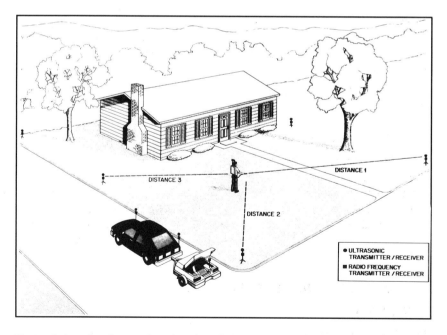

Figure 1. Locating the surveyor by triangulating delay-in-flight of ultrasonic signal from surveyor's backpack to ultrasonic receivers in survey area.

The set-up requires system calibration to determine the speed of sound in air under the atmospheric conditions of the survey. The location of the stationary receivers must also be specified. Calibration is achieved by setting a second portable crystal at a fixed distance from a stationary receiver. The system is turned on for 30 sec (e.g., 30 measurements), and an algorithm in the PC calculates the time of flight of sound in air.

A schematic of the area to be surveyed may be loaded into the PC memory prior to the survey. At least two points on the schematic are identified on the area to be surveyed. Other stationary receivers are placed relative to these fixed locations, so that locations of all stationary receivers are stored in the PC memory. Stationary receivers are placed so that a surveyor can see at least three of them at any time. The maximum effective distance between a surveyor and a stationary receiver is about 80 m.

System set-up usually takes 20 to 30 min. Two people are required to conduct the survey; one operates the PC and master receivers, the other conducts the survey. The PC operator monitors progress by watching the PC display; a point appears once per second on the schematic. The PC operator can then inform the surveyor if an area being surveyed has not received adequate coverage. As the surveyor scans the area, the PC reads time-of-flight data from the 15 stationary receivers once per second, determines which signals are valid, computes the surveyor's location, plots the location on the PC display, and stores all raw data.

USRADS Hardware

The USRAD system has five primary hardware components. The surveyor's backpack contains the ultrasonic transmitter, the radiation survey measurement interface, the rf telemetry link to the PC, and a hand-held terminal with a microcomputer chip. The ultrasonic transmitter is a lead-zirconate-titanate crystal cylinder (5.58 cm diameter by 3.67 cm height) with a hollow core. The natural resonating frequency of this crystal is 19.5 kHz, pulsed for 10 msec per second. A specific customized interface was developed to allow the individual electric pulses processed in the portable radiation detection survey instrument to sum for 1 sec. The pulses are then routed to the rf link for transmission to the master receiver at the start of the next ultrasonic pulse. The embedded PC, the master timing device for the system, is operated by the surveyor using a hand-held terminal.

The PC contains 640K random access memory, a math coprocessor, and hard disc. A plug-in interface card was custom-designed to automatically enter data from the master receiver into the PC. A portable generator provides power for the PC and master receiver.

USRADS Software

A digitized schematic of the area to be surveyed can be stored in and displayed on the PC, using commercially available computer-assisted drafting software. Data are added to this information during the survey. As the surveyor traverses the area, past and present positions are displayed. Software programs check incoming information and alert the PC operator and surveyor if errors are detected in the survey or position data. All data are permanently stored on the hard disk every 30 sec.

Data may be analyzed in the field using several software packages. Real-time location display assures the surveyor that sufficient data are obtained to characterize the area. Data may be viewed in several formats. Raw data are converted to appropriate units and displayed or printed in tabular or graphic format.

TERRAIN CONDUCTIVITY MEASUREMENTS

The terrain conductivity instrument (EM-31) is a valuable tool in geophysics because it responds to any change in the average electrical conductance of the ground. Examples of such effectors are: buried metal, soil moisture and clay content, and chemicals in ground water, such as salts and metal ions. The instrument has been used in hazardous-waste surveys to locate trenches, burial areas, and changes in subterranean formations.

Operation

The EM-31 terrain conductivity device (Figure 2) was developed by Geonics (Mississauga, Ontario, Canada). A transmitter coil at one end broadcasts an alternating electromagnetic field that induces electrical eddy currents in the ground. A receiver coil in the other end detects both the primary field generated by the transmitter and the secondary field generated by eddy currents induced in the ground. The eddy currents create an alternating magnetic field that is the same frequency but is shifted in phase and reduced in amplitude compared to the transmitted wave; the more conductive the ground, the larger the eddy current and the larger the secondary field. The ratio of secondary field to primary field strength is used to calculate electrical conductivity of the ground. Depth of induced eddy currents, and hence survey depth, is controlled by the spacing between transmitter and receiver coils. Coil separation is fixed at 3.66 m in the EM-31, limiting maximum sensing depth to about 3 m.

Figure 2. Surveyor uses terrain conductivity instrument to locate underground objects. Ultra Sonic Ranging and Data System (USRADS) automates geophysical survey of hazardous-waste sites.

For homogeneous soils, the amplitude of the electric currents induced by the EM-31's transmitter is directly proportional to the electrical conductivity of the soil. When buried objects are present, however, the EM-31's response is a function of object size, depth, orientation, and electrical conductivity, as well as the electrical conductivity of the surrounding soil. EM-31 data alone cannot fully characterize the object; in complex areas, interpretation is limited to contouring or plotting profiles of the data and denoting departures from background.

Background

The EM-31/USRAD system was used to detect waste trenches in the 93,000-m^2 solid-waste storage area 4 (SWSA 4) at Oak Ridge, Tennessee. From 1951 to 1959, the landfill accepted low-level radioactive waste, including paper, glassware, scrap metal, laboratory-animal carcasses, and large pieces of equipment. Most waste was buried in trenches ranging from 15-122 m long, 29 m wide, and 2-4 m deep. Disposal methods at the time were inadequate: compacting the fill with backhoes and bulldozers ruptured some canisters containing radioactive waste; fill material was more permeable than the surrounding clayey wastes; the burial ground sloped steeply, and some trenches were dug along a dip. Water entered the uphill end of the trench, flowed along the trench, and pooled until the bottom end filled. Contaminated seeps formed at the surface, as in a water-filled bathtub that has been tipped on end. These trenches are of special concern because they bring contaminated leachate to the surface, where it flows rapidly above ground to nearby streams and is carried off site. In contrast, contaminant transport by ground water in this area is very slow.

Surveying

Trenches were identified and surveyed, and coordinates were digitized into the USRAD system. Using the EM-31/USRAD system (Figure 2), the surveyor took continuous measurements while traversing the area, with about 1.5 m distance between passes.

Survey Results

An isopleth map of data from SWSA 4 is shown in Figure 3. The contoured, in-phase data clearly show the trench responsible for the seep, as well as the smaller hot spot, running roughly west to east, along the predominant ground slope. Other linear anomalies run from northwest to southeast; they are presumably also trenches but are probably drier and may contain less metal. For certain configurations of source coil, receiver coil, and buried metal object, the EM-31 will read zero or may even report negative conductance, thus explaining the small, localized conductivity lows seen occasionally over the trenches.

The general course of the trench in question could also be traced by following a 10-cm depression, probably caused by settling of trench fill material. An advantage of the USRAD system is that it can also be used as a straightforward surveying instrument. The computer logs the surveyor's position while "walking the outline" of a building, the edges of a road, a fence line, etc.

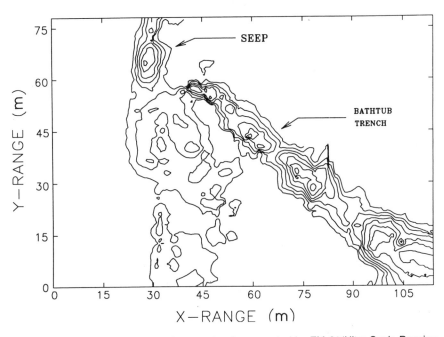

Figure 3. Isopleth map of hazardous-waste site generated by EM-31/Ultra Sonic Ranging and Data System (USRADS).

SUMMARY

The EM-31/USRAD system was successfully used to map an underground trench. Data used to generate a high-quality isopleth contour map were introduced directly into a field microcomputer. Although initially time-consuming, setting up the system prior to the survey has been reduced to about 30 min.

We believe the EM-31/USRAD system will significantly enhance previously available geophysical techniques that provide information about subterranean physical formation. By automating survey techniques, more data can be introduced directly into a computer, free from errors of transcription. The process saves time, produces high-quality data, and makes surveying more cost-effective.

ACKNOWLEDGMENT

Work sponsored by Division of Facility and Site Decommissioning Projects, U.S. Department of Energy, under contract DC-AC05-84OR-21400 with Martin Marietta Energy Systems, Inc.

SAFETY-NET CONCEPT—AN EXTRA STEP IN ENVIRONMENTAL MONITORING

L. E. Sage,[1] M. Kachur,[1] K. E. Shank,[2] and J. Palms[3]

[1] The Academy of Natural Sciences of Philadelphia, Division of Environmental Research, Philadelphia, Pennsylvania

[2] Environment and Chemistry Group, Pennsylvania Power & Light Company, Allentown, Pennsylvania

[3] Physics Department, Emory University, Altanta, Georgia and Georgia State University, Atlanta, Georgia

Key Words: *Monitoring, ecosystem, radionuclide, pathway*

ABSTRACT

In 1979, a monitoring program, designed by the Academy of Natural Sciences, was implemented at the Pennsylvania Power and Light Company nuclear station in rural Pennsylvania. The program had three objectives: (1) provide an independent level of public confidence concerning the ecological significance of radionuclides released to the environment; (2) understand the transport and fate of radionuclides in the environment; (3) develop monitoring methods that are responsive to cumulative radiation in the environment.

This program focuses on biological receptors that concentrate radionuclides and increase detection sensitivity in all segments of the environment. The aquatic environment is monitored in the conventional manner by sampling fish tissues and in a less traditional manner by sampling the finer river sediments and periphytic diatoms. The terrestrial environment is monitored by sampling home vegetable gardens, forest vegetation, lichens, and game mammals. A primary goal is to establish ecological linkages, for example, between radionuclides, tree leaves, leaf litter, humus, and fungi. These linkages extend, through food, to game mammals, thence to humans. Eight years of experimental results are presented.

INTRODUCTION

The Academy of Natural Sciences of Philadelphia, in collaboration with Emory University of Atlanta, Georgia, developed an ecological monitoring and research program for the Pennsylvania Power and Light Company at its Susquehanna Steam Electric Station (SSES), Berwick, Pennsylvania (Palms et al., 1989). The program is site specific, based on ecological characterization of the region, and is an adjunct to the Technical Specifications Radiological Environmental Monitoring

75

Program (REMP) for the SSES. Although both programs assess the possible environmental impact of station operations, the adjunct "Safety Net Program" provides an independent, academic assessment of radionuclide releases to the environment from SSES by scientists from five academic institutions. The program is charged with expanding our understanding of the environmental fate of radionuclides, especially in food pathways leading to people (Boone et al., 1981); the hypothetical dose to people is calculated for relevant components. The program also develops innovative techniques for monitoring radionuclides near a nuclear power station.

The greatest value of continuous monitoring, and the principal focus of the Safety Net Program, is the ability to examine environmental trends relative to potential impacts of the facility. To provide preoperational data, the program was initiated several years before the station became operational. Data are examined yearly across stations, and for selected stations across years, to distinguish between short-term fluctuation and long-term trends. Many biological receptors that have been studied since 1979 were chosen for their efficiency in accumulating radionuclides and their role in radionuclide transport to people. Through pilot studies, environmental components which prove effective as monitoring tools are incorporated in the program design; those which prove ineffective are eliminated.

RESULTS

Because the majority of controlled radionuclide releases from SSES are waterborne and discharged into the Susquehanna River, we monitored radionuclides in the aquatic environment to determine their fate and assess pathways that could lead to people. Flocculated river sediments (floc) and periphyton (mainly diatoms) growing on glass slides in diatometers are highly efficient accumulators of radionuclides (ANSP, 1989). Comparison of SSES monthly waterborne release data with mean monthly radionuclide concentrations in periphyton and floc collected 400 m downriver from the water discharge diffuser pipe indicates the general bioaccumulation of anthropogenic radionuclides (Figure 1). Accumulation by periphyton was more efficient than that by floc (Palms et al., 1989). Aquatic components that were less effective in accumulating radionuclides included coarse sediments, aquatic insects, freshwater mussels and crayfish; these are no longer sampled on a regular basis.

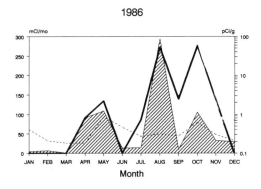

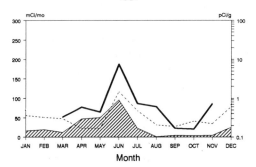

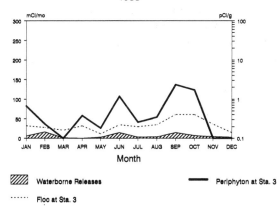

Figure 1. Mean concentrations (pCi/g dry wt), by month, for gamma-ray-emitting anthropogenic radionuclides (mCi) in flocculated sediment and periphyton samples collected near the Susquehanna Steam Electric Station, Pennsylvania, 1986-1988.

Because fish are consumed by people, they provide a direct radiological pathway to people. Representative carnivorous, omnivorous, and benthic feeder fish are sampled, and these tissues are analyzed; only low levels of anthropogenic radionuclides have been detected. In 1988, the hypothetical dose to people of 0.18 mrem/kg (wet weight) of fish consumed (Palms et al., 1989) was almost entirely from naturally occurring radionuclides.

Airborne releases from SSES have been insignificant; to date, few, if any, anthropogenic radionuclides attributable to station operations have been detected in the various terrestrial components monitored. Controlled experimental garden plots were planted and maintained consistent with regional gardening practices. Surface soil and the edible portions of beans, cabbage, carrots, corn, potatoes, tomatoes, and several leafy vegetable crops were sampled from three plots around the perimeter of the facility and at a control location. For these items, the dose to people in 1988 ranged from 0.041 mrem/kg (wet) of corn consumed to 0.16 mrem/kg (wet) of cabbage consumed (Palms et al., 1989) and was also due almost entirely to naturally occurring radionuclides.

Various forest studies were useful in determining radionuclide transfer through environmental pathways and, ultimately, to people. In 1986, upper-canopy-level leaves from trees collected fallout radionuclides following the Chernobyl accident in the Soviet Union (Figure 2A and B). Wash-off by rains and autumn leaf fall transported radionuclides to litter on the forest floor. Gradual decomposition of leaf fall to compact humus concentrated radionuclides per unit volume. Naturally occurring and anthropogenic radionuclides were incorporated by fungal mycelia growing in humus and were concentrated in fruiting structures, e.g., mushrooms (Figure 3). If a human consumed mushrooms with the maximum concentration of radionuclides measured in 1988, a dose of 0.49 mrem/kg (wet) would be received, with ^{137}Cs being the major contributor to that dose (Palms et al., 1989).

Through other studies, transfer of radionuclides through the forest ecosystem was traced further up the food chain (Figure 3). Literature sources (Flyger and Gates, 1982) and gut analyses (ANSP, 1989) confirm that gray squirrels eat fungi. Radionuclide concentrations were often greater in squirrels than in the fungi they ate, suggesting probable biomagnification. A pilot study is currently underway using lichens as a biomonitor of airborne radionuclide deposition. Lichens are effective bioaccumulators, as demonstrated by their accumulation of radio-nuclides resulting from the Chernobyl accident.

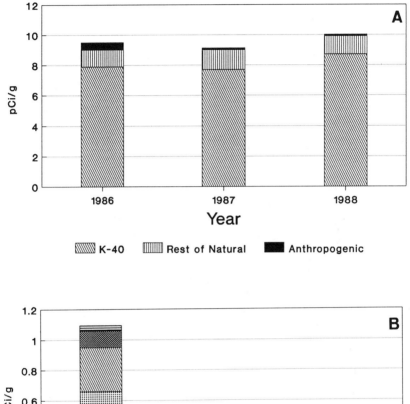

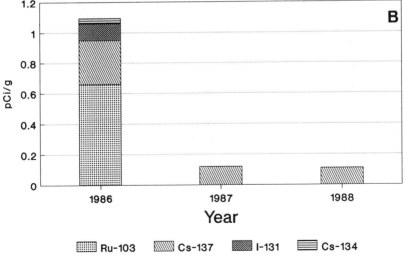

Figure 2. Annual mean concentrations (pCi/g dry wt) of: A, gamma-ray-emitting radionuclides and B, gamma-ray-emitting anthropogenic radionuclides in canopy leaves collected near the Susquehanna Steam Electric Station, Pennsylvania, 1986-1988.

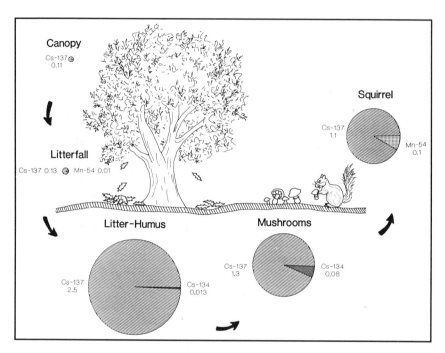

Figure 3. Annual mean concentrations (pCi/g dry wt) of gamma-ray-emitting anthropogenic radionuclides in canopy leaves, litterfall, litter-humus, mushroom, and squirrel muscle samples collected near the Susquehanna Steam Electric Station, Pennsylvania, 1988.

DISCUSSION

Nuclear generation of electrical power has met public resistance even though it has distinct environmental and economical advantages over other power generation options. Recently, there have been calls for corporate environmentalism, defined as attitude and performance commitments that place corporate environmental stewardship in line with public desires and expectations. To meet the energy needs of an expanding population, the electric power industry must convince an environmentally concerned public that industry seeks an environmental partnership. Integrating long-term studies of biological systems into site-specific environmental monitoring programs can provide useful and innovative approaches to determining the environmental fate of radionuclides, especially in food pathways leading to people. Such programs have scientific value and also provide objective information to the public.

ACKNOWLEDGMENT

Dr. Ruth Patrick of the Academy of Natural Sciences of Philadelphia coordinated the development of the original program and directed it from 1979 through 1986.

REFERENCES

ANSP. 1989. Radiological and Ecological Studies in the Vicinity of the Susquehanna Steam Electric Station for the Pennsylvania Power and Light Company, Report No. 89-15, 490 pp. Academy of Natural Sciences of Philadelphia, Philadelphia, PA.

Boone, F., Y. Ng, and J. Palms. 1981. Terrestrial pathways of radionuclide particulates. *Health Phys.* *41*:735-747.

Flyger, V. and J. E. Gates. 1982. Fox and gray squirrels-*Sciurus niger, S. carolinensis,* and allies, pp. 209-229. In: *Wild Mammals of North America.* Johns Hopkins University Press, Baltimore, MD.

Palms, J. M., B. K. Tanner, and R. N. Coleman. 1989. Radiological and Ecological Studies in the Vicinity of the Susquehanna Steam Electric Station, Report EMP-ANSP-89-1. Emory University, Atlanta, GA.

REGULATORY REQUIREMENTS FOR GROUND-WATER MONITORING NETWORKS AT HAZARDOUS-WASTE SITES

J. F. Keller

Pacific Northwest Laboratory, Richland, Washington

Key Words: *Ground water, monitoring, hazardous waste*

ABSTRACT

In the absence of an explicit national legislative mandate to protect ground-water quality and because there is no coordination between federal and state agencies, those responsible for hazardous-waste management and cleanup must utilize a number of statutes and regulations as guidance for detecting, correcting, and preventing ground-water contamination. For example, the current regulatory framework provides no clear guidance for compliance. I will present an integrated approach to protect ground-water resources through the use of various standards and classifications, based on a comprehensive regulatory and policy analysis. Information presented can be used to develop ground-water quality protection programs, assess regulatory compliance, and characterize sites for potential remediation and corrective action. Regulation-based ground-water monitoring networks can be developed to address these concerns in a technically feasible yet cost-effective manner.

BACKGROUND

About half the U.S. population depends on ground water for drinking. Contaminated ground water has been found in every state (The Conservation Foundation, 1987), underscoring the need to protect this resource. Owners and operator of hazardous-waste sites will be required to develop programs to monitor nearby ground-water sources. Contamination may not be evident for years after waste disposal. Ground water is an important environmental pathway that extends beyond hazardous-waste site boundaries by connecting with noncontaminated ground and surface waters.

Ground-water monitoring programs at hazardous-waste sites (both active and inactive) must integrate site-specific technical needs with regulatory requirements. Monitoring requirements for each site must be determined by a team of hydrologists, geologists, regulatory analysts, and other experts. This team should understand the regulatory and technical needs, choose regulatory standards and classifications most suitable to the specific situation, and initiate discussions with regulators to develop the best monitoring program to best protect the resource.

Many federal and state environmental pollution control statutes and regulations are relevant to such programs. Statutes and regulations reviewed in this paper include the Resource Conservation and Recovery Act (RCRA, 1984; the Comprehensive Environmental Response, Liability, and Compensation Act (CERCLA, 1986); the Safe Drinking Water Act (SDWA, 1986); the Clean Water Act (CWA, 1987); the Low Level Radioactive Waste Policy Act (LLRWPA, 1980); and the Nuclear Waste Policy Act (NWPA, 1982).

SPECIFIC STATUTES AND REGULATIONS

RCRA established monitoring requirements for hazardous and solid-waste facilities that might leach contaminants into ground water. Under RCRA, operators of such facilities must implement programs to determine the site's impact on ground-water quality. RCRA contains guidelines for establishing ground-water monitoring systems, applying protection standards, and determining points of compliance (EPA, 1988a).

CERCLA requires ground-water monitoring in connection with cleanup activities. Monitoring begins when the site is characterized to determine type, rate, and extent of contamination. Monitoring continues through planning stages to provide information necessary to design a site cleanup plan. After cleanup, ground-water monitoring is needed to determine if it was a success (EPA, 1988b).

The SDWA protects drinking water by setting standards (SDWA, 1986). The standards are often used to ensure that ground-water protection is appropriately considered at active and inactive hazardous-waste sites (CERCLA, 1986). Strategies, policies, and guidelines such as those developed under the wellhead protection (SDWA, 1986) and the sole-source aquifer programs of SDWA (EPA, 1988c) can be used to develop comprehensive ground-water cleanup and protection programs.

The CWA is the U.S. Environmental Protection Agency's (EPA) mechanism for helping states develop and implement ground-water protection strategies. In addition to surface-water standards, the CWA contains guidelines for controlling and monitoring discharges to surface waters from a single point (point source discharge). Recent amendments to the CWA authorized EPA to establish a program for managing discharges in surface waters from multiple sources (nonpoint source).

The LLRWPA implements regulations (EPA, 1988d) apply to release of radionuclides into ground water. The regulations are of particular interest to managers of facilities handling radioactive or mixed radioactive wastes. NWPA requirements apply to release of high-level or transuranic radionuclides into ground water (NRC, 1988). In addition to regulatory requirements, operators must understand the technical requirements associated with their specific hazardous-waste site.

TECHNICAL REQUIREMENTS

To evaluate potential migration of hazardous-waste constituents from the site to an aquifer, the following must be determined:

- water balance: precipitation, evapotranspiration, runoff, and infiltration;
- unsaturated zone characteristics: geologic materials, physical properties, and depth to ground water;
- saturated zone characteristics: geologic materials, physical properties, quantity and chemical quality, rate of ground-water flow, and ground-water discharge points;
- proximity of facility to supply wells or to surface water: proximity of users and rate at which ground water is withdrawn;
- volume, physical, and chemical characteristics of waste, including potential for migration and behavior and persistence of contaminants in the ground-water environment;
- hydrogeological characteristics of site and surrounding land;
- interaction among ground-water systems and between ground-water and surface-water systems.

The following must also be determined: (1) current and future ground-water or surface-water uses, including any established water-quality standards; (2) existing quality of ground or surface water, including other contaminant sources and their cumulative impact on water quality; (3) potential for health risk; (4) potential for damage to ecological systems, including wildlife, crops, vegetation, and physical structures; (5) persistence and permanence of potential adverse effects (EPA, 1988a).

REGULATORY REQUIREMENTS

Regulatory requirements for a monitoring program at hazardous-waste sites will be discussed in terms of ground-water classifications and protection standards. Both classifications and applicable standards must be understood to design a comprehensive ground-water protection program.

Ground-Water Classifications

Classifications from EPA, the SDWA, and the LLRWPA are available in a general guidance document (EPA, 1986). EPA's proposed hierarchical protection policy is based on the value, use, and vulnerability of potentially affected ground water. This classification system affects the level of protection or remediation to be applied under RCRA and CERCLA. For example, in certain aquifer classifications, CERCLA may require that the water be cleaned to drinking quality. EPA estimates that 83 to 94% ground-water classification determinations would be in this category.

The SDWA also contains classifications under its wellhead protection area program (SDWA, 1986) that relate to water entering public wells. Individual states must develop programs to protect such water supplies from contamination.

Under the LLRWPA, proposed standards require that low-level waste (LLW) be managed and disposed of so that radioactivity levels in certain ground-water classifications do not increase (EPA, 1988d).

Table 1 gives ground-water classifications, standards, and requirements associated with each statute scheme. The CWA, CERCLA, RCRA, and NWPA do not specifically address ground-water classification systems.

Ground-Water Protection Standards

The SDWA and RCRA regulations could be used to ensure that ground-water protection is appropriately considered at active and inactive hazardous-waste sites (Table 2). CERCLA relies on applicable or relevant and appropriate requirements (ARAR) as standards. Standards presented in Table 2 could be used as ARAR for cleanup of inactive waste sites. Although CWA standards are not particularly useful for ground-water monitoring, they will be useful for monitoring ground- and surface-water connections. Temperature, biological oxygen demand, turbidity, pH, and total coliform count are examples of CWA standards. Although the NWPA contains no specific standards, the allowable dose of 25 mrem/yr for all pathways will be important to managers responsible for radioactive mixed-waste sites. The LLRWPA contains no specific standards but limits exposure for one classification to 4 mrem/yr (Table 1).

Table 1. Ground-water classifications as given by U.S. Environmental Protection Agency (EPA), Safe Drinking Water Act (SDWA), and Low-Level Radioactive Waste Policy Act (LLRWPA).

Organization or Act	Standards	Classification Review Area[a]
Environmental Protection Agency Groundwater Classification Guidelines		
Class I	Drinking water	2-mile radius[b]
Class II	Drinking water	2-mile radius[b]
Class III	Less than drinking water (i.e., total dissolved-solids concentration over 10,000 mg/L or contaminated by naturally occurring conditions).	2-mile radius[b]
Safe Drinking Water Act		
Wellhead Protection Program	None to date[c]	2-mile radius
Sole Source Aquifer Program	None to date	None to date
Low Level Radioactive Waste Policy Act		
Class I	No increase in radioactivity levels	None
High-Yield Class II	No increase above 4 mrem per year	None
All Other Class II	No increase above 25 mrem per year	None
Class III	No more than 25 mrem per year	None

[a] A defined surface location and the underlying subsurface to which ground-water classification schemes are applied.
[b] Expanded for sites with high ground-water flow velocities.
[c] Individual states will determine wellhead protection area requirements.

Table 2. Examples of potential ground-water protection standards as given by the Resource Conservation and Recovery Act (RCRA) and the Safe Drinking Water Act (SDWA).[a]

	Maximum Amounts Allowable		
	RCRA[b,c]	SDWA[d]	
	(mg/L)	MCL (mg/L)[e]	MCLG (mg/L)[e]
Heavy Metals			
Arsenic	0.05	0.05	0.05[f]
Barium	1.0	1.0	1.5[f]
Cadmium	0.01	0.010	0.005
Chromium	0.05	0.05	0.12
Fluoride	1.4-2.4	4.0	4.0
Lead	0.05	0.5	—
	—	0.005[g]	zero[g]
Mercury	0.002	0.02	0.003[f]
Nitrate (as N)	10.0	10.0	10.0[f]
Nitrite (as N)	—	—	1.0[f]
Selenium	0.01	0.01	0.45[f]
Silver	0.05	0.05	—
Pesticides			
Endrin	0.0002	0.0002	—
Lindane	0.004	0.004	0.0002[h]
Methoxychlor	0.1	0.1	0.34[h]
Toxaphene	0.005	0.005	zero[h]
2,4-D	0.1	0.1	0.07[h]
2,4,5-TP Silvex	0.01	0.01	0.052[h]
Radionuclides			
Radium-226 and -228	5 pCi/L	5 pCi/L	—
Alpha Activity [i]	15 pCi/L	15 pCi/L	—
Beta Activity	4 mrem/yr [j]	—	—
Manmade			
radioactivity	—	4 mrem/yr	—
Total Trihalomethanes	—	0.01	—
Volatile Organic			
Chemicals			
Benzene	—	0.005	0
Vinyl chloride	—	0.002	0
Carbon tetrachloride	—	0.005	0
1,2 Dichloroethane	—	0.005	0
Trichloromethane	—	0.005	0
1,1-Dichloroethylene	—	0.007	0.007
1,1,1-Trichloromethane	—	0.20	0.20
Para-Dichlorobenzene	—	0.075	0.075

[a] Other standards are available in the RCRA (1984) and SDWA (1986) regulations.
[b] Resource Conservation and Recovery Act of 1976 and the Hazardous and Solid Waste Amendments of 1984.
[c] EPA (1988a, 1988e).
[d] Safe Drinking Water Act of 1986.
[e] Maximum contaminant levels (MCL) and MCL goals (EPA, 1988e).
[f] Proposed federal regulations at 40 CFR 141.51 (50 FR 46936, November 13, 1985).
[g] Proposed federal regulations at new subpart I of 40 CFR 141 (53 FR 31516, August 18, 1988).
[h] Proposed federal regulations at 40 CFR 141.50b (50 FR 46936, November 13, 1985).
[i] EPA (1988e) and SDWA MCL exclude radon and uranium.
[j] EPA (1988a). No further explanation (whole-body dose, dose equivalent, etc.) is given in the regulation.

CONCLUSIONS

EPA and state regulatory agencies have not clearly defined the applicability of ground-water classification and protection standards to active and inactive hazardous-waste sites. Thus, operators of such sites should consider the entire ground-water classification and standards scheme in developing protection and monitoring programs. As EPA and the states develop ground-water protection strategies, operators of hazardous-waste sites should track regulatory changes and integrate them in their technical programs.

ACKNOWLEDGMENT

Work supported by the U.S. DOE under Contract DE-AC06-76RLO 1830.

REFERENCES

Clean Water Act. 1987. U.S. Code Title 33, Sec. 1251 et seq.

CERCLA. 1986. Comprehensive Environmental Response, Compensation, and Liability Act and the Superfund Amendments and Reauthorization Act. U.S. Code Title 42, Sec. 9601 et seq.

The Conservation Foundation. 1987. Groundwater Protection: Saving the Unseen Resource and A Guide to Groundwater Pollution: Problems, Causes, and Government Responses. The Conservation Foundation, Washington, DC.

EPA. 1986. Guidelines for Groundwater Classification under the EPA Groundwater Protection Strategy. U.S. Environmental Protection Agency, Office of Groundwater Protection, Washington, DC.

EPA. 1988a. Final and Interim Status Standards for Owners and Operators of Hazardous Waste Treatment, Storage, and Disposal Facilities, 40 CFR 264-265. U.S. Environmental Protection Agency, Washington, DC.

EPA. 1988b. National Oil and Hazardous Substances Pollution Contingency Plan, 40 CFR 300. U.S. Environmental Protection Agency, Washington, DC.

EPA. 1988c. Sole Source Aquifers, 40 CFR 149. U.S. Environmental Protection Agency, Washington, DC.

EPA. 1988d. Environmental Standards for the Management, Storage, and Disposal of Low-Level Radioactive Waste, 40 CFR 193. U.S. Environmental Protection Agency, Washington, DC.

EPA. 1988e. Criteria for Classification of Solid Waste Disposal Facilities and Practices, 40 CFR 257. U.S. Environmental Protection Agency, Washington, DC.

Low Level Radioactive Waste Policy Act. 1980. U.S. Code Title 42, Sec. 2021b et seq.

NRC. 1988. Disposal of High-Level Radioactive Wastes in Geologic Repositories, 10 CFR 60. U.S. Nuclear Regulatory Commission, Washington, DC.

Nuclear Waste Policy Act. 1982. U.S. Code Title 42, Sec. 10101 et seq.

Resource Conservation and Recovery Act of 1976 (RCRA) and the Hazardous and Solid Waste Amendments of 1984. 1984. U.S. Code Title 42, Sec. 6901 et seq.

Safe Drinking Water Act. 1986. U.S. Code Title 42 Sec. 300f et seq.

APPLICABLE OR RELEVANT AND APPROPRIATE REQUIREMENTS (ARAR) FOR RADIOACTIVE MIXED WASTE

J. F. Keller and M. G. Woodruff

Pacific Northwest Laboratory, Richland, Washington

Key Words: *CERCLA, ARAR, mixed waste, site remediation*

ABSTRACT

The Resource Conservation and Recovery Act (RCRA) and the Comprehensive Environmental, Response, Compensation, and Liability Act (CERCLA) subject federal facilities to a complex regulatory framework for managing radioactive mixed wastes. Currently, no single regulation specifically addresses all aspects of radioactive mixed-waste management and cleanup. Without specific guidance, management of such wastes falls under the purview of numerous statutes and regulations relative to radioactive and chemical waste, and water- and air-quality protection. We will review the environmental pollution control and radioactive waste-management statutes and regulations that might contain applicable or relevant and appropriate requirements (ARAR) as defined under CERCLA. These requirements apply to four exposure pathways: air, ground water, surface water, and soil. We will also provide a framework to integrate the chemical- and radioactive-waste management requirements for these pathways. Examples of mixed-waste management scenarios will be given to illustrate the application of this framework to waste management and/or cleanup decision-making.

INTRODUCTION

We will identify potential cleanup standards for chemical and radioactive contaminants at radioactive mixed-waste (RMW) sites. RMW contains materials defined as hazardous under the Resource Conservation and Recovery Act (RCRA, 1976) and radioactive materials regulated under the Atomic Energy Act (AEA, 1954). Examples of RMW include waste oils, scintillation fluids, some defense reprocessing wastes, and organic solvents. We will focus on major federal standards that may apply to a broad range of sites.

Many waste sites that are contaminated with both chemicals and radionuclides will be cleaned up under the Comprehensive Environmental Response, Compensation, and Liability Act (CERCLA, 1980). Section 121 of CERCLA requires that federal and state statutes and regulations be reviewed to identify requirements that are either legally applicable or relevant and appropriate to an RMW site and to the contaminants of interest. These Applicable or Relevant and Appropriate Requirements (ARAR) are then used as cleanup targets in the design of site remediation programs. However, ARAR are only one aspect of site remediation planning. Although not reviewed in this paper, standards and criteria contained in other sources, such as guidance documents, must also be considered. The burden of identifying ARAR for a given site rests on those with technical knowledge of the site and on those who will conduct the cleanup.

Determining the target cleanup level for each contaminant is critical to developing and implementing remediation plans for hazardous-waste sites. The process is complicated by the lack of specific standards for the media and contaminants of interest. For RMW sites, the process is further complicated because most chemical standards are given as concentration limits, while most environmental radiation protection standards are given as dose limits. Even when concentration limits exist for specific radionuclides, overall or pathway-specific dose limits that are ARAR may also exist, but meeting concentration limits may not ensure that dose limits are met.

As overall chemical risk standards are developed, these issues will complicate the setting of target cleanup levels for chemicals. In such cases, concentration standards must be used in site-specific transport and exposure models to determine if overall exposure or risk limits are met. The same process must be used to determine target cleanup levels for radionuclides and chemicals where there are no concentration standards. Negotiations with regulators will help determine the acceptability of model results and the proposed concentration standards for each site.

FRAMEWORK FOR RMW MANAGEMENT

Radioactive waste that also contains chemical components has only recently become a dual RCRA/AEA regulatory regime; thus, RMW management is not specifically addressed under a single statute. Several statutes and regulations related to radioactive and chemical waste management, and air- and water-quality protection, must be consulted when determining ARAR for chemical and radioactive constituents at RMW sites.

Potential concentration and dose standards that could be used as ARAR are discussed below. Those identified are most relevant to RMW sites and should be considered on a site-specific basis during remediation planning. Only federal statutes, regulations, and guidance documents are reviewed here. However, state regulations and guidance must also be consulted to determine all ARAR for a given site. State requirements, which are often more stringent than federal requirements, are critical to ARAR development.

FEDERAL ARAR FOR CHEMICAL AND RADIOACTIVE CONSTITUENTS

Radioactive constituents are regulated under CERCLA, the Safe Drinking Water Act (SDWA, 1986), and the Clean Air Act (CAA, 1977). Because these statutes and their implementing regulations do not provide guidance on all radionuclides found at RMW sites, the following should also be consulted in developing ARAR: the AEA (1954), the Nuclear Waste Policy Act (NWPA, 1982), the Low Level Radioactive Waste Policy Act (LLRWPA, 1980), and the Uranium Mill Tailings Radiation Control Act (UMTRCA, 1978).

Chemical constituents of RMW are subject to several hazardous-waste management and general environmental protection statutes and regulations, including CERCLA, RCRA, SDWA, CAA, and the Clean Water Act (CWA, 1987).

POTENTIAL ARAR

This section discusses quantitative standards taken from statutes and regulations listed above, and from related guidance documents. Some standards apply only to specific exposure pathways, e.g., air, surface water, ground water, or soil, while others apply to exposures from all pathways. Table 1 shows selected examples of potential ground-water ARAR that are relevant to RMW sites and potential ARAR for radioactive materials. Table 2 shows potential air ARAR for radioactive materials, and Table 3 contains examples of potential air ARAR for chemical contaminants. Tables 4 and 5 show potential ARAR for surface-water and soil exposure pathways, respectively; Table 6 lists potential ARAR that apply to all exposure pathways. Table 7 contains some additional sources that should be consulted in determining ARAR for RMW sites. The only soil standard (Table 5) is for radium-226 at uranium mill tailings sites. Thus, all soil cleanup levels must be developed using transport and exposure modeling. Research to develop more generic soil cleanup standards would benefit RMW site remediation efforts. Also, determining ARAR for a site, early interaction with regulators is important to clarify whether the concentration or dose limit takes precedence where both exist.

Table 1. Potential Applicable or Relevant and Appropriate Requirements (ARAR) for ground water.

Hazardous Constituents[c]	RCRA[a] (mg/L)[d]	SDWA[b] MCL (mg/L)	SDWA[b] MCLG (mg/L)
Heavy Metals			
Arsenic	0.05	0.05	0.05
Barium	1.0	1.0	1.5
Cadmium	0.01	0.010	0.005
Chromium	0.05	0.05	0.12
Fluoride	1.4-2.4	4.0	4.0
Lead	0.05	0.5	—
Mercury	0.002	0.02	0.003
Nitrate	10.0	10.0	10.0
Nitrite	—	—	1.0
Selenium	0.01	0.01	0.45
Silver	0.05	0.05	—
Pesticides			
Endrin	0.0002	0.0002	—
Lindane	0.004	0.004	0.0002
Methoxychlor	0.1	0.1	0.34
Toxaphene	0.005	0.005	0
2,4-D	0.1	0.1	0.07
2,4,5-TP Silvex	0.01	0.01	0.052
Total Trihalomethanes	—	0.01	—
Volatile Organic Chemicals			
Benzene	—	0.005	0
Vinyl chloride	—	0.002	0
Carbon tetrachloride	—	0.005	0
1,2 Dichloroethane	—	0.005	0
Trichloromethane	—	0.005	0
1,1-Dichloroethylene	—	0.007	0.007
1,1,1-Trichloromethane	—	0.20	0.20
Para-Dichlorobenzene	—	0.075	0.075

Radioactive Constituents	RCRA	SDWA MCL	40 CFR 191.16[e]
Radium-226 and -228	5 pCi/L[f]	5 pCi/L	5 pCi/L
Alpha activity[g]	15 pCi/L	15 pCi/L	15 pCi/L
Beta activity	4 mrem/yr[h]	—	—
Beta/gamma activity	—	4 mrem/yr dose equivalent to whole body or any internal organ[i]	4 mrem/yr dose equivalent to whole body or any internal organ[j]

[a] EPA (1988a, 1988b, 1988j)
[b] Maximum contaminant levels (MCL) and MCL Goals (EPA, 1988c).
[c] Other standards are available in the RCRA and SDWA regulations.
[d] Milligrams per liter.
[e] EPA (1988d). The ground-water protection standards were vacated by the U.S. First Circuit Court of Appeals and remanded to EPA for further consideration. New standards are under development.
[f] Picocuries per liter.
[g] EPA (1988a) and SDWA MCLs exclude radon and uranium. EPA (1988d) excludes radon.
[h] EPA (1988b). No further explanation (whole-body dose, dose equivalent, etc.) is given in the regulation.
[i] Assumes daily consumption of 2 liters. The average annual concentration assumed to produce a whole-body or organ dose of 4 mrem/yr is 20,000 pCi/L for tritium and 8 pCi/L for strontium-90.
[j] Assumes daily consumption of 2 L.

Table 2. Potential Applicable or Relevant and Appropriate Requirements (ARAR) for radioactive materials in air.

Radioactive Constituents	CAA		AEA	UMTRCA
Constituents or Dose	Current NESHAPS[a]	Proposed NESHAPS[b]	10 CFR 20 Appendix B, Table 2[c]	40 CFR 192[d]
Dose due to air emissions (radionuclides other than radon).	25 mrem/yr, whole body or 75 mrem/yr, critical organ (Subparts H, I).	0.03, 3, or 10 mrem/yr effective dose equivalent (Subparts H, I).		
Radon-222		5,500 or 1,500 Ci/yr emission limit, or 5,000 Ci/yr emitted 30 m above ground level (Subpart B).		20 pCi/m²s release rate. Increase of 0.5 pCi/L annual average air concentrations.
Radon decay product concentration in habitable or occupied buildings.		0.02, 2, 6, or 20 pCi/m²s (Subparts Q, R, S, T).		
Gamma radiation level in habitable or occupied buildings.				
Po-210 (emission controls assumed to also limit Pb-210 emissions).	21 Ci/yr emission limit (Subpart K).	0.006, 0.6, or 10 Ci/yr (Subpart K).		
257 individual radionuclides, natural U and Th, and other radionuclides if not included in the 257 listed.			Concentration in air above natural background in effluents to unrestricted area: 2×10^{-14} to 1×10^{-4} μCi/mL[f]	

[a] National Emission Standards for Hazardous Air Pollutants (EPA, 1988e). Currently, the Subpart H and I requirements contain an alternate limit for all pathways; see Table 5.
[b] Several alternate approaches to standard development are described in the proposed rule.
[c] Standards for Protection Against Radiation (NRC, 1988).
[d] Health and Environmental Protection Standards for Uranium and Thorium Mill Tailings (EPA, 1988f).
[e] A Working Level (WL) is any combination of short-lived radon decay products in 1 liter of air that will result in the ultimate emission of 130 billion electron volts.
[f] Higher effluent concentrations may be approved if it is unlikely that an individual would be exposed to concentrations exceeding these limits.

Table 3. Potential Applicable and Relevant Appropriate Requirements (ARAR) for chemical contaminants in air.

Hazardous Constituents	Clean Air Act	
	40 CFR 51[a]	NESHAPS[b]
Asbestos	—	No visible emission[c]
Beryllium	—	10 g/24 hr[d]
Carbon monoxide	100 tpy[d]	—
Lead	0.6 tpy[d]	—
Mercury	—	2300 g/24 hr[d]
Nitrogen oxides	40 tpy[d]	—
Ozone	40 tpy of volatile organic compounds[d]	—
Sulfur dioxide	40 tpy[d]	—

[a] Requirements for Preparation, Adoption, and Submittal of Implementation Plans (EPA, 1988g).
[b] National Emission Standards for Hazardous Air Pollutants (EPA 1988e).
[c] This standard is for demolition and renovation.
[d] Significant increases in net emissions must not equal or exceed any of these rates. tpy = tons per year.

Table 4. Potential Applicable and Relevant Appropriate Requirements (ARAR) for radioactive constituents in surface water.[a]

Constituent or Dose	Standard	Source
245 individual radio-nuclides, natural U and Th, and other radio-nuclides if not included in the 245 listed.	Concentration in water above natural background in effluents to unrestricted areas: 1×10^{-2} to 3×10^{-8} μCi/ml.[b]	NRC (1988, Appendix B, Table II)

[a] No specific hazardous standards are set in federal Clean Water Act regulations. Effluent standards are set in facility permits. In addition, water quality criteria for each surface water body are based on a surface-water classification scheme.
[b] Higher concentrations in effluents may be approved if it is unlikely that an individual would be exposed to concentrations exceeding these limits.

Table 5. Potential Applicable and Relevant Appropriate Requirements (ARAR) for soil.

Constituent[a]	Uranium Mill Tailings Radiation Control Act Standard[b]
Radium-226	Averaged over 100-m² area:

- 5 pCi/g[c] above background, averaged over first 15 cm of soil

- 15 pCi/g above background, averaged over 15-cm-thick layer of soil more than 15 cm below the surface.

[a] No hazardous standards exist.
[b] EPA (1988f, Subpart B).
[c] pCi/g = picocuries per gram.

Table 6. Potential Applicable and Relevant Appropriate Requirements (ARAR) for all exposure pathways.[a]

Standard[b]	Source
Hazardous Constituents	
10⁻⁴ to 10⁻⁷ lifetime cancer risk	Superfund Public Health Evaluation Manual
Radioactive Constituents	
25 mrem/year whole-body dose	EPA (1988h)
75 mrem/year thyroid	
25 mrem/year any other organ	
25 mrem/year whole-body dose	
75 mrem/year thyroid	EPA (1988d)
25 mrem/year any other critical organ	(applicable to NRC facilities)
25 mrem/year whole-body dose	
75 mrem/year any critical organ	
100 mrem/year continuous exposure	EPA (1988d)
500 mrem in a year infrequent exposure	(applicable to DOE facilities)
25 mrem/year whole-body dose	EPA (1988d) (alternate standards for DOE facilities)
500 mrem in any one calendar year, 2 mrem in any one hour, 100 mrem in any 7 consecutive days due to radiation levels in unrestricted areas.	EPA (1988i)
	NRC (1988)

[a] None of the statutes or regulations reviewed contain soil standards for hazardous or radioactive constituents.
[b] Applies to combined dose equivalent from LLW management and storage and from all operations covered by 40 CFR 190 (EPA 1988h).

Table 7. Additional Sources of Potential Applicable or Relevant and Appropriate Requirements (ARAR).

° Agency for Toxic Substances Disease Registry (ATSDR) is developing standards for various pathways for use when performing health assessments.[a]

° U.S. Environmental Protection Agency is developing standards for sludges and soil debris.[a]

° Toxic Substances Control Act (TSCA, 1976) and its implementing regulations.

° Federal Insecticide, Fungicide, and Rodenticide Act (FIFRA, 1986) and its implementing regulations.

° Superfund Public Health Evaluation Manual (EPA, 1986).

° State statutes, regulations, and guidance documents.

[a] Operators of hazardous-waste sites should track the development of these standards.

ACKNOWLEDGMENT

Work supported by the U.S. Department of Energy under Contract DE-AC06-76RLO 1830.

REFERENCES

AEA. 1954. Atomic Energy Act. U.S. Code Title 42, Sec. 2011 et seq.

CAA. 1977. Clean Air Act. U.S. Code Title 42, Sec. 7401 et seq.

CERCLA. 1980. Comprehensive Environmental, Response, Compensation, and Liability Act of 1980 (CERCLA) and the Superfund Amendments and Reauthorization Act of 1986. U.S. Code Title 42, Sec. 9601 et seq.

CWA. 1987. Clean Water Act. U.S. Code Title 33, Sec. 1251 et seq.

EPA. 1986. Superfund Public Health Evaluation Manual, EPA/540/1-86/060. U.S. Environmental Protection Agency, Washington, DC.

EPA. 1988a. Criteria for Classification of Solid Waste Disposal Facilities and Practices, 40 CFR 257. U.S. Environmental Protection Agency, Washington, DC.

EPA. 1988b. Interim Status Standards for Owners and Operators of Hazardous Waste Treatment, Storage, and Disposal Facilities, 40 CFR 265. U.S. Environmental Protection Agency, Washington, DC.

EPA. 1988c. National Primary Drinking Water Regulations, 40 CFR 141. U.S. Environmental Protection Agency, Washington, DC.

EPA. 1988d. Environmental Radiation Protection Standards for Management and Disposal of Spent Nuclear Fuel, High-Level and Transuranic Radioactive Wastes, 40 CFR 191. U.S. Environmental Protection Agency, Washington, DC.

EPA. 1988e. National Emission Standards for Hazardous Air Pollutants, 40 CFR 61. U.S. Environmental Protection Agency, Washington, DC.

EPA. 1988f. Health and Environmental Protection Standards for Uranium and Thorium Mill Tailings, 40 CFR 192. U.S. Environmental Protection Agency, Washington, DC.

EPA. 1988g. Requirements for Preparation, Adoption, and Submittal of Implementation Plans, 40 CFR 51. U.S. Environmental Protection Agency, Washington, DC.

EPA. 1988h. Environmental Radiation Protection Standards for Nuclear Power Operations, 40 CFR 190. U.S. Environmental Protection Agency, Washington, DC.

EPA. 1988i. Environmental Standards for the Management, Storage, and Disposal of Low-Level Radioactive Waste (Draft), 40 CFR 193. U.S. Environmental Protection Agency, Washington, DC.

EPA. 1988j. Standards for Owners and Operators of Hazardous Waste Treatment, Storage, and Disposal Facilities, 40 CFR 264. U.S. Environmental Protection Agency, Washington, DC.

Federal Insecticide, Fungicide, and Rodenticide Act of 1986. U.S. Code Title 7, Sec. 136 et seq.

LLRWPA. 1980. Low Level Radioactive Waste Policy Act. U.S. Code Title 42, Sec. 2021b et seq.

NRC. 1988. Standards for Protection Against Radiation, 10 CFR 20. U.S. Nuclear Regulatory Commission, Washington, DC.

NWPA. 1982. Nuclear Waste Policy Act. U.S. Code Title 42, Sec. 10101 et seq.

RCRA. 1976. Resource Conservation and Recovery Act of 1976 (RCRA) and the Hazardous and Solid Waste Amendments of 1984. U.S. Code Title 42, Sec. 6901 et seq.

SDWA. 1986. Safe Drinking Water Act. U.S. Code Title 42, Sec. 300f et seq.

Toxic Substances Control Act of 1976. U.S. Code Title 15, Sec. 2601 et seq.

UMTRCA. 1978. Uranium Mill Tailings Radiation Control Act. 1978. U.S. Code Title 42, Sec. 7901 et seq.

IMPLEMENTATION OF COMPREHENSIVE ENVIRONMENTAL RESPONSE, COMPENSATION, AND LIABILITY ACT (CERCLA) HEALTH AUTHORITY BY THE AGENCY FOR TOXIC SUBSTANCES AND DISEASE REGISTRY

M. R. Siegel

Pacific Northwest Laboratory, Richland, Washington

Key Words: *ATSDR, CERCLA, public health, health assessments*

ABSTRACT

The Superfund Amendments and Reauthorization Act (SARA) of 1986 greatly expanded the health authority of the Comprehensive Environmental Response, Compensation, and Liability Act. One of the federal agencies most affected by SARA is the Agency for Toxic Substances and Disease Registry (ATSDR) of the U.S. Public Health Service. Among other responsibilities, ATSDR was mandated to conduct health assessments within strict time frames for each site on or proposed for the U.S. Environmental Protection Agency's National Priorities List. I will review ATSDR's efforts to address this new statutory mandate, especially for federal facilities, and will focus on different conceptual frameworks for implementing the health assessment program.

BACKGROUND

Formation of the Agency for Toxic Substances and Disease Registry (ATSDR) was authorized under the original Comprehensive Environmental Response, Compensation, and Liability Act (CERCLA or Superfund; see 42 U.S. Code 9604*) in 1980. Like its sister agency, the Centers for Disease Control (CDC), ATSDR is part of the U.S. Public Health Service (PHS), a component of the Department of Health and Human Services. ATSDR's 1989 fiscal year budget was $44.5 million, and it employed 175 individuals.

With passage of the Superfund Amendments and Reauthorization Act (SARA; see U.S. Public Law 99-499*) in 1986, Congress showed increased interest in the relationship between hazardous-waste sites

---

*Can be found in most law libraries.

and human health. The amended section 104(i) of CERCLA (or Superfund) [see 42 U.S. Code 9604* (i)] mandated ATSDR to conduct health assessments at every site on, or proposed for the National Priorities List (NPL); establish priority lists of hazardous substances at Superfund sites; produce toxicological profiles for each substance on this list; and conduct health studies related to hazardous substances.

SARA set forth a specific framework to conduct health assessments at Superfund sites. Prior to 1986, ATSDR only conducted health assessments in response to requests from the U.S. Environmental Protection Agency (EPA). Under the amended CERCLA, the responsibility to conduct health assessments at all NPL sites became mandatory. ATSDR was required to conduct health assessments, by December 10, 1988, for 887 sites on or proposed for NPL when SARA was passed. In addition, ATSDR is required to complete a health assessment within 1 yr for every new site proposed for inclusion in NPL. For example, in January 1987, EPA proposed to add 64 new sites to NPL; ATSDR was required to complete health assessments for these sites by January 1988.

ATSDR defines a health assessment as

"... the evaluation of data and information on release of hazardous substances into the environment in order to: assess any current or future impact on public health, develop health advisories or other recommendations, and identify studies or actions needed to evaluate and mitigate or prevent human health effects." [Health Assessments and Health Effects Studies of Hazardous Substances Releases and Facilities, see 53 Fed. Reg. 32259 (1988) (to be codified as 42 CFR 90*)]

Section 104(i)(6)(G) of CERCLA [see 42 U.S. Code 9604 (i)(6)(G)] specifies that the health assessments are to assist in determining (1) whether action should be taken to reduce human exposure to hazardous substances, and (2) if additional information on human exposure and associated health risks is needed and whether health effects studies for the site should be conducted.

ATSDR has attempted to standardize the format and conclusions of all health assessments [Agency for Toxic Substances and Disease Registry. Health Assessment Format, Guidelines and Methodology. ATSDR, Atlanta, GA]. Generally, the assessment should contain a

---

*Can be found in most law libraries.

description of the site location, on- and offsite contamination, physical hazards, populations at risk, and land use. The assessment should also describe environmental and human exposure pathways, conclusions and recommendations concerning public health implications, and future data-gathering needs. ATSDR can issue health advisories when specific sites are believed to pose an acute risk to public health.

CERCLA identifies additional health effects studies: pilot studies, epidemiological studies, health surveillance programs, and registries. However, conducting these additional studies is discretionary.

ATSDR encountered numerous difficulties implementing SARA. In fiscal year 1986, ATSDR had an annual budget of about $30 million and 75 employees, mostly assigned to other PHS agencies. In addition, ATSDR suffered an identity crisis in how it was perceived by other federal agencies, Congress, and the public. A common misconception was that ATSDR was a component of CDC or EPA.

ATSDR is dependent on EPA, which serves as trustee for Superfund and must approve annual funding requests. Thus, ATSDR must justify its funding requests, and thereby its policy objectives, to an agency which is itself competing for limited Superfund dollars. Accordingly, faced with limited staff and budgets, and with these factors largely controlled by competing agencies, ATSDR has been hindered in its efforts to meet its statutory mandates.

CONCEPTUAL MODELS FOR HEALTH ASSESSMENTS

Two different conceptual models could have been adopted by ATSDR to guide implementation of its health assessment responsibilities. The models differ primarily in timing of health assessments and their potential impacts on the EPA remediation process.

The first model emphasizes early identification and intervention to address potential public health problems at a site; health assessments would be completed within 1 yr. Advantages are that public health issues are addressed early in the Superfund process to minimize possible mortality and morbidity, and public health concerns are identified that influence EPA data-gathering and other activities at the site. Early intervention enables decision-makers to prioritize sites so resources can be dedicated to those posing the most serious health risks. Unfortunately, there is often little information available during the initial assessment, thereby limiting ATSDR's ability to make definitive judgments concerning risks.

The second model concentrates health assessment activity later in the Superfund process, generally during or after remedial investigation/ feasibility studies (RI/FS). Minimum effort is directed to addressing the 1-yr statutory requirement for newly proposed sites; resources are dedicated to a comprehensive review of RI/FS data when they become available. Advantages are that ATSDR can base its recommendations on more complete information that could help EPA select and prioritize remedial alternatives across sites. Disadvantages are that this model minimizes ATSDR's ability to influence EPA's data gathering at sites and reduces the possibility of early public health interventions. Furthermore, it is more resource-intensive because of its commitment to conduct full health assessments based on RI/FS data, regardless of the magnitude of health risks posed by each site.

Although elements of one model could be incorporated in the other, the models differ concerning the role and implementation of the health assessment responsibilities of ATSDR. Given sufficient resources, ATSDR could devote adequate attention to both early health assessments and those conducted during or following RI/FS. However, limited resources force ATSDR to focus efforts in one area or the other. Generally, ATSDR has favored the second model, with emphasis on conducting assessments based on RI/FS data for all sites.

IMPLEMENTATION OF SITE-SPECIFIC HEALTH RESPONSIBILITIES BY ATSDR

The requirement that ATSDR conduct health assessments within 1 yr of the date sites are proposed for NPL posed a dilemma. Usually, a site's nomination to NPL is based on little more than EPA's preliminary assessment/site investigation, which frequently does not include detailed information on environmental pathways and potential human exposures. Thus, soon after passage of SARA, ATSDR had to decide which conceptual model to follow to implement its health assessment role. Waiting until complete environmental characterization data were available following the RI/FS would ignore the statutory mandate to conduct assessments within 1 yr of a site's addition to NPL. Complying with this statutory requirement meant ATSDR had to make its best judgment based on incomplete information.

During 1986 and 1987, ATSDR generally viewed the two alternatives as mutually exclusive and chose to defer most health assessments until RI/FS data were available. However, this approach changed as ATSDR faced its first statutory deadline on January 20, 1988. One year previously, EPA had issued its Update 6 list, proposing to add 64 new sites to NPL. Under the amended CERCLA, ATSDR had 1 yr to complete health assessments for these sites. The agency decided to meet all health assessment-related deadlines, including the 1-yr requirement for newly proposed sites and the December 10, 1988, deadline for existing NPL sites.

Accordingly, ATSDR created the concept of "preliminary" health assessment to identify those completed prior to the availability of RI/FS data. Thus, ATSDR claimed to meet the deadlines of both January 20, 1988 (for the 64 Update 6 sites), and December 10, 1988 (for the remaining 887 sites) by preparing draft "preliminary" and "full" health assessments. Of 951 sites, 504 involved "preliminary" assessments and 282 were "full" assessments. Another 165 assessments were conducted before October, 1986 (Memorandum from Barry L. Johnson, Associate Administrator, ATSDR, to Walter R. Dowdle, Acting ATSDR Administrator, May 19, 1989), many of which were in draft form at deadline and, as of June, 1989, many were not final. ATSDR maintains that the drafts satisfy the statutory requirements.

Although ATSDR issued "preliminary" health assessments, its programmatic emphasis and resources currently remain committed to conducting "full" health assessments for every site, even if the "preliminary" health assessment indicates little cause for public concern (Statement by James O. Mason, Administrator, ATSDR, before the Committee on Energy and Commerce, Subcommittee on Oversight and Investigations, U.S. House of Representatives, June 20, 1988).

ATSDR has since missed the June 24, 1989 deadline and has estimated that it would address only 135 of 229 sites on EPA's Update 7 list for inclusions in the NPL [Letter from Walter R. Dowdle, Acting Administrator, ATSDR, to Rep. Richard A. Gephardt, June 16, 1989].

HEALTH ASSESSMENT FINDINGS

Congress had hoped to address through SARA the extent to which hazardous waste sites pose a risk to public health. Based on ATSDR's work to date, it is impossible to answer this question other than in general terms. ATSDR estimated that about 80% of all NPL sites have a potential pathway for human exposure to hazardous substances, and that 10% of the NPL sites present a potential exposure pathway of sufficient concern to warrant further health studies [Letter from Walter R. Dowdle, Acting Administrator, ATSDR, to Rep. Richard A. Gephardt, June 16, 1989]. Although ATSDR has characterized risks posed by individual sites, it has not compiled and analyzed information on a national basis. ATSDR has recommended emergency action at several sites, but there is no information available on the number of health advisories issued. ATSDR has not prepared guidelines or criteria for issuing health advisories at specific sites.

IMPACT OF HEALTH ASSESSMENTS ON FEDERAL FACILITIES AND SITE REMEDIATION

With the passage of SARA, many observers believed that ATSDR health assessments would influence EPA site remediation, tort litigation involving toxic substances, and community and government awareness of public health risks at hazardous-waste sites so that citizens could become more involved in the Superfund process. This was especially true for federal facilities, which generally are more complex than other Superfund sites and may represent greater public health risks. ATSDR has not yet fulfilled these expectations.

The magnitude of the statutory mandate, limitations in staff and other resources, competing program responsibilities, and its conceptual approach to conducting health assessments have limited ATSDR's ability to effectively address many of the more complex federal facilities. For example, ATSDR's health assessment for the U.S. Department of Energy (DOE) Rocky Flats site in Colorado simply evaluates a proposed incinerator test burn [Memorandum from Steven D. Von Allmen to the Record, October 18, 1988 (Establishment of Preliminary Health Assessment Equivalency for the Rocky Flats NPL Site, Golden, Colorado)]. It does not satisfy the statutory requirement for addressing public health risks posed by the entire site or the need for further health studies. The final health assessment for the U.S. Army Rocky Mountain Arsenal, outside Denver, Colorado, did not respond to detailed comments from the Army, the U.S. Department of Justice, or the State of Colorado [Agency for Toxic Substances and Disease Registry, 1988. Preliminary Health Assessment for Rocky Mountain Arsenal. ATSDR, Atlanta, GA]. ATSDR missed the statutory deadline for preparing health assessments for the Hanford DOE site in Washington State. It is not certain how ATSDR will address the 52 federal facilities nominated by EPA for NPL in July 1989. Given ATSDR's current approach, its health assessments are likely to have minimal impact on federal facilities.

For some NPL sites, ATSDR's health assessments have contributed to a better understanding of potential public health risks. However, ATSDR's continued emphasis on "full" health assessments after the

RI/FS stage rather than "preliminary" assessments early in the process has clearly affected its ability to address complex federal facilities in accordance with CERCLA requirements. In an era of resource limitations, ATSDR must evaluate and implement a health assessment model that effectively addresses the CERCLA mandate by identifying public health problems when meaningful intervention can occur.

ACKNOWLEDGMENT

Work supported by the U.S. Department of Energy under contract DE-AC06-76RLO 1830.

ENVIRONMENTAL MONITORING FOR LOW-LEVEL RADIOACTIVE WASTE-DISPOSAL FACILITIES

E. Y. Shum, R. J. Starmer, K. Westbrook, and M. H. Young

U.S. Nuclear Regulatory Commission, Washington, DC

Key Words: *Environmental monitoring, LLW disposal*

ABSTRACT

The U.S. Nuclear Regulatory Commission prepared a Branch Technical Position (BTP) paper on environmental monitoring of a low-level radioactive waste-disposal facility. The BTP provides guidance on what is required in Section 61.53 of 10 CFR Part 61 for those submitting a license application. Guidance is also provided on choosing constituents to measure, setting action levels, relating measurements to appropriate actions in a corrective action plan, and quality assurance. The environmental monitoring program generally consists of three phases: preoperational, operational, and postoperational. Each phase should be designed to fulfill specific objectives defined in the BTP. During the preoperational phase, program objectives are to provide site characterization information, demonstrate site suitability and acceptability, and obtain background or baseline information. Emphasis during the operational phase is on measurement shifts. Monitoring data are obtained to demonstrate compliance with regulations, with dose limits of 10 CFR Part 61, or with applicable U.S. Environmental Protection Agency standards. Data are also used to update important pathway parameters to improve predictions of site performance and to provide a record of performance for public information. The postoperational phase emphasizes measurements to demonstrate compliance with site closure requirements and continued compliance with the performance objective for release. Data are used to support evaluation of long-term impacts to the general public and for public information.

INTRODUCTION

The Atomic Energy Act of 1954 and the Energy Reorganization Act of 1974 assign the responsibility for licensing and regulating commercial nuclear facilities to the U.S. Nuclear Regulatory Commission (NRC). Licensing requirements for near-surface disposal of low-level radioactive wastes (LLW) are given in Part 61 of Title 10 of the Code of Federal Regulations (NRC, 1989). The basic NRC requirement for near-surface LLW disposal-site monitoring is given in 10 CFR 61.53 (NRC, 1989). The regulation calls for environmental monitoring during preoperational, operational, and postoperational stages of a facility.

The NRC is preparing a Branch Technical Position (BTP) paper to provide general guidance to applicants, their consultants, and regulatory authorities on designing a monitoring program for LLW disposal facilities. The BTP is not a handbook of detailed or mandatory procedures. The primary objective of environmental monitoring is to provide assurance that the performance objectives in 10 CFR Part 61 (NRC, 1989) are met. Because each site has unique topography, meteorology, demography, and geohydrogeology, a detailed environmental monitoring program for an LLW disposal facility must be tailored to the site-specific operating and environmental conditions.

In designing an environmental monitoring program, there is no substitute for good professional judgment, combined with a thorough knowledge of the local environment (ICRP, 1984). This paper summarizes the BTP and provides insight into the opinions and expectations of NRC for acceptance review of the applicant's environmental monitoring program. For more detailed design information and guidance on implementing an environmental monitoring program, NRC has provided references (DOE, 1988, 1989; NRC, 1982, 1989) in the BTP.

ENVIRONMENTAL MONITORING PROGRAM OBJECTIVES

Regulatory Requirements

Requirements pertaining to an environmental monitoring program are described in 10 CFR Section 61.53 (NRC, 1989), "Environmental Monitoring":

(a) At the time a license application is submitted, the applicant shall have conducted a preoperational monitoring program to provide basic environmental data on disposal site characteristics. The applicant shall obtain information about the ecology, meteorology, climate, hydrology, geology, geochemistry, and seismology of the dispoal site. For those characteristics subject to seasonal variation, data must cover at least a twelve month period.

(b) The licensee must plan to take corrective measures if migration of radionuclides would indicate that the performance objectives of Subpart C may not be met.

(c) During land disposal facility site construction and operation, the licensee shall maintain a monitoring program. Measurements and observations must be recorded to provide data to evaluate the potential health and environmental impacts during construction and operation of the facility and to enable evaluation of long-term effects and the need for mitigative measures. The monitoring system must provide early warning of radionuclide releases from the disposal site, before they leave the site boundary.

(d) After the disposal site is closed, the licensee responsible for postoperational surveillance site shall maintain a monitoring system based on operating history and the closure and stabilization of the disposal site. The monitoring system must provide early warning of radionuclide releases from the disposal site before they leave the site boundary.

OBJECTIVES OF ENVIRONMENTAL MONITORING PROGRAM

Principal objectives of the three phases of environmental monitoring for an LLW disposal facility are:

Preoperational

1. Provide site characterization information.
2. Demonstrate site suitability and acceptability.
3. Obtain background or baseline data.

Operational

1. Demonstrate compliance with applicable environmental radiation standards.
2. Obtain data on critical pathway parameters to more accurately evaluate radiation dose to the public.
3. Provide records for public information.

Postoperational

1. Demonstrate compliance with site-closure requirements.
2. Provide data to support long-term impact evaluation, e.g., on ground water.
3. Provide records for site closure and public information.

GENERAL GUIDANCE ON PREOPERATIONAL ENVIRONMENTAL MONITORING

The primary purpose of preoperational monitoring is to characterize the site environment, i.e., collect new or existing monitoring data to evaluate the geological, hydrogeological, climatological, ecological, radiological, and nonradioactive environments of the site and surrounding area. Characterization is needed to demonstrate the site's acceptability and suitability for LLW disposal, compared with that of alternative sites, in the applicant's site-selection process. In the preoperational phase, environmental media are sampled and analyzed to provide background or baseline data. Some environmental sampling data can be used for long-term impact assessment. For some characteristics, generally those subject to seasonal changes, the program must continue for at least 1 yr and should extend through NRC's license review period of 12 to 15 mo. Typical environmental measurements are summarized in Table 1.

Table 1. Site characteristics and typical environmental monitoring measurements.

Site Characteristics	Typical Measurements
Meteorology/Climatology	Windspeed and direction; stability; precipitation; temperature; evaporation
Ground-water hydrology	Rate and direction of ground-water movement; water-table elevation; movement of infiltrate; identification of aquifers and ground-water systems; hydraulic conductivity; background contaminant levels
Surface-water hydrology	Runoff, infiltration rates; erosion rates; surface-water discharge rates; surface-water quality
Geology/Seismology	Stratigraphy, tectonics, seismicity; surface and trench mapping; geophysical borehole logging
Geochemistry/Hydrochemistry	Water quality, ion-exchange capacity, Eh-pH, distribution coefficient
Ecology	Plant and animal inventory (domestic, commercial, and natural)
Demography	Population distribution by distance and sectors
Land use	Inventory of agricultural, recreational, commercial, and other uses
Background radiation	Direct radiation; soil, air, and water concentration levels.

GENERAL GUIDANCE ON OPERATIONAL ENVIRONMENTAL MONITORING

The principal purposes of the operational environmental program are to monitor site performance and demonstrate compliance with applicable standards. The following discussion will emphasize radiological aspects of operation. Nonradiological aspects are discussed only to the extent that they affect transport of radionuclides and serve as early warning indicators of waste migration into ground water.

Considerations in Design of Operational Environmental-Monitoring Program

Pathway Analysis. Knowledge of waste migration pathways is important when designing an operational monitoring program. Pathway analysis, consisting of (1) pathway identification, (2) pathway modeling, and (3) dose calculation, can identify the critical pathways for human exposure. The operational program monitors critical pathways by selecting appropriate environmental sampling media and locations to ensure that human exposures can be measured or calculated as accurately as possible. Critical pathways depend on waste stream characteristics, facility operation and design, and site environmental factors. The detail, or level, of monitoring for a particular pathway depends on the need to demonstrate compliance with applicable standards.

Critical Nuclides and Groups. "Critical" nuclides and groups refer to radionuclides most subject to release and the human population groups potentially subject to greatest exposure. To identify critical radionuclides, characteristics of the wastes to be buried at the facility must be known.

Measurement of Parameters in the Environment

Physical Parameters. Data collected to characterize fundamental variables of the site, such as the geology, ecology, hydrology, etc., may not be collected during the operational phase. However, time-variant variables, such as wind speed and direction, precipitation and evaporation data, important in dose assessment, should be collected at intervals and evaluated periodically.

Radiological Measurements. Radiological measurements include those for direct radiation, and contaminants in air, ground and surface waters, soil, sediment, flora, and fauna. Sample locations, sampling frequency, and radionuclide measurements are site-specific and are determined on a case-by-case basis. Generally, samples should be collected to determine background levels, areas of maximum impact, where people can be exposed, and where measurements can be useful in interpreting results of the overall monitoring program. Sampling depends on the critical pathway determination, which is site-specific, and on compliance requirements. Determination of radionuclides to be measured depends on waste characterization, pathway considerations, and compliance requirements.

Action Levels

The applicant should set action levels on key environmental media to provide early warning and ensure that mitigating measures are taken in a timely manner and in compliance with 10 CFR 61.53(b) (NRC, 1989). The following action levels should be considered: (1) *Triggering Level*: the concentration of radioactivity or chemical indicators above which an investigation is required. (2) *Reporting Level*: the concentration of radioactivity or chemicals that exceeds or is about to exceed regulatory standards. A report should be sent to NRC, or the appropriate state agency, describing the investigation, findings, and mitigating measures taken to correct the problem.

GENERAL GUIDANCE ON POSTOPERATIONAL ENVIRONMENTAL MONITORING

After closure of an LLW disposal site, buildings and land should have been decommissioned, and residual contamination should have been reduced to acceptable levels. Disposal units should be capped to limit infiltration, protect intruders, and prevent biological intrusion. The site is then placed under institutional control. Postoperational monitoring ensures that the site continues to meet closure requirements.

Physical surveillance should be conducted periodically after site closure and any required repairs should be made to maintain site integrity (e.g., repairing and maintaining the perimeter fence, backfilling subsidence of trenches, and repairing damage caused by erosion).

After site closure, the primary path for radionuclide release to the environment is through ground water. The operational ground-water monitoring program should be continued during the inititial period after site closure and can be gradually reduced if no potential problem is identified. Analysis of chemical indicators and radioactivity should continue. If subsurface water reaches the ground surface and eventually enters streams, rivers, or lakes, these should be monitored. Vegetation (particularly deep-rooted plants) should be sampled periodically to evaluate potential uptake of radionuclides. Burrowing animals or animal feces should be sampled and analyzed to evaluate whether the biological barrier remains effective.

QUALITY ASSURANCE/QUALITY CONTROL (QA/QC)

The applicant's environmental monitoring program should include a QA/QC program to identify deficiencies in environmental sampling and measurement. Corrective action can then be taken, and regulatory agencies and the public can be assured that results of the monitoring program are valid. The applicant should refer to NRC's Regulatory Guide 4.15 (NRC, 1979) and NUREG-0945 (NRC, 1989) for the design of a QA/QC program.

REFERENCES

DOE. 1988. Site Characterization Handbook - National Low-Level Waste Management Program, DOE/LLW-67T. U.S. Department of Energy, Washington, DC.

DOE. 1989. Low-Level Radioactive Waste Management Handbook Series - Environmental Monitoring for Low-Level Waste-Disposal Site, DOE/LLW-13Tg. U.S. Department of Energy, Washington, DC.

ICRP. 1984. Principles of Monitoring for Radiation Protection of the Population, Publication 43. International Commission on Radiological Protection. Pergamon Press, New York.

NRC. 1979. Quality Assurance for Radiological Monitoring Program (Normal Operations) - Effluent Streams and the Environment, Regulatory Guide 4.15. U.S. Nuclear Regulatory Commission, Washington, DC.

NRC. 1982. Branch Technical Position - Low-Level Waste Licensing Branch - Site Suitability, Selection and Characterization, NUREG-0902. U.S. Nuclear Regulatory Commission, Washington, DC.

NRC. 1988. Recommendations to the NRC for Review Criteria for Alternative Methods of Low-Level Radioactive Waste Disposal Environmental Monitoring and Surveillance Program, NUREG/CR-5054. U.S. Nuclear Regulatory Commission, Washington, DC.

NRC. 1989. Quality Assurance Guidance for Low-level Waste Disposal Facility, NUREG-1293. U.S. Nuclear Regulatory Commission, Washington, DC.

NRC. 1989. Licensing Requirements for Land Disposal of Radioactive Waste, Code of Federal Regulations, Title 10, Part 61. U.S. Nuclear Regulatory Commission, Washington, DC.

DEVELOPMENT OF CLOSURE CRITERIA FOR INACTIVE RADIOACTIVE WASTE-DISPOSAL SITES AT OAK RIDGE NATIONAL LABORATORY

D. C. Kocher

Oak Ridge National Laboratory, Oak Ridge, Tennessee

Key Words: *Remedial action, ARAR, closure criteria, radioactive waste disposal, health protection standards*

ABSTRACT

The Comprehensive Environmental Response, Compensation, and Liability Act (CERCLA) specifies that the U.S. Department of Energy shall comply with the procedural and substantive requirements of CERCLA regarding cleanup of inactive waste-disposal sites. Remedial actions require a level of control for hazardous substances that at least attains legally applicable or relevant and appropriate requirements (ARAR). This requirement may be waived if compliance with ARAR results in greater risk to human health and the environment than alternatives or is technically impractical. I will review potential ARAR for cleanup of inactive radioactive waste-disposal sites and propose a set of closure criteria for such sites at Oak Ridge National Laboratory. Important potential ARAR include federal standards for radiation protection of the public, radioactivity in drinking water, and near-surface land disposal of radioactive wastes. Proposed criteria for cleanup of inactive radioactive waste-disposal sites are: (1) a limit of 0.25 mSv on annual effective dose equivalent for offsite individuals; (2) limits of 1 mSv for continuous exposures and 5 mSv for occasional exposures on annual effective dose equivalent for inadvertent intruders, following loss of institutional controls over disposal sites; and (3) limits on concentrations of radionuclides in potable ground and surface waters in accordance with federal drinking-water standards, to the extent reasonably achievable.

INTRODUCTION

More than 130 sites at Oak Ridge National Laboratory (ORNL) have been contaminated with radioactive, hazardous chemical, or mixed radioactive and hazardous chemical materials over the past 45 yr (Trabalka and Myrick, 1987; ORNL, 1987). I will propose criteria for cleanup and closure of sites at ORNL, principally those used for disposal of radioactive wastes. Closure criteria for sites contaminated with hazardous chemicals are not considered.

The Comprehensive Environmental Response, Compensation, and Liability Act (CERCLA) of 1980 (Public Law 96-510), as amended by the Superfund Amendments and Reauthorization Act of 1986 (Public Law 99-499), specifies that the Department of Energy (DOE) shall comply with requirements of CERCLA regarding cleanup of inactive waste-disposal sites. Furthermore, the Environmental Protection Agency (EPA) intends to include the Oak Ridge site on the National Priorities List for remediation (EPA, 1989a).

Although CERCLA includes standards for cleanup of environmental contamination to protect human health and the environment, quantitative criteria defining acceptable levels of hazardous substances in the environment are not specified. Rather, CERCLA specifies that remedial actions shall require a level or standard of control for hazardous substances which at least attains legally applicable or relevant and appropriate requirements (ARAR). This requirement may be waived, for example, if compliance with ARAR will result in greater risk to human health and the environment than alternatives for remediation or if compliance is technically impractical.

Specific numerical goals for cleanup of hazardous substances have not been applied uniformly at all CERCLA sites (Baes and Marland, 1989). Rather, cost and feasibility have been the key factors in determining the extent to which cleanup complies with legal requirements. Additional factors have included public opinion, acceptance by the state, and participation of the potentially responsible party in remediation. Thus, implementation of CERCLA requirements has been more a process of negotiating acceptable cleanup levels based on site-specific situations than a predetermined result based on generally applicable numerical criteria for protecting human health and the environment.

Contrary to most past practices in implementing CERCLA requirements, I will assume it is desirable when planning for remedial actions to establish, a priori, specific numerical criteria that define an acceptable result for site remediation and protect human health and the environment. I will first discuss the important potential ARAR for site cleanup. Because Tennessee has not established distinct requirements that could apply to site cleanup at ORNL, I will focus on federal requirements. Based on these ARAR, I will propose quantitative criteria for site closure that protect (1) the offsite public, (2) inadvertent intruders at disposal sites following loss of active institutional control, and (3) potable ground and surface waters.

DISCUSSION OF POTENTIAL ARAR

Federal standards for limiting radiation dose to the public or levels of radioactivity in the environment (Mills et al., 1988; Kocher, 1988) can be divided into two categories: (1) radiation protection standards that are generally applicable to all sources of exposure, exclusive of natural background and medical procedures; and (2) environmental radiation standards that apply only to specific sources of exposure. Although environmental radiation standards have been developed for many sources, no standards apply specifically to cleanup of inactive radioactive waste-disposal sites.

Directly Applicable Standards

Two standards are directly applicable to cleanup of inactive radioactive waste-disposal sites at ORNL: (1) Nuclear Regulatory Commission (NRC) standards for radiation protection of the public, and (2) EPA standards for radioactivity in drinking water.

NRC's current radiation protection standards for the public (NRC, 1988a) limit annual dose equivalents to the whole body to 5 mSv (0.5 rem). These standards are being revised (NRC, 1986), and the final standards may specify a limit on annual effective dose equivalent of 1 mSv (0.1 rem), with annual effective dose equivalents up to 5 mSv (0.5 rem) permitted only under unusual circumstances (NRC, 1988b). The same dose limits are incorporated in impending DOE requirements for radiation protection of the public (DOE, 1988a).

EPA's interim standards for radioactivity in drinking water (EPA, 1988) apply only to community water systems and at the point of use rather than at the source. The standards specify (1) concentration limits of 0.2 Bq/L (5 pCi/L) for ^{226}Ra and ^{228}Ra combined and 0.6 Bq/L (15 pCi/L) for gross alpha activity, including radium but excluding radon and uranium, and (2) a limit on annual dose equivalent of 0.04 mSv (4 mrem) to the whole body or any organ from manmade, beta/gamma-emitting radionuclides. Although these standards are being revised (EPA, 1986), a proposed standard has not been issued. Impending DOE requirements (DOE, 1988a) also specify a limit on annual effective dose equivalent from DOE site drinking-water supplies of 0.04 mSv (4 mrem), excluding naturally occurring radionuclides.

Potential Relevant and Appropriate Requirements

Although EPA standards for radioactivity in drinking water apply only to community water systems (EPA, 1988), CERCLA specifies that these standards are relevant and appropriate for cleanup of sites regulated under CERCLA. Thus, the concentration and dose limits given above may be used to limit contamination of ground water or surface waters at or near inactive radioactive waste-disposal sites, particularly if: (1) sources could supply drinking water for individuals or populations, (2) cleanup to standards is technically achievable and would not result in greater risk to human health and the environment than cleanup to less stringent levels, and (3) cleanup cost is reasonable in relation to the potential benefits to human health.

Standards for near-surface land disposal of radioactive wastes at operating or future facilities are probably relevant and appropriate for cleanup of inactive sites, because previously contaminated sites and current or future facilities involve similar disposal systems and wastes with similar hazards. Current NRC standards (NRC, 1988c) specify limits on annual dose equivalent to the offsite public of 0.25 mSv (25 mrem) to the whole body, 0.75 mSv (75 mrem) to the thyroid, or 0.25 mSv (25 mrem) to any other organ. The standards also implicitly incorporate dose limits for inadvertent intruders, following loss of active institutional control, that are consistent with NRC's current radiation protection standards for the public (NRC, 1988a). Thus, NRC standards for land disposal of radioactive wastes establish the precedent that inadvertent intruders may be afforded less protection than offsite individuals, provided intruders do not receive doses exceeding limits specified in radiation protection standards for the public.

Standards have been developed for disposal of low-level radioactive wastes at DOE sites (DOE, 1988b). DOE requirements are consistent with NRC standards in that they specify (1) a limit on annual effective dose equivalent to offsite individuals of 0.25 mSv (25 mrem) and (2) limits on annual effective dose equivalent to inadvertent intruders of 1 mSv (0.1 rem) for continuous exposure and 5 mSv (0.5 rem) for occasional exposure. The latter requirement conforms to impending NRC radiation protection standards discussed earlier.

EPA is developing standards for land disposal of low-level radioactive wastes and naturally occurring and accelerator-produced radioactive materials (NARM) (EPA, 1989b; EPA, 1989c). Consistent with NRC standards and DOE requirements, EPA intends to propose a limit on annual effective dose equivalent to offsite individuals of 0.25 mSv (25 mrem).

EPA may also propose requirements (EPA, 1989b; EPA, 1989c) for protection of ground water at land disposal sites as follows: (1) No increase in levels of radioactivity for Class I ground waters, which are irreplaceable sources of drinking water for a substantial population and/or are ecologically vital. (2) For Class II ground waters, which could or do provide the primary source for a community water system, a limit on annual effective dose equivalent to individuals from manmade radionuclides of 0.04 mSv (4 mrem), assuming ingestion of 2 L/day, and a concentration limit for radium of 0.2 Bq/L (5 pCi/L). (3) A limit on annual effective dose equivalent of 0.25 mSv (25 mrem) from all exposure pathways from contamination of Class IIIA or IIIB ground waters, which are not potable but are interconnected to adjacent Class I or II ground and/or surface waters. These potential ground-water protection requirements would be important potential ARAR for cleanup of inactive radioactive waste-disposal sites.

EPA's draft standards for low-level waste disposal (EPA, 1989b) do not address protection of inadvertent intruders. However, draft standards for disposal of NARM (EPA, 1989c) incorporate a level of protection for inadvertent intruders that is consistent with NRC's standards for land disposal of radioactive wastes (NRC, 1988c).

PROPOSED RADIOLOGICAL CRITERIA FOR SITE CLOSURE

Based on impending NRC standards for radiation protection of the public, EPA standards for radioactivity in drinking water, and current NRC and draft EPA standards for near-surface land disposal of radioactive wastes, the following radiological criteria are proposed for closure of inactive radioactive waste-disposal sites at ORNL:

- for offsite individuals beyond any boundary at which active institutional control is maintained, a limit on annual effective dose equivalent from all exposure pathways of 0.25 mSv (25 mrem);

- for inadvertent intruders following loss of active institutional control, limits on annual effective dose equivalent from all exposure pathways of 1 mSv (0.1 rem) for continuous exposure and 5 mSv (0. 5 rem) for occasional exposure; and

- to the extent reasonably achievable, limits on concentrations of radionuclides in ground and surface waters in accordance with federal drinking-water standards and ground-water protection requirements.

The closure criteria for inactive radioactive waste-disposal sites at ORNL would be the same as requirements that will be placed on new low-level waste-disposal facilities at all DOE sites (DOE, 1988b) for protection of human health and the environment.

Two aspects of the proposed closure criteria should be emphasized. First, these criteria would be used to determine *a priori* the need for and acceptability of remedial actions at radioactively contaminated sites. Second, because previous waste-disposal practices at ORNL were not subject to the requirements for protection of ground and surface waters that will apply to future disposals, cleanup of potential sources to current or future standards would be required only if compliance is technically achievable and the resulting benefits exceed costs. Even if drinking-water standards and ground-water protection requirements were not reasonably achievable at ORNL, the requirements for limiting dose from all exposure pathways to offsite individuals and inadvertent intruders would ensure adequate protection of public health from consumption of drinking water at or near contaminated sites.

Cleanup of contaminated sites is not the only means of complying with the proposed closure criteria. Appropriate remedial actions could include (1) extending the period of active institutional control over disposal sites beyond 100 yr, (2) maintaining active institutional control at locations well beyond the boundary of contaminated sites, and (3) use of passive institutional controls, e.g., public records and marker systems at disposal sites to reduce public risk, particularly to inadvertent intruders.

ACKNOWLEDGMENT

Work supported by U.S. Department of Energy under Contract DE-AC05-84OR 21400 with Martin Marietta Energy Systems, Inc.

REFERENCES

Baes, C. F. III and G. Marland. 1989. Evaluation of Cleanup Records for Remedial Action at CERCLA Sites Based on a Review of EPA Records of Decision, ORNL-6479. Oak Ridge National Laboratory, Oak Ridge, TN.

DOE. 1988a. Radiation Protection of the Public and the Environment, Draft Order 5400.xx. U.S. Department of Energy, Washington, DC.

DOE. 1988b. Management of low-level waste, Chapter III. In: Radioactive Waste Management, Order 5820.2A. U.S. Department of Energy, Washington, DC.

EPA. 1986. Water Pollution Control; National Primary Drinking Water Regulations; Radionuclides, Advance Notice of Proposed Rulemaking, 40 CFR Part 141. *Fed. Reg. 51*:34836-34862.

EPA. 1988. National Interim Primary Drinking Water Regulations, Part 141, pp. 526-587. In: Code of Federal Regulations, Title 40, Parts 100 to 149. U.S. Government Printing Office, Washington, DC.

EPA. 1989a. National Priorities List for Uncontrolled Hazardous Waste Sites: Update #9 - Federal Facility Sites, Proposed Rule, 40 CFR Part 300. *Fed. Reg.* *54*:29820-29825.

EPA. 1989b. Environmental Standards for Management and Land Disposal of Low-Level Radioactive Wastes, Draft Proposed Rule, 40 CFR Part 193. U.S. Environmental Protection Agency, Washington, DC.

EPA. 1989c. Land Disposal of Naturally Occurring and Accelerator-Produced Radioactive Materials (NARM), Draft Proposed Rule, 40 CFR Part 764. U.S. Environmental Protection Agency, Washington, DC.

Kocher, D. C. 1988. Review of radiation protection and environmental radiation standards for the public. *Nucl. Saf.* *29*:463-475.

Mills, W. A., D. S. Flack, F. J. Arsenault, and E. F. Conti. 1988. A Compendium of Major U.S. Radiation Protection Standards and Guides: Legal and Technical Facts, ORAU 88/F-111. Oak Ridge Associated Universities, Oak Ridge, TN.

NRC. 1986. Standards for Protection Against Radiation, Proposed Rule, 10 CFR Parts 19, 20, 30, 31, 32, 34, 40, 50, 61, and 70. *Fed. Reg.* *51*:1092-1216.

NRC. 1988a. Standards for Protection Against Radiation, Part 20, pp. 264-302. In: Code of Federal Regulations, Title 10, Parts 0 to 50. U.S. Government Printing Office, Washington, DC.

NRC. 1988b. Standards for Protection Against Radiation, Part 20, Draft Final Rule. Nuclear Regulatory Commission, Washington, DC.

NRC. 1988c. Licensing Requirements for Land Disposal of Radioactive Waste, Part 61, pp. 92-116. In: Code of Federal Regulations, Title 10, Parts 51 to 199. U.S. Government Printing Office, Washington, DC.

ORNL. 1987. RCRA Facilities Assessment (RFA) - Oak Ridge National Laboratory, ORNL/RAP-12/Vl. Oak Ridge National Laboratory, Oak Ridge, TN.

Trabalka, J. R., and T. E. Myrick. 1987. ORNL Remedial Action Program Strategy (FY 1987-FY 1992), ORNL/TM-l0244. Oak Ridge National Laboratory, Oak Ridge, TN.

EFFECTIVENESS OF INTERIM REMEDIAL ACTIONS AT THE NIAGARA FALLS STORAGE SITE

J. S. Devgun,[1] N. J. Beskid,[1] W. M. Seay,[2] and E. McNamee[3]

[1]Argonne National Laboratory, Argonne, Illinois

[2]U.S. Department of Energy, Oak Ridge, Tennessee

[3]Bechtel National, Inc., Oak Ridge, Tennessee

Key Words: *Radioactive, remedial actions, NFSS*

ABSTRACT

There are 190,000 m³ of contaminated soils, wastes, and residues stored at the Niagara Falls Storage Site (NFSS). The residues have a volume of 18,000 m³ and contain about 1930 Ci of ^{226}Ra, which accounts for most of the radioactivity. Since 1980, actions have been taken to minimize potential radiological risks and prevent radionuclide migration. Interim actions included capping vents, sealing pipes, relocating the perimeter fence (to limit radon risk), transferring and consolidating wastes, upgrading storage buildings, constructing a clay cutoff wall (to limit potential ground-water transport of contaminants), treating and releasing contaminated water, using a synthetic liner, and using an interim clay cap. An interim waste containment facility was completed in 1986.

Environmental monitoring showed a decrease in radon concentrations and in external gamma radiation from 1982 to 1986; levels have been stable since 1986. Uranium and radium concentrations in surface water have decreased; very low concentrations have been detected in stream sediments, and concentrations in ground water have remained stable. Recent monitoring showed that NFSS is in compliance with the U.S. Department of Energy's (DOE's) radiation protection standards.

SITE BACKGROUND

The Niagara Falls Storage Site (NFSS) is located in northwestern New York in Lewiston Township, Niagara County, approximately 6.4 km south of Lake Ontario and 16 km north of Niagara Falls. The site occupies approximately 77.4 ha in a generally rural setting and is bordered by a hazardous-waste disposal site, a sanitary landfill, and vacant land. Figure 1 shows the key features of the site, including the numbers and locations of various old buildings that are no longer in existence. The nearest permanent residence is 1.1 km to the southwest.

125

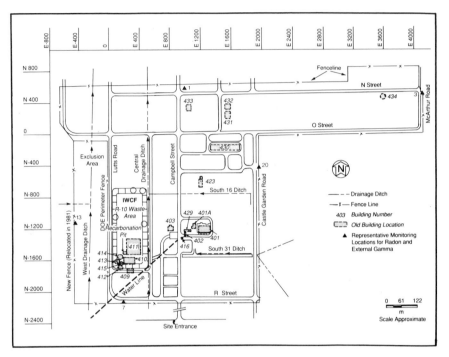

Figure 1. Niagara Falls storage site (NFSS).

The climate of the area is classified as humid continental; normal yearly temperatures range from -3.9 to 24.4°C; mean annual precipitation is 80 cm. Wind is predominantly from the southwest, with an average monthly wind speed ranging from 15.9 to 23 km/h. The site is generally level, sloping gently to the northwest. Soils are predominantly silty loams underlaid by clayey glacial till and lacustrine clay. Surface water from the site discharges via the Central Drainage Ditch and its tributary ditches into Four Mile Creek, located northwest of the site (BNI, 1989).

NFSS is a remnant of the original 612-ha site used during World War II by the Manhattan Engineer District (MED) project and was part of the U.S. Department of the Army's Lake Ontario Ordnance Works (LOOW). The site's major use since 1944 has been for storage and transitory storage of radioactive residues from uranium processing during the MED and subsequent Atomic Energy Commission projects. The site is currently managed by the DOE under its Formerly Utilized Site Remedial Action Program (previously under Surplus Facilities Management Program).

Composition of residues and waste materials at NFSS is given in DOE (1986); primary radionuclides are ^{238}U, ^{226}Ra, and associated radioactive decay products. The major contaminant is ^{226}Ra. Materials stored at the site consist of low-grade residues and by-products from the Linde Air Products Division, Union Carbide Corporation, Tonawanda, New York (L-300, L-50, and R-10 residues) and from the sampling plant in Middlesex, New Jersey (F-32 residues). The L-30 and L-50 residues were stored in Buildings 411, 413, and 414; F-32 residues were stored in the recarbonation pit directly west of Building 411. R-10 residues and associated iron cake were stored in the open, north of Building 411. The small quantity of Middlesex sands resulting from decontamination activities at the sampling plant was stored in Building 410. In 1949, pitchblende (K-65) residues from uranium extraction at a St. Louis, Missouri, plant were transported to the LOOW in drums; some were stored outdoors along existing roads and rail lines; others were stored in Building 410. From 1950 to 1952, the K-65 residues were transferred to a renovated concrete water tower (Building 434).

About 190,000 m^3 of contaminated soils, wastes, and residues are stored at NFSS. The residue inventory includes: 3891 short tons (tn) K-65, 8227 tn L-30, 1878 tn L-50, 138 tn F-32, and 8235 tn R-10 (BCL, 1981). About 2 tn of Middlesex sands are also stored at the site. The residues, about 18,000 m^3, account for most of the radioactivity, primarily from ^{226}Ra. The K-65 residues, which account for about 95% of the ^{226}Ra content, are estimated to contain about 1830 Ci of ^{226}Ra (Letter from G. P. Turi, U.S. Department of Energy, Washington, D.C. to R. Hargrove, U.S. Environmental Protection Agency, New York, NY, March 13, 1987). The amount of uranium remaining in residues and wastes after extraction from the ores is low: <30 Ci in residues and <1 Ci in wastes (DOE, 1986).

INTERIM REMEDIAL ACTIONS AND THEIR EFFECTIVENESS

Over the past 3 yr, several interim actions were taken at NFSS. Overall, these actions reduced radon release levels from above DOE guidelines to near background. Beginning in 1984, wastes were consolidated; following this action, gamma exposure rates declined to stable, low levels when the Interim Waste Containment Facility (IWCF) was completed in 1986.

Inhalation of radon and gamma irradiation are the only significant exposure pathways at or near NFSS. Figures 2 and 3 show declines in radon and gamma exposure rates during the years when interim remedial actions were taken, eventually culminating in waste consolidation in the IWCF. Radon levels, including background, which has ranged from 0.3 to 1 pCi/L over the past several years, are shown in Figure 2. Gamma exposure rates that can be attributed to radioactive materials at NFSS are shown in Figure 3. The background levels, 64 to 91 mR/yr, were subtracted from the readings.

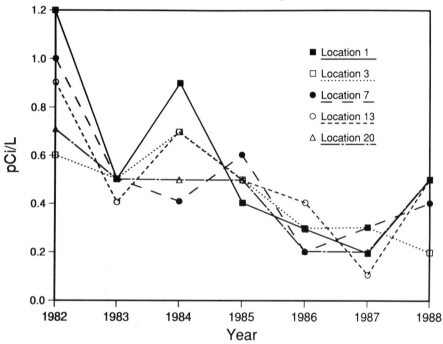

Figure 2. Radon levels (annual averages) at representative NFSS boundary locations.

The current monitoring network includes 35 radon detectors and 33 thermoluminescent dosimeters to measure gamma radiation. Average annual concentrations of total uranium in surface water where the Central Drainage Ditch exits NFSS have decreased from 108 pCi/L in 1982 to 10 pCi/L in 1988. Radium concentrations at the same location have remained low, ranging from 1.5 pCi/L in 1982 to 1.0 pCi/L in 1988. Average concentrations in sediments were 2 pCi/g (dry) for uranium and 0.9 pCi/g for radium in 1988; these are near-background levels. Total uranium and radium in ground water have generally remained stable. For example, along the eastern and western edges of the northern NFSS boundary, uranium concentration is about 4 pCi/L and that for radium is about 0.4 pCi/L. Only one well on the western perimeter of IWCF has shown elevated uranium (about 55 pCi/L). The well is located in a sand lens (a small deposit of sand of finite extent in a formation of clay or other geologic stratum); radioactive contamination may reflect contaminated solids in or near the well (BNI, 1989). The current ground water monitoring network consists of 48 onsite wells.

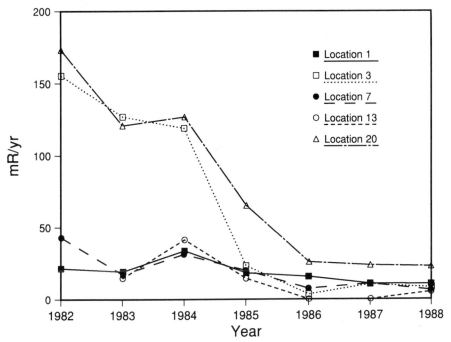

Figure 3. Gamma exposure rates (annual averages) at representative NFSS boundary locations.

A radiological survey of NFSS conducted in 1979 served as the basis for initial interim remedial action planning (BCL, 1981). Bechtel National, Inc., DOE's project management contractor, has implemented interim remedial actions since 1981 and currently maintains the site and conducts environmental monitoring (BNI, 1989).

Since 1980, actions have been taken at the NFSS to minimize radiological risks and prevent migration of residues. For example, the vent on top of Building 434 (the former water tower where K-65 residues were stored) was capped to reduce radon emissions, and pipes penetrating the walls of residue storage buildings were sealed or resealed to prevent radionuclide migration. Because radon levels (5 to 7 pCi/L; NLO, 1981) exceeded the DOE limit (3 pCi/L; DOE, 1987), the site fence was relocated, in 1981, 152.4 m to the west, to create an exclusion area and protect the public. Radon levels at the new boundary were below applicable guidelines. Also in 1981, 342 m³ of excavated material, contaminated with ^{238}U and decay products, from a triangle-shaped property adjacent to NFSS, was placed in storage at the site.

To further reduce radon levels, Buildings 413 and 414 (used to store L-50 residues) were upgraded and sealed in 1982. To prevent further migration of residues, contaminated soil near the R-10 pile was moved onto the pile, and a dike and cutoff wall were constructed around the R-10 area. The R-10 pile was then covered with an ethylene propylene diene monomer (EPDM) liner. This action effectively reduced radon concentrations at the old site boundary (along Lutts Road, Figure 1) to below DOE guidelines.

In 1983 and 1984, the EPDM liner was removed, additional contaminated soils and rubble from on and off site were placed on the pile, and the pile was covered with the first layer of an interim clay cap. These actions constituted the origin of the IWCF. In 1984, 93% of K-65 residues were transferred from Building 434 to Building 411 inside the IWCF.

Transfer of K-65 residues from Building 434 to the IWCF was completed in 1985. Other actions included demolition of Building 434, completion of remedial action on properties near the site, and continued installation of the cap over waste in the IWCF. These actions involved excavating 10,640 m³ of contaminated materials from on and off site, transferring 1,102 m³ of building rubble to the IWCF, and discharging 12 million L of treated, impounded water in accordance with New York State Department of Environmental Conservation (NYSDEC) permit requirements. In 1986, another 25.8 million L of contaminated water were treated and released; four of six water treatment ponds were reclaimed and reduced to grade.

The cap over the IWCF was completed in 1986. The facility covers 4 ha and is enclosed within a dike and cutoff wall, each constructed of compacted clay. The cutoff wall extends a minimum of 45 cm into an underlying clay unit. The dike and cutoff wall, in conjunction with the engineered earthen cap, enclose waste in a clay envelope that prevents migration of contaminants. Pollution control measures used during construction of the IWCF included sedimentation barriers in excavation areas and batch discharges of treated, impounded surface water in accordance with NYSDEC requirements. In 1987, impounded water in the remaining two ponds (38.8 million L) was treated and released; the ponds were reclaimed and reduced to grade; and the NFSS was closed. The site is currently inactive except for environmental monitoring, and surveillance and maintenance of the IWCF.

In 1988, several isolated areas of residual radioactivity were excavated and placed in temporary storage until the IWCF is reopened so that additional material can be added. At present, all the residual radioactivity on site has been remediated except for one localized area, which will be remediated in the future (BNI, 1989).

CONCLUSIONS

Interim remedial actions over the past 8 yr at NFSS have reduced radon and gamma exposure. Since the IWCF was completed in 1986, exposure levels have remained stable and close to background. Remedial actions have also limited migration of radionuclides via water. Environmental monitoring shows the site is in compliance with DOE's radiation protection standards.

ACKNOWLEDGMENT

Work supported by the U.S. Department of Energy under Contract W-31-109-Eng-38.

REFERENCES

BCL. 1981. A Comprehensive Characterization and Hazard Assessment of the DOE Niagara Falls Storage Site, BMI-2074. Battelle Columbus Laboratories, Columbus, OH.

BNI. 1989. Niagara Falls Storage Site Annual Site Environmental Report, Calendar Year 1988, DOE/OR/20722-219 (Other relevant reports: 1982, No. 10-05-202-002; 1983, DOE/OR 20722-18; 1984, DOE/OR/20722-557; 1985, DOE/OR/20722-98; 1986, DOE/OR/20722-150; 1987, DOE/OR/20722-197). Bechtel National, Inc., Oak Ridge, TN.

DOE. 1986. Final Environmental Impact Statement: Long-Term Management of the Existing Radioactive Wastes and Residues at the Niagara Falls Storage Site, DOE/EIS-0109F. U.S. Department of Energy, Washington, DC.

DOE. 1987. U.S. Department of Energy Guidelines for Residual Radioactive Material at Formerly Utilized Sites. Remedial Action Program and Remote Surplus Facilities Management Program (Revision 2, March). U.S. Department of Energy, Washington, DC.

NLO. 1981. Environmental Monitoring Report for Niagara Falls Storage Site for 1979 and 1980, NLCO-OO7EV. National Lead of Ohio, Cincinnati, OH.

MONITORING STRIP-MINE RECLAMATION IN IOWA

L. Drake

Department of Geology, University of Iowa, Iowa City, Iowa

Key Words: *Strip mine, reclamation, surface mine, monitoring*

ABSTRACT

Iowa coal strip-mine spoils are unusually acid compared to those elsewhere in the Midwest. Although monitoring and reclamation regulations have been gradually implemented in Iowa over the past two decades, prereclamation monitoring is still inadequate, and surprises during reclamation are common. For example, expansion of a headwall lake basin uncovered a mine drift filled with a 50-yr accumulation of hog manure slurry, washed in from a nearby feedlot. For long-abandoned strip mines, enforcement of acid mine drainage regulations usually causes the demise of rare and endangered plant species, creating a dilemma for regulators. Short-term postreclamation monitoring usually shows that most sites have been adequately reclaimed for the first few years but may still be destined to revert to prereclamation condition. A serious deficiency is the lack of long-term studies of reclaimed areas. Reclamation methods that often lead to long-term failure are used because they usually represent the lowest per-acre bid, and there is no documentation of previous failures. Lack of information about organic matter in rebuilt "soils" is probably the cause of many of these failures. Dendrochronology is proving to be a useful tool for monitoring the long-term response of older tree plantings.

INTRODUCTION

Since 1968, I have monitored abandoned and reclaimed coal strip-mines in south-central Iowa. This paper summarizes four concerns raised by this monitoring and their possible solutions.

AVOIDING SURPRISES

Although prereclamation monitoring is now required in Iowa, once reclamation is underway, surprises are common. One example occurred during reclamation of the south Hull site, near Oskaloosa, during 1986-1987. Strip-mining during World War II left pyritic shales exposed, producing acid surface conditions, a barren landscape, and massive erosion (averaging 2 cm/yr; Esling and Drake, 1988). Underground mining had preceded strip-mining, and before reclamation started some collapse pits were observed, but no particular significance was then attached to them.

133

Part of the reclamation project was to enlarge a highwall pit into a small lake. As adjacent spoil piles were being reshaped to form the basin, a spring developed at the base. From it flowed a brown liquid, recognizable a quarter-mile downwind as ripe hog manure. One of the collapse pits across the strip mine was downslope from a feedlot; its runoff had been funneled into the pit for the last 50 yr.

The "solution" was to seal off both seep area and collapse pit with a cap of compacted shaley spoil. Rainfall in 1987 filled the lake, increasing pressure against the seal. Monitoring indicated there were no feedlot organics in the lake. As the lake filled, another leachate spring developed elsewhere in the mine which was also capped with compacted shale. We do not know whether an entire mine-drift system within the site was filled with this material, or whether capping the first spring raised the hydraulic head and redirected flow. Since then, the weather has been drier, and no additional springs have developed. Besides the potential for future breakouts, it is not known whether aquifers are being contaminated.

More comprehensive prereclamation monitoring might not only have recognized the size of the problem but would have encouraged use of less vulnerable designs. If the site had been recognized as a ground-water protection project rather than merely a reclamation project, other funding might have been available. Additional prereclamation monitoring could have included:

1. Differentiating drift-mine spoils from strip-mine spoils, which might have revealed locations of drift adits and patterns of later strip-mining through the drift-mined area.

2. Detailed mapping of surficial drainages and estimates of flow volumes, which should have revealed that the feedlot drainage had gone underground. A few monitoring wells in this drift would probably have indicated the dimensions of the problem.

3. Geophysical techniques might have provided useful information. On the nearby Rempe reclamation site, electromagnetic conductivity outlined the details of a collapsed room-and-pillar mine (Drake and Neimann, 1987). This method measures contrasts in bulk conductivity of soil, rock, and ground water. It is not known how successful this technique would be for liquid-manure-filled passages.

4. Delineation of underground mine drifts by drilling would have been informative if only a few samples (e.g., of mine water) were

required. However, in most cases, drilling is prohibitively expensive unless a mine map is available. Although maps are available for 864 underground mines in Iowa (of about 6000 known to exist), none was found for this mine.

Overall, the presence and distribution of old underground mines remains a difficult aspect of Iowa strip-mine reclamation and monitoring.

MONITORING/ENFORCEMENT DILEMMAS

Monitoring, which is frequently tied to regulatory programs, can be problematic. Regulations predate monitoring and do not adequately address discoveries made during monitoring. For example, prior to reclaiming the abandoned south Hull site in 1986-1987, monitoring showed that a small wetland (a fen bordered by wet prairie) was partially enclosed by mine spoils.

In a brief visit to the fen, bryologist Diana Horton (Botany Department, University of Iowa) located seven species of sphagnum, including two that were rare and one never before recorded in Iowa. Sphagnum communities require acid conditions, and a study of the shallow hydrology revealed that the fen was fed by acid springs (pH, 3.1-3.5) at the head of the wetland. The springs emanated from the base of a spoil ridge, behind which was a very acid pond (pH, 2.8), at an elevation 0.8 m (33 in.) higher than the springs. Leakage of acid pond water through the spoil ridge was evidently the source for the acid springs.

Although a major reclamation goal was to eliminate acid drainage, this drainage was supporting the sphagnum fen. Eliminating the acid flow would probably destroy these rare species. Earliest air photos, dated 1938, showed that the fen already existed, unplowed, prior to strip-mining. Thus, this may have been a natural sphagnum wetland that came into existence before the mine spoils created acid conditions.

Graham Tobin (Geography Department, University of Iowa) and I then cored the fen in three locations. The preagricultural soil was distinctive at depths of 203-254 mm (8-10 in.), above which were watery silts and peats. Kathy Woida (Geology Department, University of Iowa) studied spores and pollen from one core. Spore and pollen counts from samples below the preagricultural surface were sparse and dominated by sedges, which are mostly wetland species. The sparse counts indicate an oxidizing environment which destroys pollen and spores and represents very slow sediment accumulation, which is compatible with the deep, black, prairie topsoil at these levels. Above the preagricultural surface, a massive influx of ragweed pollen was indicative of the disturbed ground produced by European-style agriculture. In addition, there were high counts of Paleozoic-age spores, fossils eroded from the surrounding mine spoils. No sphagnum spores were found in any sample; perhaps they were not well preserved in this environment. In one core extending to 3.5 m (11-1/2 ft), a sample of black soil from near the bottom was radiocarbon-dated at 7120 yr, demonstrating that the site has been a wetland for at least that long. However, it is still unclear whether the sphagnum is a natural component, or whether it moved in after strip-mining created appropriately acid conditions.

When reclamation began, the spoils enclosing the wetland were smoothed into tile terraces, draining toward the wetland to retain water. The acid source pond was filled, and the surrounding landscape was covered with a thin layer of salvaged soil, limed heavily, and planted with grasses for erosion control. Rainfall was subsequently above average, the springs continued to flow, and during May 1987 the site acquired the unmistakable odor of hog manure. The springs are apparently also in hydrologic continuity with the mine system discussed earlier.

We have now entered a drought cycle, the springs have dried up, and the water table in the fen has dropped about a foot. When normal rainfall returns, the fate of the now-desiccated sphagnum community will depend on the hydrologic balance. If surface runoff dominates, flashy input will result in rapid water loss (compared to steady leakage from the former strip-mine pond) and, probably, lowering of the water table. This, in addition to the applied lime, will probably prove fatal to the sphagnum. However, if the underground system dominates, acid mine waters may flush the lime and keep the water table high. High nutrient levels (lime plus hog manure) might encourage the growth of cattails, which invade disturbed or eutrophic wetlands (Apfelbaum, 1985), and the sphagnum fen could also be choked out.

This problem is not limited to this site. Most of Iowa's ground water is very hard (high calcium and magnesium content), and most of its wetlands are enriched both mineralogically (calcareous marshes, rich fens) and by agricultural runoff (especially nitrogen and phosphorus). Acid-loving bryophytes are therefore rare. A survey of bryophyte species in abandoned Iowa strip mines showed that the occurrence and distribution of 29 mosses and 2 liverworts on spoils of varying age was related to processes of spoil revegetation (Carvey et al., 1977). A few of these species are known only from acid mine seeps. The standard strip-mine reclamation goal of eliminating acid mine drainage will also eliminate these rare species. If they were not originally native to Iowa, their loss might not be serious; if they were initially rare, it is difficult to justify their extirpation. I hope that continued long-term monitoring at the south Hull site will reveal the most important conditions that determine the success or failure of sphagnum species at reclaimed sites.

MONITORING SOIL ORGANICS

A 1972 survey of abandoned mines in the south-central Iowa coal district showed that in 22 of 38 mines, more than 50% of the surface area had a pH of 4 or less (Drake and Ririe, 1981). It has long been recognized that this degree of acidity is lethal to most plants (Limstrom, 1960). When reclaiming abandoned sites, one of the most difficult aspects is locating enough soil materials to cover the acid spoils. As little as 152-305 mm (6-12 in.) of cover will marginally support grasses (Drake, 1983), shrubs, and trees (Drake, 1986), but even this is often not available.

One remedy is to modify existing spoils so as to provide a suitable growing medium. Reclamation, in many states, has incorporated large amounts of lime, fertilizer, and organics into leveled spoils to create a "soil." The literature documents many successes from incorporating sewage sludge. Application of just powdered limestone to barren acidified soils around Sudbury, Ontario, triggered immediate colonization of native plant species (Winterhalder, 1983). This was an unusually responsive situation because these pedogenic soils had been acidified by smelter fumes and, once neutralized, there were no residual sulfide minerals to create more acidity. By contrast, strip-mine spoils can contain an abundance of sulfide minerals, which continuously weather to form more acid. Although several calculation methods are available, the correct amount of lime needed is difficult to determine because rates of acid production depend on mineralogy, grain size, depth of burial, redox conditions, and bacterial activity, and their combined effects are difficult to predict.

Attempts to create soil from strongly acidic mine wastes by incorporating lime and raw organic materials (e.g., straw) are fraught with difficulties. The Schmidt site near Knoxville, Iowa, was reclaimed using this method in 1987. In the more acid portions of the graded spoil, 44,790 kg/ha (20 tons/acre) of powdered limestone and 11,198 kg/ha (5 tons/acre) of straw were disked into the top foot of spoil, and the site was heavily fertilized. After seeding with grasses, an additional 4479 kg/ha (2 tons/acre) of straw was applied as mulch. Even this was inadequate, for several reasons. Organics in native black topsoils include colloidal humates, gums, polysaccharides, and resins, along with fine fibrils which coat and separate soil particles. The latter have a large surface area and absorb and retain water for plant use. Raw straw, which consists of large chunks of cellulose and lignin, does not offer these amenities to growing plants. In contrast, sewage sludge has been through two digestion processes and contains organics more like those in natural soil than does straw. Although straw eventually decomposes, the quantity of useful organics will be smaller than that in straw. Seven tons of straw, if composted separately, will produce less than 1 ton of compost, and part of that will be moisture. Thus in 1988, a drought year, the new seeding at the Schmidt site was practically a total loss.

Reclamation programs should include monitoring of soil organic matter. Soil micromorphology (the optical study of soil thin sections) can reveal the distribution of organic matter in reclaimed soils. Although our knowledge of the molecular chemistry of soil organics is primitive, data on cation exchange capacity and water retention might be adequate predictive monitoring tools.

NECESSITY OF LONG-TERM MONITORING

Failure of reclamation sites can be a slow, cumulative process, and long-term monitoring is required to understand the mechanisms involved. The 1968 north Hull site reclamation is an example. Reclamation goals were modest: attempt to establish a plant cover and prevent erosion. Scattered patches of loess, till, and brown shale were salvaged for a final cover. The design was intended to create a smoothed topography with little acid shale at the surface. Terracettes were included on long slopes to reduce erosion. However, to minimize costs, bulldozer operators were not continually instructed to segregate the low-acid materials. Thus, the final surface on the east half of the plot had many exposed acid patches (pH, 3.3-4.8), and the low-acid cover was thin and discontinuous. All surfaces were heavily limed and fertilized. A mixture of perennial grasses and legumes, and an oat nurse crop, were seeded over the regraded surface. Approximately 31,000 tree seedlings were planted.

Scattered "hot spots" (pH, 2.8-3.5) developed quickly, but on most of the area the oat crop retarded erosion. By late 1970, 4000 seedlings were still alive. The mine inspector reported (Ross, 1970) that 50% of the area was well covered and another 25% was fairly well covered, so there was reason for optimism that the area would, in a few years, be reclaimed for useful purposes. The acid-eroding portions were regraded, relimed, and reseeded several times in subsequent years, but with discouraging results.

More serious difficulties were observed in the third year after reclamation. Oats no longer provided cover, and many seedling roots encountered acid shale at shallow depths and perished. As vegetation slowly failed, headward erosion from the barren zones undercut healthy plants. By 1985, only small relics of the 1968 surface remained on the east side, and the gullies had enlarged to canyons 3-4.6 m (10-15 ft) deep. The area was again reclaimed in 1986-1987.

Most reclamation sites in Iowa generally look healthy during the first year. Oats, winter wheat, and annual rye need only a few rains to produce a lush green carpet that creates the impression of success. If the following summers are unusually moist or cool, even a site doomed to fail in normal weather will temporarily support grasses and trees. Ideally, plant monitoring at reclamation sites should focus on roots rather than stems and leaves. Root density, rate of elongation, depth of penetration, and available soil volume are probably the critical factors for survival.

REFERENCES

Apfelbaum, S. I. 1985. Cattail management. *Natural Areas J. 3*:9-17.

Carvey, K., D. R. Yarrar, and D. C. Glenn-Lewis. 1977. Bryophytes and revegetation of coal spoils in southern Iowa. *The Bryologist 80*:631-637.

Drake, L. D. 1983. Erosion control with prairie grasses in Iowa strip-mine reclamation, pp. 189-197. In: Proceedings, 7th North American Prairie Conference, C. L. Kucera (ed.). Southwest Missouri State University, Springfield, MO.

Drake, L. D. 1986. Survival and growth of conservation shrubs and trees with thin-cover reclamation on acid substrate, Iowa, USA. *Environ. Geochem. Health 8*:62-67.

Drake, L. D. and R. Neimann. 1987. Strip-mine reclamation in Iowa, pp. D1-D43. In: 51st Annual Tri-state Geological Field Conference Guidebook, G. R. McCormick (ed.). University of Iowa, Iowa City, IA.

Drake, L. D. and G. T. Ririe. 1981. A low-cost method of reclaiming strip-mined land in Iowa to agriculture. *Environ. Geol. 3*:267-279.

Esling, S. and L. D. Drake. 1988. Erosion of strip-mine spoil in Iowa and its implications for erosion models. *Geomorphology 1*:279-296.

Limstrom, G. A. 1960. Forestation of strip-mined land, U.S. Department of Agriculture Handbook 166:74. U.S. Government Printing Office, Washington, DC.

Ross, M. B. 1970. Project to Demonstrate the Rehabilitation of Land Affected by Surface Mining, Progress Report. Iowa Department of Mines, Des Moines, IA.

Winterhalder, K. 1983. Limestone application as a trigger factor in the revegetation of acid, metal-contaminated soils of the Sudbury area, pp. 201-212. In: Proceedings, Canadian Land Reclamation Association, 8th Annual Meeting. University of Waterloo, Waterloo, Ontario, Canada.

DECOMMISSIONING OF NUCLEAR FACILITIES INVOLVING OPERATIONS WITH URANIUM AND THORIUM

E. Y. Shum and S. M. Neuder

U.S. Nuclear Regulatory Commission, Washington, DC

Key Words: *Decommissioning, uranium-thorium, facilities*

ABSTRACT

When a licensed nuclear facility ceases operation, the U.S. Nuclear Regulatory Commission (NRC) ensures that the facility and its site are decontaminated to acceptable levels so they may safely be released for unrestricted public use. Because specific environmental standards or broad federal guidelines governing release of residual radioactive contamination have not been issued, NRC has developed *ad hoc* cleanup criteria for decommissioning nuclear facilities that involved uranium and thorium. Cleanup criteria include decontamination of buildings, equipment, and land. We will address cleanup criteria and their rationale; procedures for decommissioning uranium/thorium facilities; radiological survey designs and procedures; radiological monitoring and measurement; and cost-effectiveness to demonstrate compliance.

INTRODUCTION

In decommissioning a nuclear facility, two sets of clean-up criteria are generally applied. One set of criteria defines acceptable residual levels of radioactivity for decontaminated buildings and equipment; the other defines acceptable residual levels for land or soil. The U.S. Nuclear Regulatory Commission (NRC) has developed *ad hoc* clean-up criteria for decommissioning nuclear facilities that involved operations with uranium and thorium. We will describe NRC's criteria and procedures for decontaminating these facilities to demonstrate compliance.

CRITERIA FOR CLEANUP
Buildings and Equipment

Guidelines specifying acceptable surface contamination levels for uranium and thorium are summarized in Table 1 (NRC, 1982). NRC is currently working on revised residual contamination limits for decommissioning based on radiological dose. Prior to publication and acceptance of revised limits, the criteria cited should be used for routine decontamination of these facilities.

Table 1. Acceptable surface contamination levels (dpm/100 cm²) for uranium and thorium (NRC, 1982).[a,b]

Nuclides	Average	Maximum	Removable
U-natural, U-235, U-238 and associated decay products	5,000	15,000	1,000
Th-natural and associated decay products	1,000	3,000	20
Beta-gamma emitters	5,000	15,000	1,000

[a] Where surface contamination is by both alpha- and beta-gamma-emitting nuclides limits for each should apply independently.

[b] Average and maximum radiation levels associated with surface contamination from beta-gamma emitters should not exceed 0.2 mrad/hr at 1 cm and 1.0 mrad/hr at 1 cm, respectively, measured through less than 7 mg/cm² of total absorber.

Land

For land or soil cleanup, NRC has established target criteria (Table 2), specified as Option 1 (NRC, 1981). In establishing these criteria, NRC applied the following rationale and objectives: (1) Radiation exposure to individuals using the land must be within current NRC and U.S. Environmental Protection Agency (EPA) guidelines, including the requirement that these exposures be as low as reasonably achievable. (2) The criteria must be consistent with those currently being applied or developed for similar situations.

Clean-up criteria for natural uranium and thorium when daughters are in equilibrium are based on EPA's mill tailings clean-up standards (EPA, 1987a). Clean-up criteria for depleted and enriched uranium are based on EPA's proposed guidance on dose limits for persons exposed to transuranic elements in the general environment (EPA, 1977).

Table 2. Clean-up criteria for land and soil (NRC, 1981a).

Material	Concentration (pCi/g)
Natural thorium (Th-232 + Th-228) with daughters present and in equilibrium	10
Natural uranium (U-238 + U-234) with daughters present and in equilibrium	10
Depleted uranium, natural uranium with daughters separated	35
Enriched uranium	30

DECOMMISSIONING PROCEDURES

General requirements and procedures for decommissioning nuclear facilities are specified in NRC's final rule on decommissioning (NRC, 1988). Specific requirements for decommissioning such facilities are specified in 10 CFR Parts 30, 40 and 70, covering by-product, source material, and special nuclear material licenses. Prior to initiating decommissioning, the licensee must submit a plan for review and approval. The decommissioning plan should include the following: (1) description of decommissioning procedures, including plans for processing and disposing of radioactive waste; (2) description of procedures to ensure worker and public safety; (3) plan for a final radiation survey to determine if property is suitable for unrestricted use; (4) cost estimate to ensure that adequate funds are available before decommissioning is initiated; and (5) description of quality assurance and safeguards provisions, if appropriate for specific license, such as for special nuclear materials.

Radiological Surveys

Radiological surveillance requirements and procedures to demonstrate compliance with the criteria cited for unrestricted use of the facility and site are given below.

Buildings and Equipment. (1) All survey instruments must be calibrated by qualified personnel, using accepted practices specified in the license. (2) Instruments must have sufficient detection sensitivity to verify compliance with acceptable contamination levels. Guidance concerning sensitivity for different radiation detection instruments is included in Chapter 4, NUREG/CR-2082 (NRC, 1981b) and National Council on Radiation Protection and Measurements Report No. 50 (NCRP, 1976). (3) All indoor (floors, walls, ceilings, equipment, furniture) and outdoor areas (roofs, ground, etc.) of buildings should be surveyed, and radiation levels should be reported, in appropriate units, in a survey report. Prior to surveying, the facility should be divided into specific survey areas. Guidance concerning grid sizes and total sample size required can be found in Chapter 3, NUREG/CR-2082 (NRC, 1981b). (4) For each survey block in the grid, the following measurements should be reported: (a) direct readings for alpha and beta-gamma radiation: Average and maximum contamination levels at the surface should be reported in dpm/100 cm^2 for alpha; dpm/ 100 cm^2 and μrad/hr for beta-gamma. (b) Alpha and beta-gamma removable contamination levels determined by smear testing should be reported in dpm/100 cm^2.

Land. Acceptable sample collection and measurement procedures are described in NUREG/CR-2082 (NRC, 1981b). Prior to decommissioning, split soil samples should be sent to NRC or its contractor for analysis to compare and confirm results.

Surface. (1) Surface (0-15 cm depth) soil samples should be systematically collected from each 10-m x 10-m grid block for all "affected" areas; samples from the center and from four points midway between the center and block corners should be combined for analysis. An affected area is one with high potential for contamination from plant operations. Grid blocks for unaffected areas may be sampled and analyzed randomly. (2) Exposure rate should be measured at and 1 m above the surface at soil sampling locations directed in (1). (3) Beta-gamma radiation should be measured 1 cm above the surface at soil sampling locations. (4) Composite sediment samples should be collected from lagoons and outfalls.

Subsurface. Subsurface samples are required if there is reason to suspect contamination in outdoor areas or under buildings. Standard core-sampling techniques may be used to assess subsurface soil contamination as a function of depth. Any of the following conditions may require analysis of subsurface samples: (1) if records show radioactive material has been buried in the area; (2) if records show radioactive material (such as dry or liquid wastes) has been stored underground, or in a pond, in the area; (3) if there is any unexplainable elevated, direct survey reading in the area; (4) if creeks, streams, or underground transfer pipes were used for contaminated liquid effluent release.

Water. Samples should be taken from each source of potable water, surface water, and ground water on the site, including water in core holes drilled for subsurface soil samples. Additional onsite and offsite ground-water samples may be required if subsurface contamination is suspected.

DEMONSTRATING COMPLIANCE

NRC has considered the cost of soil analyses for radionuclides in the uranium and thorium series, and encourages the licensee to propose easy and less costly methods to demonstrate compliance. Some acceptable ways to demonstrate compliance are: (1) For natural uranium with daughters in equilibrium, ^{226}Ra can be used as the dominant radionuclide because of the easily measurable gamma peak from ^{214}Bi. (2) For natural thorium with daughters in equilibrium, ^{228}Ra or ^{228}Ac can be used as the dominant radionuclides for the reason given in (1). Radionuclides in the thorium series are strong gamma-emitters; NRC has criteria for direct gamma radiation that limits exposure to less than 10 μR/hr above background measured 1 m above the surface. If the licensee can show that 10 μR/hr can be related to a soil level of less than 5 pCi/g ^{228}Ra, direct gamma radiation measurement, which is less costly than performing specific radionuclide measurements, can be used to demonstrate surface soil compliance. (3) For depleted uranium, gross alpha activity in soil may be measured to demonstrate compliance. (4) For enriched uranium, ^{235}U can be used as the dominant radionuclide because of the easily detectable gamma peak, provided that the ratio of ^{234}U/^{235}U is accurately measured.

The criteria summarized in Table 2 apply to surface and subsurface soil decontamination. Issues arising from ground-water contamination are handled on a case-by-case basis. For example, if ground water is or could be used for drinking water, EPA's drinking-water standards for radionuclides such as ^{226}Ra and ^{228}Ra will apply. There is currently no drinking-water standard for uranium. If ground water is not used for drinking, the full pathway analysis to meet a target dose limit may be applied.

REFERENCES

EPA. 1977. Proposed Guidance on Dose Limits for Persons Exposed to Transuranium Elements in the General Environment, EPA 520/4-77-016. U.S. Environmental Protection Agency, Washington, DC.

EPA. 1987. 40 CFR Part 192: Standards for Remedial Actions of Inactive Uranium Processing Sites, 52 FR 36000-8. U.S. Environmental Protection Agency, Washington, DC.

NCRP. 1986. Environmental Radiation Measurements, NCRP Report No. 50. National Council on Radiation Protection and Measurements, Washington, DC.

NRC. 1981a. Branch Technical Position on the Disposal of Residual Thorium or Uranium, 46FR52061-3. U.S. Nuclear Regulatory Commission, Washington, DC.

NRC. 1981b. Monitoring for Compliance with Decommissioning Termination Survey Criteria, NUREG/CR-2082. U.S. Nuclear Regulatory Commission, Washington, DC.

NRC. 1982. Guidelines for Decontamination of Facilities and Equipment Prior to Release for Unrestricted Use or Termination of Licenses for Byproduct, Source, or Special Nuclear Material. U.S. Nuclear Regulatory Commission, Washington, DC.

NRC. 1988. General Requirements for Decommissioning Nuclear Facilities, 53FR24108-56. U.S. Nuclear Regulatory Commission, Washington, DC.

PROTECTIVE BARRIER DEVELOPMENT: OVERVIEW

N. R. Wing[1] and G. W. Gee[2]

[1]Westinghouse Hanford Company, Richland, Washington

[2]Pacific Northwest Laboratory, Richland, Washington

Key Words: *Technology development, in situ disposal, barriers, caps*

ABSTRACT

Protective barrier and warning marker systems are being developed to isolate wastes disposed of near the earth's surface at the Hanford Site. The barrier is designed to function in an arid to semiarid climate, to limit infiltration and percolation of water through the waste zone to near-zero, to be maintenance free, and to last up to 10,000 yr. Natural materials (e.g., fine soil, sand, gravel, riprap, clay, asphalt) have been selected to optimize barrier performance and longevity and to create an integrated structure with redundant features. These materials isolate wastes by limiting water drainage; reducing the likelihood of plant, animal, and human intrusion; controlling emission of noxious gases; and minimizing erosion. Westinghouse Hanford Company and Pacific Northwest Laboratory efforts to assess the performance of various barrier and marker designs will be discussed.

INTRODUCTION

Protective barrier and warning marker systems are being developed to isolate certain types of wastes, disposed of near the earth's surface at the Hanford Site, from the environment. The barrier and warning marker systems use layers of natural materials to create an integrated structure with redundant protective features. The natural and manufactured materials (e.g., fine soil, sand, gravel, riprap, clay, asphalt) have been selected to optimize barrier performance and longevity. Current design objectives are to isolate wastes up to 10,000 yr by limiting water drainage; reducing the likelihood of plant, animal, and human intrusion; controlling emission of noxious gases; and minimizing erosion.

FUNCTIONAL PERFORMANCE OF PROTECTIVE BARRIERS

Protective barriers consist of various materials placed in layers to form an above-grade mound directly over the waste zone. A typical barrier (Figure 1) includes (layered from top to bottom) fine soil, sand/fine gravel, and coarse materials such as pitrun gravels or crushed basalt riprap. A layer of crushed basalt riprap may also be used on the shoulder, side slopes, and toe of the structure.

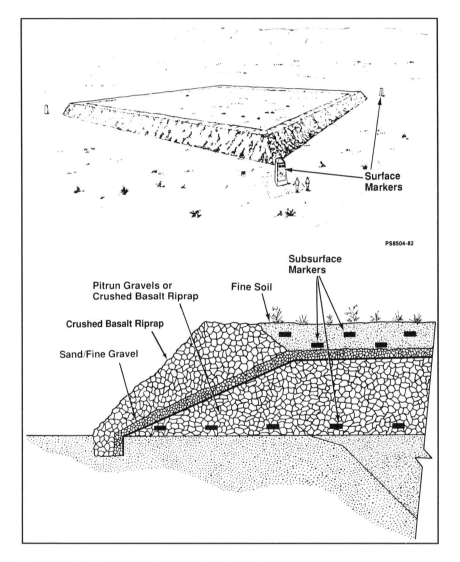

Figure 1. Typical protective barrier and warning marker system.

Each layer serves a distinct purpose (Figure 2). Fine soil stores moisture until evaporation and transpiration recycle the excess water back to the atmosphere. Fine soil also provides a substrate for plants that are necessary for transpiration. Gravels may be admixed into, or spread onto, the surface of the fine-soil layer to minimize wind and water erosion. The surface of the fine-soil layer can be designed to have a slight slope, or crown, to maximize runoff while further minimizing erosion.

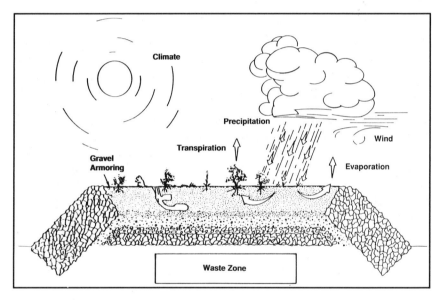

Figure 2. Functional performance of barriers.

The sand/fine-gravel layer serves a dual purpose. The textural difference at the interface between sand/fine gravel and fine soil creates a capillary break. The capillary break inhibits downward movement of moisture from the overlying unsaturated fine-soil layer. The sand/fine-gravel layer also functions as a filter to prevent fine soils from penetrating the void spaces of coarser materials below.

Coarse materials (e.g., pitrun gravels, crushed basalt riprap) are used to deter burrowing animals, deep-rooting plants, and human intruders from reaching the buried waste. Crushed basalt riprap is also used to protect against wind and water erosion of the barrier shoulder, side slope, and toe.

Low-permeability materials are also being considered for incorporation in the protective barrier design. During periods of unusually heavy or intense precipitation, the fine soil layer may not be able to completely retain and subsequently recycle all of the water to the atmosphere. Unless checked, the water would migrate through the protective barrier to the waste below. To restrict the percolating water, a low-permeability layer could be placed below the capillary break. This layer could be constructed of asphalt, clay, or chemical grout and would divert percolating water away from the waste zone. The layer would also help control emissions of noxious gases from certain wastes.

Surface markers, placed around the periphery of waste sites, will inform future generations of the nature and hazards of the buried wastes. In addition, subsurface markers, buried throughout the protective barrier, will warn people who inadvertently intrude into the barrier.

Because the barrier must perform for thousands of years without maintenance, natural materials (e.g., fine soil, sand, gravel, cobble, crushed basalt riprap, clay, asphalt) have been selected for use. Most of these materials exist in large quantities on the Hanford Site. In contrast to the natural construction materials, the ability of manmade construction materials to survive and function properly for thousands of years is not known. Because of this uncertainty, manmade construction materials are not used in protective barrier designs.

HANFORD SITE PROTECTIVE BARRIER DEVELOPMENT TEAM

Considerable development and evaluation must accompany the assessment of barrier and marker system performance. Thus, engineers and scientists from Westinghouse Hanford Company and the Pacific Northwest Laboratory formed the Hanford Site Protective Barrier Development Team in 1985. The team has overall responsibility for planning, directing, and executing development activities.

A Protective Barrier and Warning Marker System Development Plan (Adams and Wing, 1986) was prepared to organize and coordinate various activities associated with the development and testing of protective barrier and warning marker systems. Specific tasks were identified to resolve technical concerns and complete development and final design of the system (Figure 3). Test plans and detailed reports will describe future activities and results.

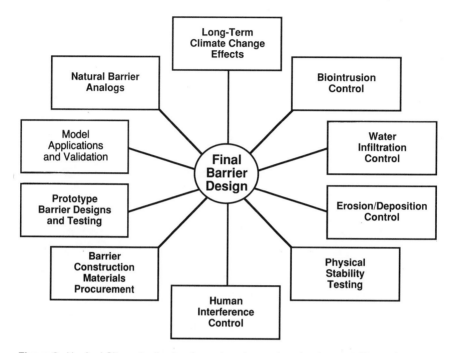

Figure 3. Hanford Site protective barrier and marker system development: Key tasks.

REFERENCE

Adams, M. R. and N. R. Wing. 1986. Protective Barrier and Warning Marker System Development Plan, RHO-RE-PL-35P. Rockwell Hanford Operations, Richland, WA.

ENVIRONMENTAL SURVEILLANCE AND RESEARCH AT THE NEVADA TEST SITE: THE BEGINNING AND THE RATIONALE

D. R. Elle, B. W. Church, and F. E. Bingham

Nevada Operations Office, U.S. Department of Energy, Las Vegas, Nevada

Key Words: *Nevada Test Site (NTS), program design, environmental monitoring, environmental impact*

ABSTRACT

Concurrently with the first nuclear-weapons tests at the Nevada Test Site (NTS) in 1951, an environmental surveillance and monitoring program was established offsite. Initial emphasis was on tracking fallout clouds and measuring external radiation exposure rates. An environmental research program was also initiated. Establishment of comprehensive programs has facilitated the ability to address issues such as the inventory and distribution of radionuclides in surface soils, reconstruction of offsite population doses, and recognition of areas requiring additional information. We have learned that a successful environmental monitoring program must be flexible and responsive to change; must address public as well as technical and regulatory concerns; and results must be continuously interpreted to ensure that all pathways are considered and that the programs are proactive in their approach.

THE BEGINNING

The Nevada Test Site (NTS), located 65 mi northwest of Las Vegas, Nevada, encompasses 1350 mi^2 in a sparsely populated region of the Mojave and Great Basin deserts. NTS is surrounded on three sides by the Nellis Air Force Bombing Ranges, which provide a buffer zone between the site and public lands. NTS was chosen as a continental proving ground for nuclear devices in 1950 to reduce expense and logistics problems associated with conducting nuclear testing in the mid-Pacific Ocean. The Nevada Operations Office (NVO) in Las Vegas was created in 1962 and assumed responsibility for operations and programs at NTS.

The first NTS nuclear detonation was an atmospheric test conducted in 1951. Testing continued periodically until 1958, when a testing moratorium was declared by President Eisenhower. After 3 yr, testing was resumed at NTS in 1961. All but five weapons tests conducted at the site since 1961 have been detonated deep underground, as prescribed by the Limited Test Ban Treaty signed in 1963. Currently, all NTS tests are limited to a maximum yield of 150 kilotons in accordance with terms of the Threshold Test Ban Treaty of 1974.

The original, primary purpose of the NTS was to provide a continental site to test nuclear devices. NTS has also been the site of many other defense- and energy-related programs, ranging from research and development efforts to commercial waste management.

WHY ENVIRONMENTAL MONITORING

From 1951 to 1962, 124 nuclear tests were conducted at NTS in which radioactive materials were released to the atmosphere. Through 1988, approximately 700 announced nuclear tests have been conducted, mostly underground, resulting in a large subsurface inventory of contamination. Above-ground testing resulted in portions of land surface being contaminated with radioactive materials having half-lives up to 24,000 yr. Thus, monitoring and surveillance programs were established. Their objective has been to measure levels and trends of radioactivity in the environment around test areas to ascertain whether testing complies with existing radiation protection standards.

As questions and legal challenges were raised by the public, monitoring programs, which had a single focus on radioactivity, had to adapt to different directions. New programs were developed to address the specific questions or issues identified. Such programs require the expertise of many individuals and organizations within the NVO system in an interdisciplinary approach to problem solving.

While the focus on radioactivity has continued, there is a growing awareness of the nonradiological products and impacts of nuclear testing programs. Enactment of laws and regulations governing hazardous materials and other chemicals has necessitated that monitoring programs be expanded to incorporate a broader spectrum of concerns.

SPECIFIC MONITORING PROGRAMS

A comprehensive offsite environmental program was established in 1951; from 1954 to 1970 the program was conducted by the U. S. Public Health Service. Since 1970, the U. S. Environmental Protection Agency, through the Environmental Monitoring and Support Laboratory of Las Vegas, has been responsible for the program. Part of this effort includes participation by local communities.

Because of concerns about local radionuclide contamination from NTS activities, an environmental surveillance program was established in 1955. In 1966, the program was redefined and modified to monitor and evaluate ambient radioactivity and environmental media at NTS, including air and water. Today, onsite environmental monitoring is largely conducted by the Reynolds Engineering and Electric Company Inc. (REECo).

In addition to these general programs, special efforts have been initiated at various times to address specific topics and concerns related to NTS activities. NVO currently has more than 17 organizations participating in the testing program (Table 1).

Table 1. Participants in DOE Nevada Test Site Programs.

CER Corporation	Wackenhut Services, Inc.
Computer Sciences Corporation	U.S. Environmental Protection Agency
Department of Defense-DNA	Pan Am World Services, Inc.
Desert Research Institute	U.S. Department of Commerce-
EG&G Energy Measurements, Inc.	NOAA/WSNSO
Fenix & Scisson, Inc.	Oak Ridge National Laboratory
Holmes & Narver, Inc.	University of California, Los Angeles
Los Alamos National Laboratory	LFE Environmental
Lawrence Livermore National Laboratory	University of Nevada, Las Vegas
Sandia National Laboratory	McClellan Central Laboratory
Reynolds Electrical & Engineering Co. Inc.	Eberline Instrument Corp.
U.S. Geological Survey	Battelle, Pacific Northwest Laboratories
Science Applications International Corp.	Battelle, Columbus Laboratory
	Air Resources Laboratory

The former above-ground test areas, which offer unique sites to study the behavior of plutonium in a desert environment, have been preserved. In 1970, studies on the behavior of radionuclides in the environment were initiated by the Nevada Applied Ecology Group (NAEG). An outgrowth of NAEG was development of an inventory and distribution of surface contamination, conducted under the Radionuclide Inventory & Distribution Project. Investigators from 16 organizations (Table 2) participated in NAEG, which has an extensive listing of publications summarizing results of these studies. The NAEG program was concluded in 1987.

Since then, interest has increased in assessing changes in the radiological and ecological conditions at NTS and in surrounding areas and in providing data needed for compliance according to applicable environmental laws. The Basic Environmental Monitoring and Compliance Program focuses on updating key parameters for use in compliance assessments.

Table 2. Participants in the Nevada Applied Ecology Group.

U.S. Environmental Protection Agency	Oak Ridge National Laboratory
University of California, Los Angeles	LFE Environmental
University of Nevada, Las Vegas	EG&G Energy Measurements
Reynolds Electrical & Engineering Co. Inc.	Holmes & Narver, Inc.
McClellan Central Laboratory	Eberline Instrument Corp.
Los Alamos National Laboratory	Battelle, Pacific Northwest Laboratories
Lawrence Livermore National Laboratory	Battelle, Columbus Laboratory
Air Resources Laboratory	Desert Research Institute

As a result of claims alleging harm from radioactive fallout and requests for historic and current fallout information, the Off-Site Radiation Exposure Review Project (ORERP) was initiated in 1979 to collect historical data and reconstruct historic radiation doses from NTS operations. The project reviews, reconstructs, and verifies historic data; conducts field work to verify predictions; and develops complex models of exposure pathways specific to identified locations. This project incorporates the expertise of several organizations.

Although concerns over surface radiation and its impacts have been the focus of much past and continuing study, subsurface radioactivity is also of interest. Data from ground-water studies, conducted for many years, have been considered in siting underground tests. In 1973, the Radionuclide Migration in Groundwater (RNM) program was initiated to develop information regarding the movement of radionuclides away from a testing area. In 1988, the RNM program became the Hydrology Radionuclide Migration Program. The original scope was expanded to include hydrologic considerations in migration studies.

Other programs to demonstrate compliance with environmental regulations or requirements have also been conducted at NTS. For example, The Desert Research Institute conducts archaeological surveys where land disturbances have taken place or will occur. Surveys of endangered wildlife species are conducted by EG&G and REECo to verify compliance with state and federal regulations.

The programs discussed above are largely independent of the testing program regarding programmatic direction and funding. However, the testing program includes additional efforts related to environmental monitoring and surveillance. For example, the National Oceanic and Atmospheric Administration operates the Weather Service Nuclear Support Office, which provides 24-hr routine and emergency weather forecasting for NTS. The U.S. Geological Survey conducts extensive programs on the geology of NTS in support of the test program. This information is also used to answer questions about hydrology and environmental transport.

The creation of new programs such as the DOE Environmental Restoration program; the passage of laws like the Resource Conservation and Recovery Act, the Comprehensive Environmental Restoration Compensation and Liability Act, and Superfund Amendment and Reauthorization Act; and the imposition of new DOE Orders mandate the expansion, modification, or adaptation of existing programs. The challenge is to identify limited resources and maximize the flexibility of existing programs to address present and future needs.

EXPERIENCE AT NTS

Programs at NTS have several unique features and have produced valuable information. Lessons learned may be particularly important as future DOE programs grow in complexity and significance.

NVO environmental programs are large and diverse. While drawing on the expertise of many specialists to address particular questions provides benefits, there can be lack of coordination or communication across projects or programs. Although the products are generally without parallel in quality, programs often duplicate efforts. Several organizations within NVO are responsible for program direction and focus on their specific needs. The absence of centralized coordination and focus may result in a lack of clarity in purpose and direction.

Given the breadth of program interests, the number of organizations participating in NTS programs continues to be large and diverse. Participants include DOE contractors from both NVO and other Field Offices, national laboratories, universities, and private consultants. This design utilizes a wide range of technical expertise and organizational potential to address a problem. However, the diversity of individuals and organizations results in real challenges in management and direction, as well as in optimal use of available funds. Without strong DOE leadership and technical direction, individual interests may supersede the collective interest in accomplishing program goals.

As individuals and organizations in NTS programs are diverse, methods of data management have been diverse. Each investigator collects data and enters them in a system, and there has been little or no coordination or standardization of data management. Consequently, there are numerous data sets; most are limited or narrowly focused, and unrelated to each other; even those within the same organization may be duplicative. The difficulty in achieving uniform quality is secondary to the need to have data immediately accessible to synthesize or assess results or conclusions of the larger program.

CONCLUSIONS

Environmental programs at NTS have produced valuable and innovative results. The NAEG program established the baseline for much of the bioenvironmental work at NTS. The ORERP program serves as the model for dose reconstruction, for involvement of the public, and for conducting external peer review in such programs. Public participation in the environmental monitoring program at town hall meetings has been an example for similar programs.

The advantages and disadvantages of multiple participant programs are clear. Without strong, coordinated management at all levels throughout a program's duration, delay and failure may occur. Coordinated data management is vital to the success of a program, as is the establishment of clear quality assurance requirements.

RADIATION-RELATED MONITORING AND ENVIRONMENTAL RESEARCH AT THE NEVADA TEST SITE

L. R. Anspaugh,[1] S. C. Black,[2] C. F. Costa,[2] D. R. Elle,[3] E. H. Essington,[4] R. O. Gilbert,[5] D. A. Gonzalez,[6] R. B. Hunter,[6] R. D. McArthur,[7] P. A. Medica,[6] T. P. O'Farrell,[8] S. E. Patton,[1] E. M. Romney,[9] J. H. Shinn,[1] and C. B. Thompson[7]

[1]Environmental Sciences Division, Lawrence Livermore National Laboratory, Livermore, California

[2]U.S. Environmental Protection Agency, Las Vegas, Nevada

[3]Nevada Operations Office, U.S. Department of Energy, Las Vegas, Nevada

[4]Los Alamos National Laboratory, Los Alamos, New Mexico

[5]Pacific Northwest Laboratory, Richland, Washington

[6]Reynolds Electrical & Engineering Co., Inc., Las Vegas, Nevada

[7]Desert Research Institute, University of Nevada System, Las Vegas, Nevada

[8]EG&G Energy Measurements Inc., Santa Barbara, California

[9]University of California, Los Angeles, California

Key Words: *Monitoring, radiological, environmental, assessments*

ABSTRACT

Beginning with the first nuclear-weapons-related tests at the Nevada Test Site (NTS) in 1951, a radiation-related monitoring program was established to determine the levels and distribution of radionuclides released. Primary methods involved survey-meter-equipped field-monitoring teams and placement of film badges and air-sampling devices at fixed locations. Beginning in the mid-1950s, more stringent standards, the results of this monitoring program, and the results of related research programs led to increased engineering efforts to reduce local fallout.

With passage of the National Environmental Policy Act and increased concern about possible effects of radiation exposure, environmental activities related to the NTS increased. There is now an extensive monitoring program at the NTS to assess radiological conditions resulting from past tests and from continued testing of nuclear-weapons devices. In populated areas near NTS, there is also a monitoring effort that relies on assistance from local communities.

Other efforts include reconstruction of radiation doses received by offsite residents during the 1950s and 1960s, determination of the current inventory and distribution of radionuclides in surface soil, and studies of the movement of radionuclides in the desert ecosystem.

INTRODUCTION

With the first nuclear-weapons test at the Nevada Test Site (NTS), a radiation-related monitoring program was initiated. Monitoring programs at NTS have evolved to meet changing concerns about possible radiation exposure and the requirements of environmental laws, regulations, and orders. We present here an overview of current radiation-related monitoring and supporting environmental research programs at NTS, a summary of results, and some requirements for future efforts.

Nuclear weapons were first tested at NTS in 1951. Until 1963, when the Limited Test Ban Treaty was signed, more than 100 nuclear devices were detonated on or near the ground (Friesen, 1985); the collective yield was about 1 megaton (Mt) (Friesen, 1985), which is equivalent to 10^{15} calories. Underground tests were also conducted during this period, a practice that continues today. In surface tests, about 3 x 10^{26} fission-product atoms were formed; most decayed rapidly, but some radionuclides, for example, ^{137}Cs (half-life, 30 yr), are still detected. Approximately 6 PBq (200 kCi) of ^{137}Cs were released to the atmosphere from these explosions. Radiation exposure to the public was estimated for each event from 1951 to 1958; collective exposure was 85,000 person-R to nearby residents in Nevada and southwestern Utah (Anspaugh and Church, 1986).

The 3500-km^2 area occupied by NTS, 105 km northwest of Las Vegas, Nevada, is of extraordinary biological interest because it straddles the boundaries of the Great Basin and Mojave Deserts. There have been ecological impacts on the site from nuclear tests as well as from natural events. From NTS land-use maps, we estimate that approximately 25% of the NTS has been and is currently being used for testing of nuclear-weapons-related devices. Included in this 25% are an extensive network of roads, support facilities, and areas fenced for the requirements of radiation control. The most widespread disturbance has been caused by subsidence craters resulting from underground tests; of secondary significance is vegetation denudation resulting from above-ground tests during the 1950s. There have been ecological impacts on the site from "natural" events as well. From records kept by the NTS Fire Chief since 1978, it has been estimated that 4% of the NTS area has been disturbed by wildfires. Other significant effects have been attributed to native animals and the intrusion of non-native plants and animals.

At present, somewhat less than 1% of the NTS land area remains fenced for the requirements of radiation control. These locations include those contaminated by fission products and by plutonium and uranium from special experiments. A variety of natural plant and animal communities is included in these exclusion zones, and they provide unique resources for ecological research.

MONITORING

Radiological monitoring at NTS began with the first nuclear explosion and became extensive with the advent of testing on towers rather than using air drops. Initially, onsite monitoring was coordinated with nuclear events; later, it was expanded to a year-round radiological monitoring program that is now managed by the Nevada Operations Office of the Department of Energy (DOE/NV). Offsite locations were monitored by the military and the Los Alamos National Laboratory through 1953. In 1954, the U.S. Public Health Service became the responsible agency; since 1970 the U.S. Environmental Protection Agency (EPA) has been responsible for the program (Grossman et al., 1986).

Currently, the onsite program conducted by Reynolds Electrical & Engineering Co. measures and monitors effluents from NTS operations (Gonzalez, 1988). Primary objectives are to collect and analyze air, water, and other media to demonstrate compliance with applicable standards and permit requirements and assess possible effects to workers and the local environment from site operations.

Ecological monitoring and research at the NTS includes study plots at both disturbed and undisturbed sites that are used to monitor the status of plants and animals. Vegetation, reptiles, and small mammals are monitored at various time intervals, depending on the disturbance involved. Large game animals, raptorial birds, migrating waterfowl, and feral horses are monitored periodically along roadways and at natural springs and manmade water sources. NTS provides habitat for the threatened desert tortoise, *Gopherus agassizii*, and seven plants that are Category 1 or 2 candidates for federal protection. Populations of some of these species of concern have been monitored since the mid-1970s. Monitoring includes population studies and identifying and determining habitat condition to evaluate effects of NTS activities.

The objective of offsite monitoring is to measure and determine trends of radioactivity in the environment surrounding NTS and to ascertain whether effluents from NTS are in compliance with radiation-protection standards. Activities include (1) surveillance of radionuclide-transport pathways (air, water, and food chains); (2) monitoring external radiation exposure through thermoluminescent dosimeter (TLD) networks and gamma-rate recorders; and (3) direct measurement of internal exposure by whole-body counting. Monitoring stations operated by local communities at 18 towns around NTS have samplers for noble gases, tritium, and particles in air, as well as TLD and gamma-rate recorders.

SUPPORTING RESEARCH

In conjunction with the passage of the National Environmental Policy Act, DOE/NV decided in 1970 to increase its investigation of potential environmental problems at NTS. The first major action supporting radiological and environmental research was formation of the Nevada Applied Ecology Group (NAEG). Subsequent programs included the Offsite Radiation Exposure Review Project (ORERP), the Radionuclide Inventory and Distribution Program (RIDP), and the Basic Environmental Compliance and Monitoring Program (BECAMP).

The NAEG was established in 1970 to coordinate ecological and radiological monitoring and other environmental programs necessary to support continued nuclear testing activities at NTS. Priority of the 16-yr program was to investigate the occurrence and effects of plutonium on NTS and surrounding areas (Dunaway and White, 1974). Research included determining contaminated locations and rates of plutonium movement in the environment and development of a dose-assessment model as a tool in evaluating radiological hazards.

The ORERP began in 1978 to reconstruct the radiation dose from previous testing to residents of Nevada, Utah, Arizona, New Mexico, and parts of California, Oregon, Idaho, Wyoming, and Colorado. Currently, both external and internal doses are being evaluated, using historical external gamma-exposure measurements, contemporary measurements of ^{137}Cs and $^{239+240}$Pu deposition, and the ^{240}Pu/^{239}Pu ratio. State-of-the-art stochastic models were developed; for example, the PATHWAY code (Whicker and Kirchner, 1987) used to model radionuclide movement through food chains.

The RIDP (1981 to 1987) assessed inventory and distribution of manmade radionuclides in NTS surface soil (McArthur and Kordas, 1983). More than 7000 *in situ* gamma radiation measurements were made over nearly 1300 km^2. These measurements, with supplementary data from aerial radiological surveys and analytical data from soil samples, provide an estimate of radionuclide inventories in surface soils.

The BECAMP began in 1986 to assess changes over time in radiological and ecological conditions at NTS and to provide information for assessing compliance with applicable environmental laws, regulations, and orders (Patton, 1988). The ongoing BECAMP uses information provided by the NAEG to design effective programs to monitor radionuclide movement in soils, to update human dose-assessment models, and to evaluate changes in NTS flora and fauna.

WHAT HAVE WE LEARNED: SCIENTIFIC FINDINGS

Monitoring and research programs have made major use of newer methods of analysis. These have been applied in developing new methods of dose reconstruction and radionuclide inventory. We have also developed comprehensive analyses of the behavior of plutonium in desert environments and have incorporated these into a dose-assessment model for this site.

Most valuable for reconstructing radiation doses and assessing current radionuclide inventories are Beck's (1980) gamma-ray transport calculations for planar, uniform, and exponentially distributed sources; his results are expressed in terms of exposure rate above a unit deposition of a single radionuclide. These, coupled with detailed calculations of source-specific, relative radionuclide abundances as a function of time (Hicks, 1982), provide the ability to deduce the complete time-dependent history of radionuclide deposition with only the additional datum of a measured external gamma-exposure rate. The gamma-ray transport calculations are also the key to field spectrometry (taking the detector to the field, rather than taking the sample to the detector), which has made possible our study of the inventory and distribution of radionuclides in surface soil at NTS.

In the mid-1970s, a new geostatistical technique, kriging, was used to estimate the spatial pattern of radionuclides in surface soil at testing areas (Gilbert and Simpson, 1985; McArthur and Kordas, 1983). Kriging uses the spatial correlation structure in data to estimate the variance of spatial patterns. Statisticians were included as members of study teams and helped design sampling plans, applied data analysis methods, and wrote major reports. The involvement of statisticians in long-term projects resulted in a more complete data base and better interpretation of historical data.

Prior to incorporation of quality assurance (QA) in monitoring programs, the credibility of environmental data at NTS was primarily the responsibility of individual investigators; quality of results was judged by peer review of project documents. The need for QA was formalized during NAEG studies and included evolution of written procedures and independent oversight of sampling, sample preparation, and analysis. Also included were analysis of replicate samples and development of standard reference materials to track performance of analytical laboratories. More recently, all programs were required by DOE Orders to include QA plans. The QA plan assists in designing study protocols to ensure data credibility and facilitate documentation of experimental design, sampling, analysis, reporting, and archiving information.

Studies of plutonium dynamics have included processes from resuspension through metabolism by range cattle. Resuspension factors (air concentration divided by areal ground contamination) were measured in the usual way and by the meteorological flux-gradient method (Anspaugh et al., 1975). Effects of surface disturbances, such as removing the pebbled desert pavement (Shinn and Homan, 1987), soil cleanup (Shinn et al., 1989), and wildfires, were recorded. Anspaugh et al. (1974) developed two models: a nonexponential time-dependent resuspension factor model and a mass-loading model. The latter is the primary basis for the U.S. Environmental Protection Agency's interim recommendations for a screening level for plutonium in soil.

The capacity for plant foliage to entrap fine particles from initial deposition or resuspension processes can make vegetation a major pathway for human exposure (Romney et al., 1963). Our studies show that, via resuspension, plants attain dry weight concentrations of plutonium that are about 10^{-1} of that found in soil; in contrast, uptake through the root system is only 10^{-4} to 10^{-6} (Romney et al., 1977, 1987). The results of these and other studies have been synthesized to provide an overall description of the ecosystem dynamics of plutonium (Gilbert et al., 1988a,b, 1989).

State-of-the-art models for estimating dose to man from radionuclides were also developed. A dose model for human exposure to $^{239+240}$Pu via inhalation and ingestion was developed by NAEG in the early 1970s (Martin and Bloom, 1977). It is currently being updated to a fully stochastic model for all major radionuclides and all exposure pathways, including external exposure. The model is now a major component of DOE/NV programs that evaluate human exposures from NTS activities.

WHAT HAVE WE LEARNED: GENERAL CONCLUSIONS

Experience has demonstrated that creative insights are essential for successful monitoring programs, especially if future environmental issues are to be anticipated. One of the greater dangers is to succumb to the mechanical collection of data; continual analysis and feedback are needed to identify for further investigation episodic events or serious data faults.

Experience from ORERP and NAEG shows that lost data are not easily retrieved. Information must be preserved through changes in organizations and for longer than the period of study. Computerized data bases in structured and protected archival systems are critical to effective synthesis of information in response to questions. Plans for preserving the integrity and completeness of data should be developed and carried out consistently in a timely manner.

The NAEG program published 15 progress reports between 1974 and 1987 (Howard and Fuller, 1987). However, to achieve scientific credibility for DOE/NV environmental programs, publishing in peer-reviewed journals was desired. Therefore, NAEG data were synthesized in major publications (for example, Gilbert et al., 1988a,b, 1989). This aspect of publishing was also emphasized in other DOE/NV programs, including RIDP, ORERP, and BECAMP.

A valuable lesson learned from the NTS offsite monitoring program is that when communities are involved, residents can independently verify information released by government agencies to the press, thus improving its credibility. In addition, monitoring program personnel who have factual knowledge about radiation and its risks at various exposure levels can supply information to residents.

ACKNOWLEDGMENT

Work supported by the U.S. Department of Energy.

REFERENCES

Anspaugh, L. R. and B. W. Church. 1986. Historical estimates of external gamma exposure and collective external exposure from testing at the Nevada Test Site. I. Test series through Hardtack, 1958. *Health Phys.* *51*:35-51.

Anspaugh, L. R., J. H. Shinn, P. L. Phelps, and N. C. Kennedy. 1975. Resuspension and redistribution of plutonium in soils. *Health Phys.* *29*:571-582.

Anspaugh, L. R., J. H. Shinn, and D. W. Wilson. 1974. Evaluation of the resuspension pathway toward protective guidelines for soil contamination with radioactivity, pp. 513-524. In: Population Dose Evaluation and Standards for Man and His Environment. International Atomic Energy Agency, Vienna.

Beck, H. L. 1980. Exposure-Rate Conversion Factors for Radionuclides Deposited on the Ground, EML-378. Environmental Measurements Laboratory, U.S. Department of Energy, New York.

Dunaway, P. B. and M. G. White (eds.) 1974. The Dynamics of Plutonium in Desert Environments, pp. 1-4, NVO-142. U.S. Department of Energy, Las Vegas, NV.

Friesen, H. N. 1985. A Perspective on Nuclear Tests in Nevada, NVO-296. U.S. Department of Energy, Las Vegas, NV.

Gilbert, R. O. and J. C. Simpson. 1985. Kriging for estimating spatial pattern of contaminants: Potential and problems. *Environ. Monit. Assess.* 5:113-135.

Gilbert, R. O., D. W. Engel, D. D. Smith, J. H. Shinn, L. R. Anspaugh, and G. R. Eisele. 1988a. Transfer of aged Pu to cattle grazing on a contaminated environment. *Health Phys.* 54:323-335.

Gilbert, R. O., J. H. Shinn, E. H. Essington, T. Tamura, E. M. Romney, K. S. Moor, and T. P. O'Farrell. 1988b. Radionuclide transport from soil to air, native vegetation, kangaroo rats and grazing cattle on Nevada Test Site. *Health Phys.* 55:869-887.

Gilbert, R. O., D. W. Engel, and L. R. Anspaugh. 1989. Transfer of aged [239+240]Pu, [238]Pu, [241]Am, and ^{137}Cs to cattle grazing a contaminated arid environment. *Sci. Tot. Environ.* 85:53-62.

Gonzalez, D. A. 1988. Onsite Environmental Report for the Nevada Test Site, DOE/NV/10327-39. Reynolds Electrical & Engineering Co., Inc., Las Vegas, NV.

Grossman, R. F., S. C. Black, R. E. Dye, D. D. Smith, D. J. Thorne, A. A. Mullen, and Nuclear Radiation Assessment Division. 1986. Off-Site Environmental Monitoring Report, Radiation Monitoring Around U.S. Nuclear Test Areas, Calendar Year 1985, EPA-600/4-86-022. U.S. Environmental Protection Agency, Las Vegas, NV.

Hicks, H. G. 1982. Calculation of the concentration of any radionuclide deposited on the ground by off-site fallout from a nuclear detonation. *Health Phys.* 42:585-600.

Howard, W. A. and R. G. Fuller (eds.). 1987. The Dynamics of Transuranics and Other Radionuclides in Natural Environments, pp. 562-563, NVO-272. U.S. Department of Energy, Las Vegas, NV.

Martin, W. E. and S. G. Bloom. 1977. Nevada Applied Ecology Group model for estimating plutonium transport and dose to man, pp. 621-706. In: Transuranics in Natural Environments, M. G. White and P. B. Dunaway (eds.), NVO-178. U.S. Department of Energy, Las Vegas, NV.

McArthur, R. D. and J. F. Kordas. 1983. Radionuclide Inventory and Distribution Program: The Galileo Area, DOE/NV/10162. Desert Research Institute, Las Vegas, NV.

Patton, S. E. 1988. Basic Environmental Compliance and Monitoring Program (BECAMP) FY 1989 Annual Work Plan, UCAR-10220-89, Lawrence Livermore National Laboratory, Livermore, CA.

Romney, E. M., R. G. Lindberg, H. A. Hawthorne, B. G. Bystrom, and K. H. Larson. 1963. Contamination of plant foliage with radioactive fallout. *Ecology 44*:343-349.

Romney, E. M., A. Wallace, P. A. T. Wieland, and J. Kinnear. 1977. Plant uptake of ^{239,240}Pu and ^{241}Am through roots from soils containing aged fallout materials, pp. 54-64. In: Environmental Plutonium on the Nevada Test Site and Environs, M. G. White and P. B. Dunaway (eds.), NVO-171. U.S. Department of Energy, Las Vegas, NV.

Romney, E. M., E. H. Essington, E. B. Fowler, T. Tamura, and R. O. Gilbert. 1987. Plutonium in the desert environment of the Nevada Test Site and the Tonopah Test Range, pp. 121-130. In: Environmental Research of Actinide Elements, J. F. Pinder, J. J. Alberts, K. W. McLeod, and R. G. Schreckhise (eds.). CONF-841142, U.S. Department of Energy, Las Vegas, NV.

Shinn, J. H. and D. N. Homan. 1987. Plutonium-aerosol emission rates and human pulmonary deposition calculations for Nuclear Site 201, Nevada Test Site, pp. 261-278. In: The Dynamics of Transuranics and Other Radionuclides in Natural Environments, W. A. Howard and R. G. Fuller (eds.), NVO-272. U.S. Department of Energy, Las Vegas, NV.

Shinn, J. H., E. H. Essington, F. L. Miller, T. P. O'Farrell, J. A. Orcutt, E. M. Romney, J. W. Shugart, and E. R. Sorum. 1989. Results of a cleanup and treatment test at the Nevada Test Site: Evaluation of vacuum removal of Pu-contaminated soil. *Health Phys. 57*:771-779.

Whicker, F. W. and T. B. Kirchner. 1987. PATHWAY: A dynamic food-chain model to predict radionuclide ingestion after fallout deposition. *Health Phys. 52*:717-737.

THE EMBRYOGENESIS OF DOSE ASSESSMENT AT HANFORD

R. F. Foster

P.O. Box 4263, Sunriver, Oregon

Key Words: *Monitoring, environment, history, Hanford*

ABSTRACT

Several significant events occurred between 1955 and 1960 that resulted in major changes in environmental monitoring at Hanford and in the initiation of comprehensive dose assessments. These included: (1) specification of dose limits for nonoccupational exposure (including internal emitters); (2) a national and international awakening to the need for managing the disposal of radioactive wastes; (3) identification of the most important radionuclides and their sources of exposure; (4) data that quantified the transfer coefficients of nuclides along environmental pathways; and (5) development of greatly improved radiation detection instrumentation. In response to a growing need, the Hanford Laboratories formed the "Environmental Studies and Evaluation" component. This group revamped the monitoring and sampling programs so that analytical results contributed directly to dose estimation. Special studies were conducted to ascertain local dietary and recreational habits that affected dose calculations and to calibrate the models. These studies involved extensive contact with the public and governmental agencies, which elicited a positive reaction.

INTRODUCTION

The Hanford Engineering Works was the first nuclear facility to release substantial amounts of radioactive effluents into the environment. Although governmental regulations did not exist at the time, responsible officials of the Manhattan Project and the Du Pont Company took the initiative to monitor these releases. The late Herb Parker was the chief architect of this effort, and senior members of his staff, notably Carl Gamertsfelder, Jack Healy, and Walt Singlevich, pioneered in implementing the monitoring and analysis work.

In the late 1940s, radiation standards were ill defined. The first environmental monitoring program was characterized by a large number of measurements of low accuracy, which covered a large area and a variety of problems at minimal expense. Liquid and gaseous effluents were sampled before release; Columbia River water was sampled near the old Hanford Ferry and in the Tri-Cities. With few exceptions, these were "grab" samples collected at weekly intervals. Ionization chambers were used to measure external radiation on site and at some offsite locations.*

Most samples were analyzed for gross beta emitters, because the common detection instrument was the thin mica end-window Geiger-Mueller (G-M) detector. Gamma spectrometers had not been perfected for routine use. Some samples were analyzed for alpha emitters and some for individual nuclides by tedious procedures. These crude beginnings evolved into more comprehensive programs as observations, research, and technical developments pointed the way.

BIOLOGICAL ATTRACTION

From the beginning, some pioneer health physicists realized that radioactive gases might be of greater concern because of inhalation than as an external radiation source in the atmosphere (Stannard, 1988). When the buildup of ^{131}I was noted on Hanford vegetation and in grazing animals, Parker recognized the significance of this additional pathway. Accordingly, he recommended revised release limits for ^{131}I from the 200-Area stacks that were based on dose to the thyroid via a vegetation pathway (Parker, 1946). This required that vegetation be routinely included in the sampling program, therefore native vegetation was obtained and composited at weekly to monthly intervals from zones on and near the site.

It is noteworthy that control of ^{131}I releases based on thyroid dose preceded any published guidelines. The National Bureau of Standards (now National Institute of Standards and Technology) Handbook 52, the first report of the Subcommittee on Permissible Internal dose of the National Committee on Radiation Protection** (NCRP), was not issued until 1953 (NCRP, 1953). Inasmuch as Parker was a member of this committee, he was able to apply the concepts as they were developed.

Karl Herde, Hanford's pioneer wildlife biologist, was likely the first to find ^{131}I in the thyroids of rabbits, goats, and sheep on the site (Stannard, 1988). This was soon after the chemical separations plants began

---

*Carey, Z. E., R. F. Foster, J. J. Fuquay, J. W. Healy, R. L. Junkins, and L. C. Schwendiman. 1959. Final Report-Radiological Evaluation Task Force, "Strictly private" report to H. M. Parker.

**Now called the National Council on Radiation Protection and Measurements.

operation. These early observations prompted opportunistic sampling of rabbits and some marginally successful, clandestine attempts to monitor the thyroids of cattle that grazed close to the site perimeter. By the early 1950s, the wildlife monitoring program had become more structured and included, in addition to rabbits, waterfowl that frequented the Columbia River and the liquid-waste disposal ponds of the chemical separations areas (Hanson and Kornberg, 1956).

Paralleling observations on rabbits and other wildlife were measurements on fish and other aquatic organisms. The first analyses were made on laboratory fish being used to evaluate the toxicity of reactor cooling water (Healy, 1946). Results were misleading, however, because the fish ate only uncontaminated laboratory food. Fish collected from the Columbia River were much more radioactive (Herde, 1947). The dominant radionuclide was determined to be ^{32}P. This was a surprise because this radionuclide was not especially abundant in reactor effluent. The fish were actually accumulating ^{32}P from food organisms that had concentrated it from river water. These observations prompted extensive exploratory sampling of fish and other organisms throughout the river (Foster and Davis, 1956).

Although Columbia River fish were also accumulating significant amounts of ^{65}Zn, this gamma emitter did not receive much attention initially because it was not efficiently detected by the G-M counters. In the late 1950s, ^{65}Zn was observed in people counted in a prototype whole-body monitor, especially in those who had recently eaten seafood harvested from near the mouth of the Columbia River. Exploratory sampling in that region confirmed an extraordinary accumulation of ^{65}Zn in shellfish. Thus, routine sampling of oysters from Willapa Bay was initiated in 1960. By this time, gamma spectroscopy was well developed and in routine use.

CONCEPTION OF DOSE EVALUATION

All early environmental monitoring was expected to enhance our knowledge about radiation exposures of people in the site environs. However, procedures for evaluating the significance of ingested and inhaled radionuclides were not developed until the mid-1950s. The seminal publication that set the stage for such evaluations was the NCRP report on "Maximum Permissible Amounts of Radioisotopes in the Human Body and Maximum Permissible Concentrations in Air and Water" (NCRP, 1953). These recommendations were immediately incorporated in "Radiation Protection Standards" for Hanford Atomic Products Operation (General Electric Co., 1958).

Provided with these guides, workers in the Radiation Protection and Biology groups estimated how much water, fish, or ducks could be consumed without exceeding the limits. The results were not dose estimates *per se* and, at the outset, such evaluations by the different groups were not combined to provide a comprehensive exposure status for individuals.

The environmental dose evaluation program evolved rapidly during the late 1950s. The potential for significant exposure could no longer be considered minor since, by 1955, eight reactors were discharging effluents to the Columbia River. Furthermore, the NCRP issued recommendations for "nonoccupational exposure" that were only one-tenth of those for radiation workers (NCRP, 1954). In 1957 and 1958, these limits were expressed even more conservatively for "persons outside of controlled areas" (Addendum to NCRP, 1954).

The time had come to change the direction of the environmental program from a demonstration that radiation contamination levels were well below some level of concern to a sophisticated analysis that accurately estimated doses to people in the environs and compared results with the new dose limits being promulgated.

Fundamental principles for calculating radiation dose from Hanford effluents were first stated by Healy when he was serving on NCRP's Subcommittee of Permissible Internal Dose (Healy, 1956). Using Healy's guidance, H. V. Clukey proposed a "Method of Calculating Columbia River Drinking Water Exposure" (Clukey, 1957) and determined that the gastrointestinal tract was the critical organ for this source.

By 1958 the basic methods had been developed, and enough field data had been accumulated to estimate the composite exposure from several Hanford sources and exposure modes. The Second Geneva Conference provided an added incentive to show that this could be done. Healy et al. (1958) presented a landmark paper, using 1957 data on radionuclides in air, water, fish, and waterfowl to estimate radiation doses to people. Their calculations used "standard man" parameters embodied in NCRP Handbook 52 (NCRP, 1953) and dietary information compiled from literature concerned mostly with U.S. populations as a whole (Soldat et al., 1986).

GESTATION PERIOD

It was apparent in 1958 that available monitoring data and knowledge of the habits of local people were inadequate for a fully satisfactory evaluation. Further, consolidation of the required data was difficult because responsibilities for the necessary parts were fragmented in six different sections of the Hanford Laboratories. Seeking resolution of these and other radiological problems, Parker established a Radiological Evaluation Task Force to make recommendations, with Jack Healy as leader. The Task Force began its work in November 1958 and submitted its "strictly private" final report a year later. Among its recommendations were major revisions to the environmental monitoring program, in sample analysis, field dosimetry, initiation of dietary surveys, and creation of a permanent "Radiological Evaluation Group."[*]

Three events of national and international significance occurred during the tenure of the Task Force which drew further attention to dose evaluation: (1) congressional hearings on industrial radioactive waste disposal; (2) an International Atomic Energy Agency (IAEA) conference in Monaco on disposal of radioactive wastes (the U.S. delegation was concerned that the Russians might create an international issue because Hanford contaminants were entering the Pacific Ocean); (3) attention directed to radioactive wastes in the Columbia River by subcommittees of the first National Academy of Sciences Biological Effects of Ionizing Radiation Committee. The congressional hearings were significant because they afforded Parker an opportunity to herald the bases of radiation protection at Hanford and Hanford's waste-disposal policy. This included a "point-of-exposure" philosophy and estimating the combined exposure from all sources of environmental radiation. (Parker, 1959). To illustrate this point, we developed a comprehensive set of diagrams that showed the many possible pathways by which people can be exposed. These were probably the first such diagrams ever developed.

Many recommendations of the Radiological Evaluation Task Force were subsequently implemented. In 1960, R. L. Junkins influenced changes in the sampling and analysis programs and helped lay the groundwork for dietary surveys. With the aid of others, he produced substantially enhanced estimates of radiation exposure in the Hanford environs for the year 1959 (Soldat et al., 1986).

---

[*]Carey, Z. E., R. F. Foster, J. J. Fuquay, J. W. Healy, R. L. Junkins, and L. C. Schwendiman. 1959. Final Report-Radiological Evaluation Task Force, "Strictly private" report to H. M. Parker.

More pervasive developments occurred in 1961, when a new organization, Environmental Studies and Evaluation, was created as a part of the Hanford Radiation Protection Section. I managed this group, which included most of the health-physics-oriented staff involved with environmental monitoring and evaluations. Its scope included design and implementation of all sample collections, field measurements, laboratory analyses, and computational procedures for evaluating exposure of people in the Hanford environs. The group was also charged with research and development studies on the "mechanism of environmental exposure."

These studies focused on determining the parameters needed to quantify ingestion rates of drinking water and local foods, especially fish, milk, and farm produce. A creel census of Columbia River fishermen showed the quantities of particular species of fish which should be used for dose estimates. A mobile whole-body counter was built and used to measure gamma emitters in Richland school children, fishermen on the banks of the Columbia River, local farm families, and residents of towns near the river mouth. Although using the whole-body counter outside the Richland community was viewed with trepidation by some, the study was received enthusiastically by cooperating state officials and the participants.

FRUITION

Information on diet and recreational habits of people who visited the whole-body counter and data from other studies were soon incorporated in the computations developed to estimate dose (Foster, 1973). Use of this information, and other details concerning the evolution of environmental monitoring at Hanford through 1984, have been described authoritatively by Soldat et al. (1986).

REFERENCES

Clukey, H. V. 1957. Method of calculating Columbia River drinking water exposure, AEC Document HW-49214. Pacific Northwest Laboratory, Richland, WA.

Foster, R. F. 1973. Observed versus theorized capacity of the environment for radioactive contaminants, pp. 593-601. In: Proceedings of the Symposium on Environmental Behavior of Radionuclides Released in the Nuclear Industry. IAEA, Vienna.

Foster, R. F. and J. J. Davis. 1956. The accumulation of radioactive substances in aquatic forms, pp. 364-67. In: Proceedings of the First International Conference on Peaceful Uses of Atomic Energy (Geneva), Vol. 13. United Nations, New York.

General Electric Co. 1958. Hanford Atomic Products Operation-Radiation Protection Standards, AEC Document HW-25457, Rev. II. Pacific Northwest Laboratory, Richland, WA.

Hanson, W. L. and H. A. Kornberg. 1956. Radioactivity in terrestrial animals near an atomic energy site, pp. 385-88. In: Proceedings of the First International Conference on Peaceful Uses of Atomic Energy (Geneva), Vol. 13. United Nations, New York.

Healy, J. W. 1946. Accumulation of radioactive elements in fish immersed in pile water, AEC Document 3-3442. Pacific Northwest Laboratory, Richland, WA.

Healy, J. W. 1956. Reactor effluent monitoring, AEC Document HW-45725. Pacific Northwest Laboratory, Richland, WA.

Healy, J. W., B. V. Andersen, H. V. Clukey, and J. K. Soldat. 1958. Radiation exposure to people in the environs of a major production atomic energy plant, pp. 309-318. In: Proceedings of the Second United Nations International Conference on the Peaceful Uses of Atomic Energy, Vol. 18. United Nations, New York.

Herde, K. E. 1947. Radioactivity in various species of fish from the Columbia and Yakima Rivers, AEC Document 3-5501. Pacific Northwest Laboratory, Richland, WA.

NCRP. 1953. Maximum permissible amounts of radioisotopes in the human body and maximum permissible concentrations in air and water. National Committee on Radiation Protection. NBS Handbook 52. U.S. Government Printing Office, Washington, DC.

NCRP. 1954. Permissible dose from external sources of ionizing radiation. National Committee on Radiation Protection. NBS Handbook 59. U.S. Government Printing Office, Washington, DC.

Parker, H. M. 1946. Tolerable concentrations of radioiodine on edible plants, AEC Document HW-7-3217. Pacific Northwest Laboratory, Richland, WA.

Parker, H. M. 1959. Hanford radioactive waste management, pp. 202-241. In: Hearings on Industrial Radioactive Waste Disposal before the Joint Committee on Atomic Energy, Congress of the United States, Vol. 1. U.S. Government Printing Office, Washington, DC.

Soldat, J. K., K. R. Price, and W. D. McCormack. 1986. Offsite radiation doses summarized from Hanford environmental monitoring reports for the years 1957-1984, PNL-5795. NTIS, Springfield, VA.

Stannard, J. N. 1988. *Radioactivity and Health - A History*. Battelle Press, Columbus, OH.

ENVIRONMENTAL MONITORING AT HANFORD BY THE STATE OF WASHINGTON

A. W. Conklin, R. R. Mooney, and J. L. Erickson

Environmental Radiation Section, Division of Radiation Protection, Department of Health, Olympia, Washington

Key Words: *Environmental monitoring, quality assurance, public health, split sampling*

ABSTRACT

The Department of Social and Health Services' Office of Radiation Protection (ORP), Washington State's radiation control agency, has a mandate to protect the public from radiation. In 1985, ORP was instructed by the legislature to establish a statewide environmental radiological base line, beginning with Hanford, to verify federal environmental programs, and to enforce federal and state Clean Air Acts. The primary mission of the agency is to protect public health by active involvement in Hanford monitoring and oversight. The state's program was designed not to duplicate but to supplement existing programs and to identify any sampling gaps or problems. Split, side-by-side, and independent samples are collected, with analysis performed by the state's own laboratory. Media sampled have included surface and drinking water, seep and ground water, fruits and vegetables, milk, soils, and air particulates; ambient radiation levels have been determined.

Special activities have included split sampling of river seeps with multiple agencies, preliminary dose assessment of early Hanford releases, investigations of [129]I in the environment and in Franklin County drinking water, verification of U.S. Department of Energy (DOE) data on erroneous alarms at the Hanford Plutonium Uranium Extraction Plant, split sampling with a DOE headquarters survey, and participation in several General Accounting Office investigations and a National Academy of Sciences review. The independence of ORP programs guarantees that the public has access to environmental data on the activities of DOE and its contractors. We will describe the interrelationship of ORP and Hanford programs and present results of ORP activities.

BACKGROUND

The Washington State Department of Health (WSDH) has dual legislative responsibilities: first as a public health agency and second as a radiation control agency (RCW, 1986). This legislation results in a monitoring agency with built-in independence because its primary mission is public health. This is important at Hanford, where the Department of Energy's (DOE) mission is weapons production and

177

radioactive waste disposal. The presence of the WSDH adds credibility to Hanford environmental monitoring results. To ensure the health and safety of the public, it is necessary not only to monitor independently but to validate other programs by assessing and verifying their data.

Environmental pathways associated with Hanford operations include: (1) the water pathway for effluents from liquid-waste disposal and (2) the air pathway for releases from fuel reprocessing, research and development activities and waste-handling and storage facilities. The State's environmental monitoring stations at Hanford are shown in Figure 1.

The air pathway is monitored under the state's Radioactive Air Emissions Program. The program was established to ensure compliance with the federal Clean Air Act, which requires federal facilities to comply with applicable state laws (WAC, 1986). DOE has now accepted the state's regulatory authority over Clean Air Act issues. The scope of the State program that is now being implemented includes: reviewing source registrations and issuing permits; reviewing new and modified source plans; environmental monitoring of air; reviewing and inspecting stack monitoring systems; reviewing emission data; evaluating models used for dose assessments; evaluating environmental monitoring and emissions reports; issuing periodic reports; investigating anomalies and accidents that potentially affect the public via air pathways; and keeping the public informed.

An effective means of verifying monitoring data collected by DOE contractors is to split and analyze the same samples where possible. Most sample splitting has been with the Pacific Northwest Laboratory, DOE's environmental monitoring contractor. Many split samples have also been obtained through a coordinated effort of the Environmental Radiation Quality Assurance Task Force, which the WSDH chairs. The Task Force includes most state and federal agencies and research organizations that conduct environmental radiation monitoring programs in the Pacific Northwest.

A unique sampling activity was conducted in 1987 in conjunction with a DOE headquarters survey, in which 10% (60) of the samples collected were split. Complete results are not yet available.

Another split sampling effort involves routine sampling of seeps, where low-level waste water from DOE waste-disposal activities empties into the Columbia River. In 1988, sampling was expanded to include

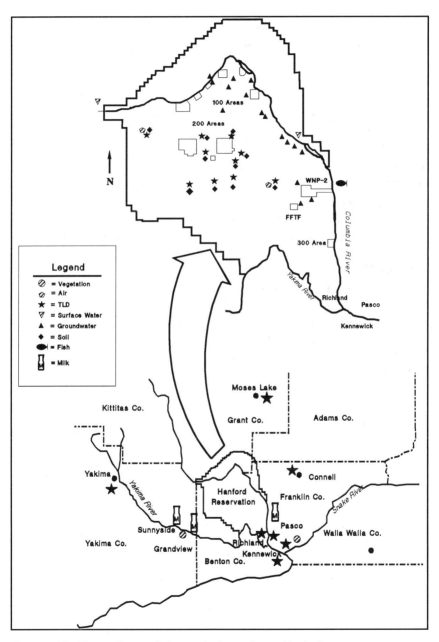

Figure 1. Washington State radiation monitoring stations at Hanford.

sediments and comparisons of data from thermoluminescent dosimeters and portable ion chambers. In addition to Task Force members, a public interest group (the Hanford Education Action League) was also invited to participate in split sampling.

At Hanford, the state's environmental monitoring efforts concentrate on ground water and river seeps that may contain contamination from soil-column disposal of liquid wastes. Although monitoring of the air pathway is minimal, expansion is planned as the Radioactive Air Emissions Program is implemented.

In addition to routine environmental monitoring at Hanford, special investigations are conducted by the state as required. Examples include:

1. **Iodine-129 in the environment:** Allegations were made that aquifer intercommunication was occurring that potentially affected the suitability of Hanford for a repository. The state assessed the available data to ensure there were no adverse health impacts from [129]I.

2. **Uranium in the Ground Water:** The state evaluated contamination that occurred when water from an active waste site flowed to an adjacent retired site, potentially driving uranium into the ground water. The investigation continued until there was assurance that removal of contaminated water was eliminating further impact.

3. **Uranium in Drinking Water:** Uranium was found in ground water used for drinking across the Columbia River from Hanford. The state investigated to assure the public that this uranium did not originate from Hanford. Isotopic analysis showed that the uranium occurred naturally.

4. **Lost Waste Sites:** A state legislator inquired whether the location of all Hanford wastes was known. The state evaluated records, concluding that selected wastes could not be accurately accounted for. DOE committed to evaluate the situation.

5. **Wastes Seeping into the Columbia River:** The state, along with other members of the Quality Assurance Task Force, continues to evaluate impacts on the Columbia River from waste management operations in the center of the reservation and from waste sites adjacent to the river.

6. **Verification of Data on Erroneous Alarms:** After continuous air monitors continued to alarm at the Plutonium-Uranium Extraction plant, the state was requested to examine data and to verify for

the public that the problem was build-up of radon daughters rather than airborne plutonium.

The state has also participated in several investigations conducted by the General Accounting Office (GAO), including one on the environment (GAO, 1986a) and one on waste management practices (GAO, 1986b). The state also provided information for a National Academy of Sciences review of Hanford's environmental monitoring programs; their report is scheduled for distribution in late 1989.

We do not contend that the state's program is technically better than that of DOE contractors. However, the state's program has credibility because its mission is to ensure public health. The state has demonstrated objectivity and a willingness both to criticize and credit DOE operations and activities.

CONCLUSION

Nuclear fuel reprocessing activities and radioactive waste disposal are publicly sensitive issues requiring the presence of an independent monitoring organization to represent the public. This is especially true at Hanford, where nuclear operations are varied and numerous, and where control of radioactivity has been lost in the past.

The WSDH, as both the public health agency and the radiation control agency, provides an additional level of independence and public credibility to verify DOE's environmental radiation monitoring program and to assure the public that it is safe.

REFERENCES

DSHS. 1986. Report to Governor Booth Gardner and the Washington State Legislature Regarding Environmental Radiation Monitoring as Required by SSB 3799. Department of Social and Health Services, Olympia, WA.

GAO. 1986a. Nuclear Safety: Environmental Issues at DOE's Nuclear Defense Facilities, GAO/RCED-86-192, Report to the Committee on Governmental Affairs, United States Senate. General Accounting Office, Washington, DC.

GAO. 1986b. Nuclear Safety: Unresolved Issues Concerning Hanford's Waste Management Practices, GAO/RCED-87-30, Report to the Committee on Governmental Affairs, United States Senate. General Accounting Office, Washington DC.

RCW. 1986. Revised Code of Washington Chapter 70.98: Nuclear Energy and Radiation. Department of Social and Health Services, Olympia, WA.

WAC. 1986. Washington Administrative Code 402-80: Monitoring and Enforcement of Air Quality and Emission Standards for Radionuclides, December 11, 1986. Washington State Legislature, Olympia, WA.

THE HANFORD ENVIRONMENTAL DOSE RECONSTRUCTION PROJECT: OVERVIEW

H. A. Haerer, M. D. Freshley, R. O. Gilbert, L. G. Morgan, B. A. Napier, R. E. Rhoads, and R. K. Woodruff

Pacific Northwest Laboratory, Richland, Washington

Key Words: *Dose reconstruction, Hanford Site, sensitivity analyses, dose distributions*

ABSTRACT

In 1988, researchers began a multiyear effort to estimate radiation doses that people could have received since 1944 at the U.S. Department of Energy's Hanford Site. The study was prompted by increasing concern about potential health effects to the public from more than 40 yr of nuclear activities. We will provide an overview of the Hanford Environmental Dose Reconstruction Project and its technical approach. The work has required development of new methods and tools for dealing with unique technical and communication challenges. Scientists are using a probabilistic, rather than the more typical deterministic, approach to generate dose distributions rather than single-point estimates. Uncertainties in input parameters are reflected in dose results. Sensitivity analyses are used to optimize project resources and define the project's scope. An independent technical steering panel directs and approves the work in a public forum.

Dose estimates are based on review and analysis of historical data related to operations, effluents, and monitoring; determination of important radionuclides; and reconstruction of source terms, environmental conditions that affected transport, concentrations in environmental media, and human elements, such as population distribution, agricultural practices, food consumption patterns, and lifestyles. A companion paper in this volume, The Hanford Environmental Dose Reconstruction Project: Technical Approach, describes the computational framework for the work.

INTRODUCTION

The objective of the Hanford Environmental Dose Reconstruction (HEDR) Project is to estimate radiation doses that the public could have received from nuclear operations at the U.S. Department of Energy's (DOE's) Hanford Site since 1944. HEDR dose estimates will be used by the U.S. Public Health Service's Centers for Disease Control in a thyroid morbidity study being conducted in counties adjacent to the Hanford Site. HEDR Project staff are currently evaluating past monitoring and assessment efforts, deciding when we have enough monitoring data, and identifying ways to make monitoring and assessment more cost-effective.

Our experiences confirm those of scientists working in the hazardous waste area; that is, addressing dose-assessment issues requires a technical and sociopolitical framework. We must move from deterministic to probabilistic radiological assessments and involve the interested public in the process. A dose assessment that is accepted by the scientific community but is not understood or accepted as credible by the public is strictly a scientific exercise. A successful dose assessment must also provide potentially affected people with information to independently evaluate impacts.

HISTORICAL BACKGROUND

HEDR was prompted by mounting concern about potential public health effects from more than 40 yr of operations at Hanford. Of particular interest was the period from startup until environmental monitoring reports were made publicly available in the late 1950s. In 1986, the Hanford Health Effects Review Panel, convened by the Centers for Disease Control at the request of the Washington State Nuclear Waste Board and the Indian Health Service, recommended that potential doses from radioactive releases at Hanford be reconstructed. The states of Oregon and Washington, representatives of three regional Indian tribes, and DOE agreed that an independent technical steering panel (TSP) should direct the HEDR Project, which is managed and conducted by the Pacific Northwest Laboratory. A TSP was subsequently selected by representatives from four Northwest universities, and the project was formally initiated in 1988.

The TSP reviews, evaluates, and approves all technical decisions and reports. Panel members include experts in various technical fields and individuals representing the states of Washington and Oregon, the Indian tribes, and the public. The TSP conducts periodic public meetings (about every 2 mo) and provides public access to the data used in reconstructing doses.

TECHNICAL APPROACH

HEDR uses an approach similar to a typical deterministic radiological dose assessment. However, HEDR uses distributions rather than point estimates as input and produces distributions rather than point estimates as results (dose estimates). Our work also differs from typical dose assessments in that it involves many years of operations and must reconstruct past conditions.

Figure 1 shows the flow of information required to estimate radiological doses; these are based on: (1) identification, review, and analysis of historical data on nuclear operations; (2) determination of radionuclides that could have contributed to dose; (3) reconstruction of the types and quantities of radiological materials released to the atmosphere, the Columbia River, and soils; (4) reconstruction of atmospheric, river, and ground-water conditions that affected the transport of radiological materials from operating facilities to offsite populations; (5) delineation of study areas; (6) review of historical measurements of radionuclides that originated at Hanford in environmental media; (7) reconstruction of agricultural practices; (8) reconstruction of general and specific population distributions; and (9) reconstruction of food consumption patterns and lifestyles.

A phased approach is being used; for example, identifying the most significant radionuclides, selecting appropriate computer models, identifying key parameters for model input, and developing preliminary dose estimates and their uncertainties for people who lived closest to the Hanford Site. Results from our initial work will support cost/benefit decisions concerning modification of the study (area and time period covered), identification of methods for improving models, and identification of additional data sources.

All major technical decisions concerning work scope and approach, including selection of radionuclides, exposure pathways, study areas and populations, time periods, computer models, methods for assessing uncertainties in dose estimates, key input parameters, and dose threshold levels, are reviewed and approved by the TSP in a public forum. Thus, the public is an integral part of the decision-making process.

Initially, the project is focussing on air emissions from 1944 through 1947 and liquid emissions from 1964 through 1966 for 10 counties surrounding the Hanford Site (about a 150-km radius; Figure 2). Preliminary doses are being estimated for the general public and for Native American populations in the study area, primarily the Yakima and Umatilla tribes.

The major surface-water pathway includes that portion of the Columbia River (about 100 river miles) between Priest Rapids Dam, immediately upstream of the site, and McNary, the first downstream dam. Radiological dose estimates for the water pathway will be compared with historical dose estimates from 1964 through 1966.

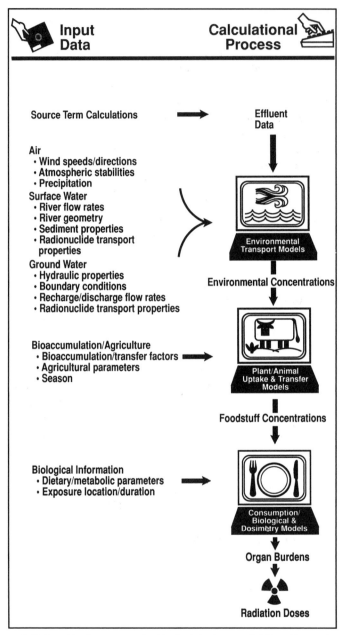

Figure 1. Data-gathering process for Hanford Environmental Dose Reconstruction.

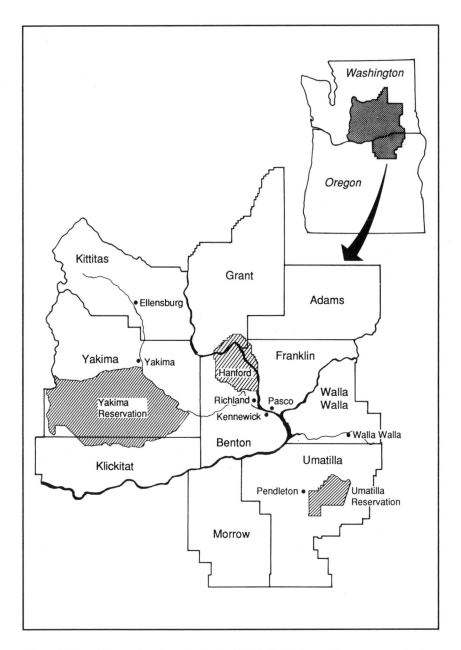

Figure 2. Map of 10 counties closest to Hanford Site, initial study area for dose reconstruction.

Figure 3 shows the relationship between our study and historical radionuclide releases to the atmosphere and radionuclides in the river. The years 1944 through 1947 were selected to study airborne emissions because more than 90% of the ^{131}I released from 1944 through 1988 occurred during that time. We are focusing on ^{131}I because it had the greatest potential contribution to radiation doses. All other important radionuclides are also being investigated in the first phase of study.

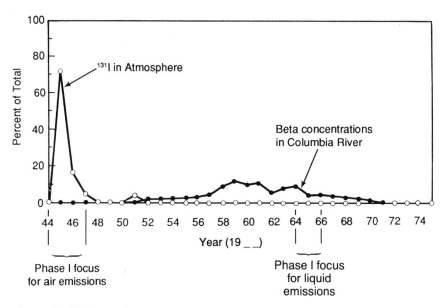

Figure 3. [131]I Releases from separations plants and total beta concentrations in the Columbia River, expressed as percents of totals from 1944-1975. Values from Anderson (1974), Essig (1970), and Hanford Site environmental monitoring reports, such as Wilson (1964), which are the basis for time periods selected for initial phase of dose reconstruction.

The years 1964 through 1966 were selected to study releases to the Columbia River primarily because extensive monitoring data were available during that period. In addition, releases to the Columbia River from 1944 through 1947 were relatively low, because only one to three reactors were operating (of the nine production reactors that operated on site in 1964), and because they operated at lower power levels than in later years. Thus, higher releases of water-transported radionuclides occurred during the late 1950s through mid-1960s. Moreover, all reactors were shut down for about 50 days in 1966, then restarted. This event provided an unusual opportunity to assess changes in radionuclide concentrations in fish, water, and sediments as related to changes in reactor emissions.

We will summarize the first phase of study for the TSP, including preliminary dose estimates and associated uncertainties, in 1990. The summary report will document the rationale for selecting radionuclides, models, parameters, study areas, and time periods for the first phase, including a comparison and evaluation of methods for analyzing sensitivity and uncertainty of preliminary dose estimates. The project is scheduled for completion in 1993.

CONCLUSIONS

HEDR uses a probabilistic approach to dose assessment that incorporates explicit evaluations of uncertainties in input parameters and dose estimates. The project assesses relative importance of input parameters using sensitivity analyses and thereby optimizes project resources in selecting radionuclides, pathways, geographic areas, time periods, and critical subpopulations. HEDR is conducted under the direction of a TSP and in full view of the public who will ultimately judge the success of the work.

ACKNOWLEDGMENT

Work supported by the U.S. Department of Energy under Contract DE-AC06-76RLO 1830.

REFERENCES

Anderson, J. D. 1974. Emitted and Decay Values of Radionuclides in Gaseous Wastes Discharged to the Atmosphere from the Separations Facilities through Calendar Year 1972, ARH-3026. Atlantic Richfield Hanford Company, Richland, WA.

Essig, T. H. 1970. Age-Dependent Radiation Dose Estimates for Residents of the Hanford Environs, 1945-1968, A special problem report submitted to the Faculty of Civil Engineering, Washington State University, for partial fulfillment of the requirements for the degree of Master of Science in Sanitary Engineering. Washington State University, Pullman, WA.

Wilson, R. H. (ed.). 1964. Evaluation of Radiological Conditions in the Vicinity of Hanford for 1963, HW-80991. General Electric Company, Richland, WA.

THE HANFORD ENVIRONMENTAL DOSE RECONSTRUCTION (HEDR) PROJECT: TECHNICAL APPROACH

B. A. Napier, M. D. Freshley, R. O. Gilbert, H. A. Haerer, L. G. Morgan, R. E. Rhoads, and R. K. Woodruff

Pacific Northwest Laboratory, Richland, Washington

Key Words: *Dose reconstruction, Hanford Site, dose distributions, uncertainty*

ABSTRACT

Historical measurements and current assessment techniques are being combined to estimate potential radiation doses to people from radioactive releases to the air, the Columbia River, soils, and ground water at the Hanford Site since 1944. Environmental contamination from these releases has been monitored, at varying levels of detail, for 45 yr. Phase I of the Hanford Environmental Reconstruction Project will estimate the magnitude of potential doses, their areal extents, and their associated uncertainties. The Phase I study area comprises 10 counties in eastern Washington and northern Oregon, within a 100-mi radius of the site, including a stretch of the Columbia River that was most significantly affected. These counties contain a range of projected and measured contaminant levels, environmental exposure pathways, and population groups. Phase I dose estimates are being developed for the periods 1944 through 1947 for air pathways and 1964 through 1966 for river pathways. Important radionuclide/pathway combinations include fission products, such as ^{131}I, in milk for early atmospheric releases and activation products, such as ^{32}P and ^{65}Zn, in fish for releases to the river. Potential doses range over several orders of magnitude within the study area. We will expand the time periods and study area in three successive phases, as warranted by results of Phase I.

INTRODUCTION

An overview of the Hanford Environmental Dose Reconstruction (HEDR) Project was given by Haerer et al. (these proceedings). We discuss here the technical approach designed to estimate radiation dose, with associated variability and uncertainty, for various populations that may have been exposed to emissions from past site operations. For hypothetical reference individuals, dose-related information is being developed, based on geographic location, age, lifestyle, ethnic group, and dietary habits. At a later time, we will ask specific individuals (real people) to help us refine this information specifically for them, so that we may more precisely estimate their doses.

The project is being conducted in phases whereby time, space, and level of detail progressively increase. Phase I focuses on the 10 counties surrounding Hanford, from 1944 through 1947 (for atmospheric releases) and 1964 through 1966 (for surface-water releases). The time periods and study area will be expanded in three successive phases as warranted by results of Phase I.

The large number of variables and potential permutations inherent in a study of this complexity, combined with the fine level of detail required to generate useful numbers, make control and manipulation of this much information a major undertaking. We describe here development of various components of the calculation, and the mathematical structure of the models.

SPATIAL AND TEMPORAL RESOLUTION

A critical task involved selecting appropriate units of spatial and temporal resolution for the calculational scheme. The census subdivisions (Figure 1), which reflect trade and service areas, principal settlements, major land uses, and physiographic differences, were selected as the grid framework. Month was selected as the unit for temporal resolution, based on the continuous nature of historical releases and the availability of atmospheric, census, dietary, and lifestyle data (Napier and Beck, 1989).

COMPUTATIONAL APPROACH

Overall radiation dose is the sum of parallel pathway calculations. A simplified conceptual logic diagram for calculating doses from atmospheric releases is shown in Figure 2 (Napier, 1990). Exposure pathways include submersion in and inhalation of contaminated air, exposure to surfaces contaminated from atmospheric deposition, and consumption of contaminated crops and animals.

Figure 3 shows a similar diagram for surface-water releases (Napier, 1990). Pathways include immersion in contaminated water, consumption of aquatic foods, and consumption of foods irrigated with contaminated water.

Sensitivity studies, conducted with increasingly sophisticated conceptual models of pathways and types of individual exposures, have been used throughout the project to focus appropriate submodels for the calculational scheme. These studies have helped identify dominant radionuclides, important parameters for calculating doses from atmospheric release of ^{131}I, and important portions of the traditional Native American diet (Napier, 1989).

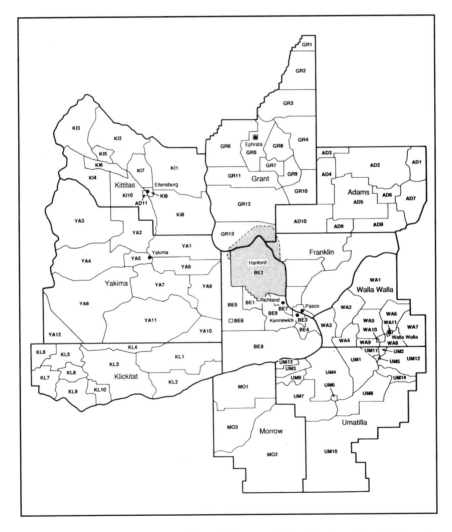

Figure 1. Census subdivisions used as grid framework for estimating historical doses to populations surrounding the Hanford Site.

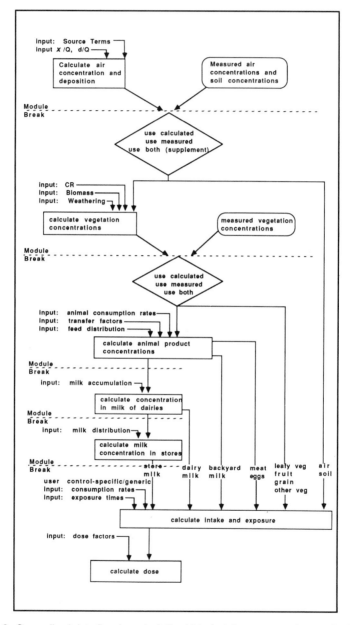

Figure 2. Generalized data flow for calculating historical doses to people near the Hanford Site from exposure via the air pathway.

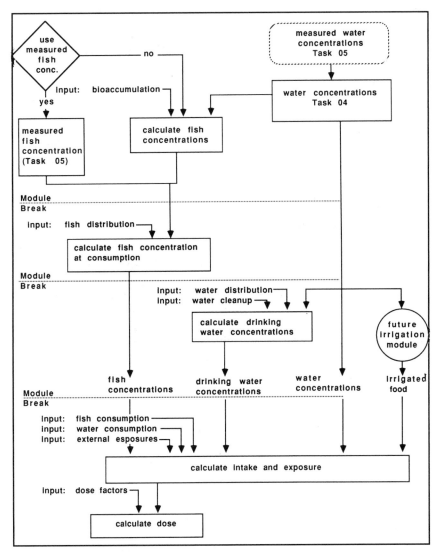

Figure 3. Generalized data flow for calculating historical doses to people near the Hanford Site from exposure via the surface-water pathway.

SOURCE-TERM DERIVATION

In Phase I, ^{131}I accounts for more than 90% of the dose from air in most cases. Atmospheric releases in the 1940s were from the two chemical separations facilities that dissolved irradiated fuel and extracted plutonium (Ballinger and Hall, 1989).

Because technology in the early years did not permit monitoring of specific radionuclides, we modeled emissions. Source-term data for atmospheric releases, including fuel irradiation history and cooling time, were prepared as vectors of total activity (per month) released for several dominant radionuclides. A triangular distribution bounded by upper and lower estimates of potential releases was used. Available effluent data for production reactors from 1964 through 1966 and measured river concentrations were used as source-term input to calculate surface-water transport.

TRANSPORT AND DEPOSITION OF RADIONUCLIDES IN THE ENVIRONMENT

No reliable monitoring data exist for areas outside the Hanford Site for 1944-1947; thus, radionuclide transport in air was modeled. The HEDR atmospheric model, adapted from a Lagrangian puff model, uses historic hourly meteorological data to provide time-integrated air concentrations, monthly averaged deposition rates, and month-end accumulations of nondepositing, chemically reactive, particulate materials (Ramsdell and Burk, 1989). Initially, data from 1983 through 1987 are being used as surrogate input. Variability is estimated as variance from individual grid point estimates. Selection of census subdivisions and atmospheric grid are interdependent and influence all other calculations.

Estimating surface-water concentrations from Hanford releases in the mid-1960s was more straightforward because site data for effluents to the river and radionuclide concentrations are available. A simple routing model was applied to effluent data, accounting for dilution in the time-varying flow of the river and decay for various travel times to locations of interest. Variability is derived from upper and lower values for each radionuclide at each sampling location and time.

To reconstruct radionuclide concentrations in vegetation, two sources are used: calculations based on source term, transport, and deposition, and environmental measurements. Variability in calculated values is accounted for in the interception fraction of the model, which varies as a function of plant biomass and moisture content (crop type and time of year). Variability in measurements is reflected using a time-and-space averaging technique (Woodruff, 1989).

RADIONUCLIDES IN FOOD PRODUCTS

Concentrations of radionuclides in animal products depend on concentrations in feed and amount of feed consumed. Four potential feeding regimes are considered for milk cows, ranging in complexity from a diet of only pasture grass to diets supplemented with hay, grain, and silage; these supplements may be from areas other than where the cow is maintained. Uncertainty in the use of feeding regimes is addressed by using distributions of possible quantities of feed consumed by the animals. Variability of the transfer of contaminants from feed to milk or other animal products is addressed using a range of transfer factors.

Some food products in the study area were purchased by distributors (most significantly, milk). Average radionuclide concentration of a distributor's product is calculated via accumulation fraction arrays, which define the fraction of product at each distribution center that originated in each census subdivision by month. Average concentration in products available from retail outlets is calculated using distribution fraction arrays, which define the fraction of product that originated at each distributor in each census subdivision. Uncertainty in reconstruction of distribution patterns is accounted for using triangular distributions of these fractions (Beck, 1989).

HUMAN FACTORS THAT INFLUENCE EXPOSURE

The model considers demographics of each census subdivision by providing estimates for individuals differentiated by age, sex, diet, and general lifestyle (Callaway, 1990). Seven age groups, divided in two sexes, will eventually be used; only adult and infant categories were investigated in Phase I (Napier and Beck, 1989).

Groups under study include the general population, Native American tribes, U.S. Army personnel stationed at Hanford, Hanford construction workers, and migrant workers. Phase I emphasizes the first two categories. Each category is subdivided into urban and rural "lifestyles."

For each subpopulation/age/lifestyle category, distributions were prepared on consumption rates of locally produced foods. Native American diets, categorized as traditional or nontraditional, were characterized after consultation with tribal members and anthropologists.

MODEL STRUCTURE

Logic diagrams (Figures 2 and 3) show module breaks for individual portions of the calculation, representing individual portions of the computer code that can be run in a stochastic simulation (also called a Monte Carlo analysis). Because of the interconnected nature of the cow-feed/milk distribution model, no doses can be calculated for individuals in a particular census subdivision without knowledge of environmental conditions in other locations. The model minimizes repetitive calculations, and accumulates information on distributions of environmental parameters for each time period (Napier, 1990).

The model structure also allows input of calculated or measured data at each step. In addition, the structure supports dose calculations for specific as well as reference individuals. This is important because we will provide doses for specific individuals to U.S. Public Health Service Center for Disease Control staff, who are conducting a parallel study on thyroid morbidity.

CONCLUSIONS

Environmental monitoring data and modeling results can be effectively combined to reconstruct historical radiation doses. Preliminary results indicate that in the early years of Hanford operations the largest doses were from ^{131}I in milk. As effluent control technology improved and more production reactors began operating, Columbia River fish became an important exposure pathway.

ACKNOWLEDGMENT

The HEDR project conceptual model is undergoing continual refinement and updating. The authors acknowledge the input of members of the HEDR Technical Steering Panel and thank the staff of the Center for Disease Control Hanford Thyroid Morbidity Study for numerous suggestions.

REFERENCES

Ballinger, M. Y., and R. A. Hall. 1989. A History of Major Hanford Operations Involving Radioactive Material, PNL-6964 HEDR. Pacific Northwest Laboratory, Richland, WA.

Beck, D. M. 1989. Milk Cow Feed Intake and Milk Production and Distribution Estimates for Phase I, PNL-7227 HEDR. Pacific Northwest Laboratory, Richland, WA.

Callaway, J. M. 1990. Estimates of Food Consumption, PNL-7260 HEDR. Pacific Northwest Laboratory, Richland, WA.

Napier, B. A. 1989. Selection of Dominant Radionuclides for Phase I of the HEDR Project, PNL-7231 HEDR. Pacific Northwest Laboratory, Richland, WA.

Napier, B. A. 1990. Computational Model Design Specification for Phase I of the Hanford Environmental Dose Reconstruction Project, PNL-7274 HEDR. Pacific Northwest Laboratory, Richland, WA.

Napier, B. A., and D. M. Beck. 1989. Defining Demographic Categories for Phase I, PNL-SA-17035 HEDR. Pacific Northwest Laboratory, Richland, WA.

Ramsdell, J. V., and K. W. Burk. 1989. Atmospheric Transport Modeling and Input Data for Phase I of the Hanford Environmental Dose Reconstruction Project, PNL-7199 HEDR. Pacific Northwest Laboratory, Richland, WA.

Woodruff, R. K. 1989. Preliminary Summaries for Vegetation, River and Drinking Water, and Fish Radionuclide Concentration Data, PNL-SA-17641 HEDR. Pacific Northwest Laboratory, Richland, WA.

METEOROLOGICAL MONITORING FOR DOSE ASSESSMENT AND EMERGENCY RESPONSE MODELING—HOW MUCH IS ENOUGH?

C. S. Glantz

Pacific Northwest Laboratory, Richland, Washington

Key Words: *Atmospheric dispersion, meteorological monitoring, emergency response, dose assessment*

ABSTRACT

Individuals responsible for emergency response or environmental/dose assessment routinely ask if there are enough meteorological data to adequately support their objectives. The answer requires detailed consideration of the intended applications, capabilities of the atmospheric dispersion model data, pollutant release characteristics, terrain in the modeling region, and size and distribution of the human population in the modeling domain. The meteorologist's detailed knowledge of, and experience in, studying atmospheric transport and diffusion can assist in determining the appropriate level of meteorological monitoring.

INTRODUCTION

At facilities that may release hazardous pollutants to the atmosphere, limited resources must be efficiently allocated among different components of environmental/dose-assessment systems (meteorological monitoring, data acquisition, computer hardware, computer software, personnel). The ability to effectively model environmental impacts has improved in recent years with increased availability of small, high-speed, relatively inexpensive computers and more sophisticated dispersion and dose-assessment models. Unfortunately, many meteorological monitoring programs have not been upgraded to provide the additional information that can be effectively utilized by new modeling systems.

In evaluating the effectiveness and appropriateness of meteorological monitoring programs, individuals responsible for planning and operating emergency response or environmental/dose-assessment programs routinely ask whether enough meteorological data are being obtained to adequately support their objectives. There is no simple answer to this question. Many factors affect the design of meteorological monitoring networks, and each must be considered when determining the number, location, and type of meteorological monitoring stations required. The objective of this paper is to discuss the factors that must be considered when developing a new meteorological monitoring program or reevaluating the adequacy of an existing program.

I will review the concept of spatial and temporal variation in meteorological parameters to illustrate why more than one monitoring station and type of measurement are needed to provide data for most atmospheric dispersion modeling applications. I will also discuss the major factors to be considered when assessing capabilities of a monitoring network.

SPATIAL AND TEMPORAL VARIATION IN THE ATMOSPHERE

Emergency response and environmental/dose assessment would be easier if the atmosphere were uniform and unchanging. In such an environment, winds measured at one location and at one time would always represent conditions throughout a modeling domain. In nature, the atmosphere is dynamic; wind speed, turbulence, and temperature vary significantly from place to place (spatial variation) and with time (temporal variation). Winds and temperature at one near-surface monitoring location are not necessarily representative of conditions several hundred meters down the road, several tens of meters aloft, or several minutes earlier or later.

Atmospheric changes occur as a result of multiscale influences. Large-scale influences (more than 100 km apart) include weather systems such as fronts and regions of high pressure. Medium-scale influences (between 2 and 100 km) include land/sea and mountain/valley circulations caused by differential solar heating and radiational cooling rates. Local-scale influences (less than 2 km) result from variations in local topography, buildings, and changes in surface roughness. In complex terrain, medium and local-scale influences are stronger and more frequently experienced than with uniform terrain.

Horizontal variations in atmospheric variables can be detected near the surface with inexpensive monitoring stations consisting of a wind vane/anemometer and temperature probe on a short tower; these stations might also have instruments for measuring other parameters. Vertical variations in atmospheric parameters are more difficult and expensive to measure than horizontal variations. Although vertical variations are often significant in atmospheric dispersion, they are seldom rigorously characterized because of the difficulties and expense associated with routine monitoring.

In recent years, traditional methods of measuring vertical variations (e.g., instrumented towers, balloon systems) have been augmented by remote sensing techniques. Remote sensing is not as vertically limited as tower-based monitoring and provides more comprehensive information than balloon systems. Remote systems, such as a Doppler acoustic sounder, can simultaneously monitor wind directions and speeds (including turbulence parameters) throughout most of the boundary layer (Mason and Moses, 1984). Although there were significant drawbacks to remote monitoring systems in the past, recent technological advances (with associated decreases in purchase and maintenance costs) have made use of the remote sensing equipment feasible for many applications.

CONSIDERATIONS WHEN PLANNING A METEOROLOGICAL MONITORING NETWORK

The number, location, and type of meteorological measurements needed for dispersion modeling depend on several factors. Some of these are obvious and easy to assess, others are frequently overlooked or are difficult to evaluate. Most important when designing or evaluating a monitoring program is that the purpose of the environmental/dose-assessment system be considered. Are data being collected for climatological purposes, for routine environmental/dose assessment, or for emergency response? For climatological assessments, one monitoring site (representative of conditions at the potential release site) may be sufficient. If the environmental impacts of long-term or routine atmospheric releases are being assessed, an expanded meteorological monitoring network may be required to provide information on long-term spatial and temporal differences in wind speed and diffusion parameters. For emergency-response applications or study of any short-term release, additional monitoring sites are often required to provide detailed information on short-term spatial and temporal variations.

Second, the quantity and quality of data provided by a monitoring network must be compatible with the meteorological data requirements of the system's dispersion models. When dispersion modeling capabilities are upgraded, increased meteorological monitoring is frequently required. It is often cheaper and easier to upgrade a system's modeling capability than to upgrade its monitoring capability; as a result, monitoring capabilities are often not upgraded to provide the data needed to take full advantage of enhanced modeling capabilities.

Managers may erroneously believe that an enhanced modeling capability will, by itself, produce improvements in environmental/dose assessments.

Other factors to consider when evaluating a meteorological monitoring program include:

- **Type and quantity of pollutants released to the atmosphere.** If a pollutant can be transported long distances in sufficient concentration to cause concern, meteorological monitoring must represent conditions throughout the potentially impacted region. Alternatively, if pollutant concentrations drop below levels of concern at short distances from the release location, limited monitoring near the release location may be sufficient.

- **Height of the pollutant release and buoyancy.** If near-surface, nonbuoyant releases are of concern, near-surface monitoring will provide the most important information for characterizing atmospheric transport. If atmospheric releases are elevated or positively buoyant (owing to vertical velocity or temperature of the effluent), transport of pollutants may be dominated by winds aloft; in such cases, near-surface wind measurements may not represent winds aloft.

- **Terrain characteristics** (e.g., topography, vegetation, and buildings). Significant spatial and temporal variations in atmospheric dispersion occur more frequently in areas with complex terrain than in areas of unchanging topography. As a result, more meteorological monitoring is required for a complex terrain environment. For a relatively flat area and a small modeling domain (e.g., 10 to 50 km wide), measurements at a single station may adequately represent conditions under most weather conditions. When terrain is more complex, additional monitoring locations are typically needed to adequately represent horizontal variations in the wind field.

- **Size of modeling domain** (e.g., large, medium, or local scales). The larger the modeling domain, the higher the probability that medium- and large-scale influences will produce significant spatial variations. Therefore, the larger the modeling domain, the more meteorological monitoring is required.

- **Distribution of human population.** Because of concern for human health, additional monitoring is frequently required to more accurately characterize potential transport along pathways leading toward populated areas.

In addition, meteorological data must be reliable and must be available when needed. Formal maintenance and quality control programs are essential to maintain data reliability. A monitoring network is of no use if equipment is off line or if measurements are grossly inaccurate. Data for emergency-response applications are useful only if available in close to real time. Data acquisition systems that record data on cassette tape or that require manual processing are inappropriate for emergency-response applications.

CONCLUSIONS

Resources must be properly distributed to maximize the performance of emergency-response and environmental/dose-assessment systems. Meteorological monitoring must be appropriate for the intended application, available dispersion models, pollutant release characteristics, terrain complexity, size of modeling domain, and distribution of local population centers. Even when properly designed, meteorological monitoring programs are effective only when data are reliable and available to users in an appropriate time frame for the intended application.

In many systems, meteorological monitoring must characterize horizontal, vertical, and temporal variations in atmospheric parameters. Recent technological innovations involving remote sensing have made feasible the real-time assessment of vertical variations in atmospheric variables. Consideration should be given to upgrading the capability of many monitoring programs to allow for characterization of vertical variations in winds and turbulence.

To more effectively allocate resources for meteorological monitoring, experienced meteorologists should be involved in the planning, development, operation, and maintenance of monitoring networks. The question of "how much is enough" can only be answered on a case-by-case basis. In some cases, the answer may involve a reduction in monitoring; in most cases, the increasing capabilities of environmental/dose-assessment models require more detailed characterizations of meteorological conditions than existing monitoring programs provide.

ACKNOWLEDGMENT

Work supported by the U.S. Department of Energy under Contract DE-AC06-76RLO 1830. Some of the information in this paper is based on lectures presented by Dr. Todd Crawford at the Advanced Studies

Institute Short Course on the Meteorological Aspects of Emergency
Response (September, 1988; Charleston, South Carolina).

REFERENCE

Mason, C. J. and H. Moses, D. 1984. Meteorological Instrumentation, pp. 81-
    135. In: Atmospheric Science and Power Production, D. Randerson (ed.),
    DOE/TIC-27601. NTIS, Springfield, VA.

THE ADDITIVITY OF RADIONUCLIDE AND CHEMICAL RISK ESTIMATES IN PERFORMANCE EVALUATION OF MIXED-WASTE SITES

J. E. Till and K. R. Meyer

Radiological Assessments Corporation, Neeses, South Carolina

Key Words: *Chemical risk, radionuclide risk, risk assessment, risk additivity*

ABSTRACT

Methods for assessing radioactive waste sites that contain chemical constituents are in the formative stages. In evaluating these sites, a key concern will be the hazard to personnel involved in cleanup work and to the general population. This paper focuses on what we have learned from pathway analysis and risk assessment about providing a combined estimate of risk from exposure to both chemicals and radionuclides. Quantitative radiation risk assessment involves a high degree of uncertainty. Chemical risk assessment generally does not provide quantitative results. Thus, it is not currently possible to develop a useful, quantitative combined risk assessment for mixed-waste sites.

INTRODUCTION

In radionuclide risk assessment, it is assumed that the dose is sufficiently low that only stochastic effects (those that occur by chance) need be considered. Stochastic effects are, mainly, cancer and genetic responses. No threshold (dose below which health effects are not observed) is assumed.

Conventional toxicological methods have been used to establish "safe" levels of exposure for chemicals presumed to have a threshold (doses below which significant nonstochastic effects such as death or severe injury are unlikely to occur). These methods cannot be used to establish safe exposure levels for chemicals that are suspected carcinogens or mutagens, because the doses are far below toxicological thresholds. As in radiation protection, chemical risk assessment involves mathematical models to extrapolate the probability of effects at relatively high exposure levels to lower levels where the actual health effect cannot be detected, either through epidemiological or experimental techniques.

With the advent of decontamination programs and cleanup of various mixed-waste sites throughout the United States, there is interest in combining risk estimates for radionuclides and those for chemicals to reflect total risk. Risk assessment evaluates known effects of radiation or chemicals on exposed individuals and populations and estimates probable effects of additional exposure. Radiation risk assessment is currently more advanced than chemical risk assessment; we will describe why.

BACKGROUND

Obtaining a reasonable risk estimate is a complicated web of equations, analytical techniques, and models. We will divide the process into several fundamental steps for clarity: hazard identification, dose-response assessment, exposure assessment, and risk characterization (NRC, 1983).

Hazard Identification

More information has been accumulated on the health effects of radiation than on any other environmental contaminant. Although there is disagreement on the effects of low radiation doses, higher doses represent a clear, measurable concern. In contrast, the likelihood of a chemical being a carcinogen is based on judgment. Initial qualitative weight-of-evidence statements are based on information about likely exposure and possible toxicity to humans (Anderson, 1983). There is no simple method or criterion to determine if a chemical is a human health hazard.

The U.S. Environmental Protection Agency (EPA) classification system for carcinogens is adapted from the International Agency for Research on Cancer (IARC) approach for judging the weight of evidence for human and animal data (EPA, 1986). The IARC Group 1 chemicals correspond to the EPA Group A (Table 1), which includes those shown to be carcinogens in humans. IARC Groups 2A, 2B, and 3 correspond to EPA Groups B, C, and D, respectively. EPA has a fifth group that includes chemicals shown to be noncarcinogens in humans.

IARC selects chemicals for evaluation based mainly on: known or suspected (derived from human, animal, or other laboratory data) human carcinogenicity. The selection is highly biased, and the group of over 500 compounds evaluated cannot be compared to a random sample of all chemicals.

Table 1. International Agency for Research on Cancer (IARC) and U.S. Environmental Protection Agency (EPA) classification system for carcinogenicity in humans.

IARC	EPA	Description
Group 1	Group A	Carcinogen in humans
Group 2A	Group B	Probable carcinogen in humans
Group 2B	Group C	Possible carcinogen in humans
Group 3	Group D	Not classifiable as carcinogen
	Group E	Evidence of noncarcinogenicity

Every year, over 400,000 new organic compounds are synthesized worldwide. Over 1,000 of these compounds will eventually be in use and will be disposed of in mixed-waste sites (Woo et al., 1985). Few of these new products can be adequately tested for carcinogenicity. Human data (case reports or epidemiological studies) are available for only a limited number of compounds (Saracci, 1981).

Table 2 shows 13 chemicals and 5 industrial processes classified as human carcinogens. Except for the three drugs, exposure is occupational (Saracci, 1981). Tables 3 and 4 show chemicals from IARC Groups 2 and 3; their carcinogenicity is debatable.

Table 2. Chemicals and industrial processes carcinogenic for humans (Group 1).[a]

4-Aminobiphenyl

Arsenic and certain arsenic compounds

Asbestos

Manufacture of auramine

Benzene

N, N-bis (2-chloroethyl) -
2-naphthyl-amine (chlornaphazine)

Bis (chloromethyl) ether and
chloromethyl methyl ether

Chromium and certain chromium
compounds

Diethylstilbestrol

Underground hematite mining

Manufacture of isopropyl alcohol by
the strong acid process

Melphalan

Mustard gas

2-Naphthylamine

Nickel refining

Soots, tars, and mineral oils

Vinyl chloride

[a]Adapted from Saracci, 1981.

Table 3. Chemicals which are probably carcinogenic to humans (Group 2).[a]

Subgroup A — Higher Degree of Human Evidence

Aflatoxins	Cyclophosphamide
Cadmium and certain cadmium compounds	Nickel and certain nickel compounds
Chlorambucil	Tris (1-aziridinyl) phosphone sulphide (thiotepa)

Subgroup B — Lower Degree of Human Evidence

Acrylonitrile	Dimethyl sulfate
Amitrole (aminotriazole)	Ethylene oxide
Auramine	Iron dextran complex
Beryllium and certain beryllium compounds	Oxymetholone
Carbon tetrachloride	Phenacetin
Dimethyl carbamoyl chloride	Polychlorinated biphenyls

[a]Adapted from Saracci, 1981.

Table 4. Chemicals not classified as carcinogens in humans (Group 3).[a]

Chloramphenicol	Isopropyl oils
Chlordane/heptachlor	Lead and certain lead compounds
Chloroprene	Phenobarbitone
Dichlorodiphenyltrichloroethane (DDT)	N-Phenyl-2-naphthylamine
Dieldrin	Phenytoin
Epichlorohydrin	Reserpine
Hematite	Styrene
Hexachlorocyclohexane (technical-grade HCH/lindane)	Trichloroethylene
Isoniazid	Tris (aziridinyl)-1-para-benzoquinone (triaziquone)

[a]Adapted from Saracci, 1981.

Dose-Response Assessment

Risk estimates for low-level radiation are determined by studying large population groups that have been exposed to high radiation doses. These include the Hiroshima and Nagasaki bomb survivors, patients who were medically exposed, and occupationally exposed populations. Several scientific committees reviewed these data and estimated the risk from exposure to low doses. Figure 1 shows a typical radiation dose-response relationship. There is considerable evidence to support a linear relationship between dose and risk, although a linear-quadratic model is supported by some studies (for example, BEIR, 1980). Even with the large data base for radiation risk assessment, there is disagreement between models because of the large uncertainty associated with the exact shape of the dose-response curves at low doses (100 μSv to 5 mSv).

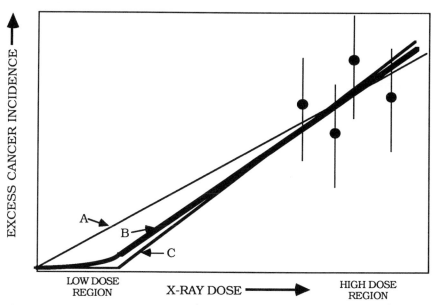

Figure 1. Radiation dose-response extrapolation (adapted from Hall, 1984). A = Linear extrapolation model, B = linear quadratic extrapolation model, C = threshold response model.

Other dose-response models have been developed. For example, the U.S. Department of Energy (DOE) combined absolute and relative risk models from BEIR (1980) to estimate health effects from the Chernobyl accident (Goldman et al., 1987). Using recent data on organ sensitivity and dose response, they provided three estimates of the risk range: an upper, a best (central), and a lower estimate. The bottom of the range for each is zero.

Dose-response assessment for chemicals usually involves extrapolation from high exposures (of experimental animals, or exposures in epidemiological studies) to the lower human exposure levels expected in the environment. Unfortunately, the data are extremely limited and, most importantly, good epidemiological data are lacking, particularly for newly developed chemicals. These data are not likely to become available because of current emphasis on safety and worker protection. Also, actual dose is not usually measured for chemicals, and complex, poorly understood factors can modify the effect by orders of magnitude.

If data are available at doses equivalent to environmental exposures, the curve that best fits should be used (EPA, 1986). Most often there is no biological justification to support the choice of model to describe actual chemical risk. The model recommended by EPA for risk extrapolation to low levels is the linear nonthreshold model of Crump (1981). This model is not used to establish actual risks but to set reasonable upper bounds. Generally, no attempt is made to pinpoint risks within the broad bounds defined at the upper limit by a dose-response model and, at the lower limit, near-zero (EPA, 1986).

Exposure Assessment

Personnel are routinely monitored for radiation by personal dosimetry, bioassay, and whole-body counting. In contrast, no one approach to assess chemical exposure is appropriate for all cases (Albert, 1985).

Each waste site has a unique physical setting and chemical profile. Extensive monitoring data are generally available only for certain pollutants, pesticides, and a few heavy metals (Nisbet, 1981). Carcinogenic responses to chemicals may differ with exposure pathway (ingestion, inhalation, absorption), term of exposure (chronic or acute), and metabolism. Inside the body a chemical may be translocated to a particular organ, stored, activated to a carcinogenic form, or excreted. Thus, it is unlikely that two assessments of exposure to the same chemical will be identical (OSTP, 1985).

Another complicating factor is the assignment of separate responsibilities within government for environmental monitoring (air, water, and waste sites), food, drugs, consumer products, and the workplace. In each area, specialized estimating techniques, data sources, and expertise have been developed. Each federal agency tends to focus on those aspects of exposure that are relevant to the laws it administers (OSTP, 1985), and there is little coordination among government agencies.

For the 18 most frequently observed chemical contaminants at 929 chemical storage facilities, only arsenic has both a drinking-water and human-health standard. Only seven others have either drinking-water standards (lead, manganese, chromium, mercury) or human-health criteria (trichloroethylene, tetrachloroethylene, benzene). Clearly, much more information is required for standard setting and risk assessment.

Many chemicals can be detected in the body: lead in blood, cadmium in urine, and polychloride biphenyl compounds (PCB) in serum are well-accepted indices of exposure. Unfortunately, the number of chemicals that can be detected is small compared to the number and types of chemicals released. Furthermore, bioassays indicate only that the chemical is present in the body and not the amount.

Maximum measured or estimated exposure concentration is used to obtain a "worst case" risk estimate. Although incorrect, the highest concentration present is used routinely to quantify risk. Adding upper bounds serves only to compound this conservatism, which stems from adopting the linear no-threshold model (and the need to extrapolate from animal data).

Risk Characterization

The results of exposure and dose-response assessments are combined to quantitatively estimate carcinogenic risk. For example, lifetime risk from 10 mGy whole-body irradiation is about 280 additional fatal cancers per million persons (BEIR, 1980). Based on the DOE model used for Chernobyl, 230 additional fatal cancers per million persons would be expected from exposure to 10 mGy (Goldman et al., 1987). For both estimates, the additional cancers from whole-body irradiation represent an increase of about 0.015%, well within the variability of natural cancer mortality. Even with the extensive data base, quantitative estimation of carcinogenic risk from low-dose, low linear energy transfer (LET) radiation is subject to numerous uncertainties (BEIR, 1980). Unlike sampling variation, these uncertainties cannot easily be summarized in probabilistic terms. Thus, there is more emphasis on the estimation method than on the estimate obtained.

For chemicals, no established procedure exists for making "most likely" or "best" estimates of risk within the range of uncertainty defined by upper and lower limits (EPA, 1986). Nevertheless, quantitative risk assessment has been applied to provide information for making policy decisions regarding public health. For example, by law EPA is required to list hazardous air pollutants and regulate sources as necessary. A potency index, defined as an upper-bound unit risk estimate and a qualitative weight-of-evidence statement, is given for each chemical (Anderson, 1983).

Table 5 shows unit risk estimates for chemicals that might present a hazard to humans in air. Most are also identified as probable or possible human carcinogens by IARC and EPA (Tables 2 and 3). The upper-bound unit risk is defined as the increased individual lifetime risk for a 70-kg individual, breathing air containing 1 $\mu g/m^3$ of chemical for a 70-yr life span. Exponents of the risk estimates range over a billionfold, from 10^8 to 10^{-1}.

Table 5. Upper-bound unit risk estimates for suspected carcinogenic air pollutants.[a, b]

Chemical	Upper-Bound Unit Risk Estimates
Acrylonitrile	7×10^{-5}
Allyl chloride	5×10^{-8}
Arsenic	4×10^{-3}
Benzene	7×10^{-6}
Beryllium	6×10^{-4}
Diethylnitrosamine (DEN)	2×10^{-2}
Dimethylnitrosamine (DMN)	5×10^{-3}
Ethylene dibromide	6×10^{-5}
Ethylene dichloride	7×10^{-6}
Ethylene oxide	2×10^{-4}
Formaldehyde	5×10^{-5}
Manganese	4×10^{-4}
Nickel	6×10^{-4}
N-nitroso-N-ethylurea (NEU)	1×10^{-2}
N-nitroso-N-methylurea (NRU)	7×10^{-1}
Perchloroethylene	2×10^{-6}
Trichloroethylene	3×10^{-6}
Vinyl chloride	4×10^{-6}
Vinylidene chloride	4×10^{-5}

[a]Unit risk is excess lifetime risk associated with a 70-kg person breathing 1 $\mu g/m^3$ of chemical over a 70-yr life span.
[b]From Anderson, 1983.

Based on responses in humans, some chemicals with the best evidence for carcinogenicity have relatively low potencies (for example, vinyl chloride and benzene, with unit risks of 10^{-6}). Therefore, EPA emphasizes that numerical estimates should be accompanied by the various assumptions and uncertainties on which they are based. There is a tendency to use risk estimates and ignore the biomedical evidence, or to treat suspected carcinogens as if they were known to be human carcinogens. In some cases, upper-bound estimates have been treated as actual risk estimates, and uncertainty estimates have been ignored.

RISK ESTIMATION PROCEDURES

Combining risk estimates for different agents has been considered for some time. EPA recommends (EPA, 1986), and others concur, that the possibility of interaction among several chemical carcinogens can be ignored and the risks summed (EPA, 1986; Albert, 1985).

Several approaches have been suggested to estimate risks from combined exposure to different carcinogens (e.g., radiation and chemicals). In one system (NRC, 1983), carcinogens are ranked. Scores are assigned for number of species affected, number of histologically different types of neoplasms, spontaneous incidence of neoplasms, amount and duration of treatment required for a specified response, malignancy of induced tumors, and genotoxicity in a battery of short-term bioassays. These methods produce a variety of end points rather than a risk estimate.

Another approach to estimating combined risk relates mutagenicity of a chemical to the amount of radiation that would produce an equal effect. A "rem-equivalent" chemical dose (REC) produces genetic damage equal to that from 1 rem (10 mSv) chronic radiation exposure (Crow, 1973). The REC was introduced not to estimate risk but as a guide to set standards. Because there were accepted radiation standards, NRC hoped that chemical risks could be evaluated by comparing chemical effects to those from radiation. However, chemicals produce various biochemical effects that are different from those produced by radiation. Most radiation-induced mutations include chromosomal breakage; some chemicals induce point mutations and changes in DNA. Although radiation damage can be measured in tissues, that is not currently the case with chemicals. A newer method, discussed below, may provide valuable information in this area.

Molecular dosimetry, a step toward detecting and measuring chemicals in tissues, is based on the relationship among altered genetic material, DNA, and carcinogenesis. The presence of carcinogen-altered DNA or DNA adducts may indicate persistent damage at the molecular level from exposure to chemicals (EPA, 1986). DNA adducts have been measured in cells and tissues from people occupationally exposed to carcinogenic polycyclic aromatic hydrocarbons (Harris et al., 1987).

CONCLUSIONS

There is currently no rationale or mathematical justification for combining radiation and chemical risk estimates. The major gaps in risk assessment of mixed waste reflect limitations in the process of chemical risk assessment.

There is no simple method or criterion for determining whether a chemical is a human health hazard. Radiation risk assessment estimates actual harm that could occur under the conditions of exposure. Many chemicals produce a spectrum of lesions that is different from that produced by radiation. Often, carcinogenicity is assumed because a substance is related to a chemical class in which another substance is a known carcinogen. There is currently no easy way to directly measure the damage from exposure to chemicals in human cells.

The data base for chemicals is inadequate for establishing dose-response relationships in humans. The data most appropriate for estimating cancer risk are from epidemiological studies. Many investigators believe that no defensible epidemiological study has been made on potential health effects to residents near hazardous waste-disposal sites (Corn and Breysse, 1985). Nor have there been acceptable studies on genetic effects in offspring of adult females exposed to a chemical mutagen.

The concept of radiation dose allows extrapolations from one exposure condition to another that are impossible with chemicals. Radiation dose, regardless of its source, produces biological effects (cancer and genetic effects) proportional to that dose (with quantifible modifiers). This is not the case for chemical risk assessment.

Exposure assessment methods for various chemicals do not necessarily provide an equivalent result because of different chemical properties, behavior (persistence and reactivity) in the environment, and route of initial exposure. A large number of potential carcinogens are unlikely to occur in the environment in quantities such that humans would be equally exposed to them all. If one agent dominates the calculated risk for an individual or population, other carcinogenic agents can be ignored until exposure to the dominant agent is reduced.

Radiation doses can be related to natural background; there is no easily measured background exposure for chemicals. Risk can be compared among chemicals, but a quantitative assessment is not possible. While the biological response to radiation generally follows well-defined physical and chemical processes at the molecular and cellular level, responses to chemicals often vary. Many chemical carcinogens require metabolic activation and the presence of cocarcinogens or tumor promoters to produce an effect.

Because epidemiological data are minimal, accurate evaluation of human risk from chemicals requires detailed exposure, dose, and response studies in the laboratory. Continued research in molecular dosimetry is essential. Although laboratory animal data can provide an approximation of chemical risk to humans, the expense, difficulty, and inaccuracy in extrapolating from animal data make this solution impractical. We must develop methods to rapidly screen chemicals and to understand the mechanisms and biochemical effects of carcinogens and mutagens. We must also develop models to simulate the interaction of chemicals with biological systems at the molecular level, especially in humans. Such investigations should lead to a statistically acceptable and scientifically sound procedure for chemical risk assessment and should result in an acceptable method for combining risks from radionuclides and chemicals.

REFERENCES

Albert, R. E. 1985. U.S. Environmental Protection Agency revised interim guidelines for the health assessment of suspect carcinogens, pp. 307-329. In: Risk Quantification and Regulatory Policy, Banbury Report 19. D. G. Hoel, R. Merrill and F. P. Perera (eds.). Cold Spring Harbor Laboratory, Cold Spring Harbor, NY.

Anderson, E. L. 1983. Quantitative approaches in use to assess cancer risk, Report of Carcinogen Assessment Group of U.S. EPA. *Risk Anal.* *3*:277-295.

BEIR (Biological Effects of Ionizing Radiation). 1980. The Effects on Populations of Exposure to Low Levels of Ionizing Radiation. National Academy Press, Washington, DC.

Corn, M. and P. N. Breysse. 1985. Human exposure estimates for hazardous waste site risk assessment, pp. 283-291. In: Risk Quantification and Regulatory Policy, Banbury Report 19. D. G. Hoel, R. Merrill and F. P. Perera (eds.). Cold Spring Harbor Laboratory, Cold Spring Harbor, NY.

Crow, J. F. 1973. The evaluation of chemical mutagenicity data in relation to population risks: Impact of various types of genetic damage and risk assessment. *Environ. Health Perspect.* 6:1-5.

Crump, K. S. 1981. An improved procedure for low-dose carcinogenic risk assessment for animal data. *J. Environ. Pathol. Toxicol.* 52:675-684.

EPA. 1986. Guidelines for Carcinogen Risk Assessment. *Fed. Reg.* 51:33992-34003.

Goldman, M., R. J. Catlin, and L. R. Anspaugh. 1987. Health and Environmental Consequences of the Chernobyl Nuclear Power Plant Accident, Report to the U.S. Department of Energy from the Interlaboratory Task Group on Health and Environmental Aspects of the Soviet Nuclear Accident, DOE/ER-0332. U.S. Department of Energy, Washington, DC.

Hall, E. J. 1984. *Radiation and Life*, pp. 30-36. Pergamon Press, London.

Harris, C. C., A. Weston, J. C. Willey, G. E. Trivers, and D. L. Mann. 1987. Biochemical and molecular epidemiology of human cancer: Indicators of carcinogen exposure, DNA damage, and genetic predisposition. *Environ. Health Perspect.* 75:109-119.

NRC. 1983. Identifying and Estimating the Genetic Impact of Chemical Mutagens. Committee on Chemical Environmental Mutagens — Board of Toxicology and Environmental Health Hazards, Commission on Life Sciences, National Research Council. National Academy Press, Washington, DC.

OSTP (Office of Science and Technology Policy). 1985. Chemical Carcinogens: A Review of the Science and Its Associated Principles. *Fed. Reg.* 50:10372-10442.

Saracci, R. 1981. The IARC Monograph Program on the evaluation of the carcinogenic risk of chemicals to humans as a contribution to the identification of occupational carcinogens, pp. 165-176. In: Quantification of Occupational Cancer, R. Peto and M. Schneiderman (eds.), Banbury Report 9. Cold Spring Harbor Laboratory, Cold Spring Harbor, NY.

Woo, Y. T., J. F. Arcos, and S. Y. Lai. 1985. Predicting carcinogenicity of chemicals from their structure, pp. 2-25. In: Handbook of Carcinogen Testing, H. A. Milman and E. K. Weisburger (eds.). Noyes Publication, Park Ridge, NJ.

ENVIRONMENTAL MONITORING DATA FOR EVALUATING ATMOSPHERIC MODELING RESULTS

J. G. Droppo, Jr.

Pacific Northwest Laboratory, Richland, Washington

Key Words: *Monitoring, modeling, environmental, and atmospheric*

ABSTRACT

Modeling results are often used to assess radionuclide exposures from atmospheric releases. Routine air monitoring has been conducted at many Department of Energy (DOE) facilities. In applying the Multimedia Environmental Pollutant Assessment System as part of DOE's Environmental Survey, these monitoring data were useful in evaluating modeling results. An example illustrates comparison of monitoring and modeled atmospheric data at DOE sites.

INTRODUCTION

A comprehensive assessment of hazardous materials released to the environment can be difficult. Actual and/or potential environmental issues need to be defined, e.g., types of release, transport pathways, and exposure scenarios, and an assessment approach needs to be selected. Options include making measurements, simulating impact with environmental models, or a combination of the two.

Simulation of environmental concentration patterns from atmospheric emission rates relies on models. Often, the validity of model applications for such efforts can be checked using historical monitoring data that have been routinely obtained at major Department of Energy (DOE) facilities. Availability of these data allows use of measured values to calibrate spatial and temporal exposure patterns generated with models.

Checking the validity of a model application generally requires special runs to generate air concentrations that correspond to the monitored values. The time period for monitored results can vary from hours to years and may not match the period of interest for assessment. Similarly, the emissions and receptor grid for monitored values and the assessment may be different. This paper considers the use of monitoring data from DOE facilities to validate models.

219

When data are available, we can compare the modeled and monitored air concentrations. Standard statistical techniques can be used to check correlations and quantify the comparison. Graphical analysis of the data often provides valuable insights that complement statistical information.

Absolute agreement between modeled and monitored air concentrations generally indicates a good simulation of atmospheric processes. However, agreement at a single point does not ensure that the model simulates environmental conditions at other locations. Conversely, disagreement in modeled and monitored air concentrations at one point does not necessarily mean the model is not simulating the local pattern of atmospheric concentrations. Comparisons must consider both magnitude and spatial pattern of air concentrations. The former is mainly a function of emission rate; the latter is a function of atmospheric transport and dispersion processes.

The work discussed here was part of a model testing effort conducted for a human health assessment model, Multimedia Environmental Pollutant Assessment System (MEPAS), developed by the Pacific Northwest Laboratory for DOE (Whelan et al., 1987; Droppo et al., 1989). A brief overview is given below, followed by an example using monitoring data to evaluate model performance.

MODELED ENVIRONMENTAL CONCENTRATIONS

The overall magnitude of modeled air concentrations depends on the emission rate. Spatial concentration patterns depend on release characteristics near the source and on atmospheric transport and dispersion processes downwind. Except for emissions from large areas, predicted air concentration patterns from a single source are generally characterized as having relatively large environmental gradients.

Variations in concentration near the source depend on several factors, including the manner of release. Elevated releases tend to result in low concentrations close to the source, with peak near-surface concentrations farther downwind. Ground-level releases usually result in highest concentrations closest to the source. Ground-level releases from a vent (or other small area) result in a much sharper decrease in concentration near the source than do releases from a larger area; for a large uniform area source, environmental gradients may be very small.

Because of natural atmospheric dispersion, concentrations in a contaminant plume decline sharply as a function of distance from a facility. In Gaussian dispersion models such as MEPAS, the decrease is characterized by empirical dispersion parameters expressed as a function of downwind distance. Removal processes can further decrease concentrations with increasing distance from the source. MEPAS contains modules for estimating rates of removal by wet and dry deposition. Wet deposition refers to washout of a plume by precipitation. Dry deposition refers to contaminant removal by impacting, settling, reacting, sorbing, or diffusing onto the earth's surface.

Airborne reactions can either decrease or increase concentration as a function of distance from a release. Although MEPAS allows for input of a material's decay rate, such reactions are often difficult to predict accurately because of synergistic and photochemical effects. In the discussion below, a nonreactive airborne constituent has been assumed.

Nonuniform wind patterns that occur with complex terrain can change the effect expected in concentration patterns. Although MEPAS incorporates first-order corrections, modeling detailed concentration patterns in complex terrain can be difficult. Monitored environmental concentrations can be useful for this purpose.

Alternative contaminant sources in the region may also affect observed environmental gradients. Monitored values include contributions from the source in question, other nearby sources, and background concentration resulting from distant sources.

Where monitored values are used to validate a model application, their validity must be ensured. The following discussion will assume the correctness of monitored values and is limited to a release of nonreactive contaminants from a single source. In more complex situations, the effect of additional factors on environmental gradients needs to be considered.

CONCENTRATION COMPARISONS

Major variations in long-term average modeled and monitored concentrations normally reflect the distance between the source and monitoring location. After ground-level concentrations peak, long-term average concentrations usually decrease as a function of distance from the source. Depending on local dispersion climatology, different concentrations are expected for different wind directions.

Background is the ambient contaminant concentration that would exist if the source of interest had no emissions. The monitored value is the sum of the background and the increment in concentrations from the source. Modeled concentrations correspond to the increment. As the background contribution to the ambient values monitored in the air around a facility becomes larger, these monitored values will demonstrate smaller fractional changes with distance from the facility. The absence of a significant decrease in monitored values with distance from the source usually indicates that the effect of facility emissions on ambient air is small. Under simple flow conditions and low background contaminant concentrations, monitored values decrease with distance from the source after ground-level concentrations have peaked, but only in a single direction. Because monitoring stations are not usually located in a single direction from the facility, a simple plot of concentrations with distance will exhibit scatter relative to varying dispersion conditions.

A plot of computed and measured values provides an indication of how closely the two match. For perfect fit, the points should fall on a line from the origin with a 1:1 slope. The ratio of computed and monitored concentrations may be plotted as a function of distance. This plot excludes directional differences in dispersion and allows analysis for model bias as a function of distance.

CASE STUDY

Activities at the Mound facility near Miamisburg, Ohio, are sources of radioactive air emissions to the atmosphere (Carfagno and Farmer, 1986). Plutonium is a heat source for radioisotope thermoelectric generators, and tritium is separated and enriched at the Mound facility. Thus, atmospheric emissions of plutonium are routinely monitored.

Two sets of ^{238}Pu concentrations were predicted using 4 yr of onsite data and 5 yr of data from a regional weather station about 19 km north of the Mound facility. Onsite data were reported without stability information and were therefore modeled only with atmospheric D-stability data (i.e., neutral dispersion conditions); the regional station data contained stability frequency information. Figure 1 is a comparison of measured and calculated ^{238}Pu concentrations for stack releases in 1985. The two data sets give equivalent concentration predictions.

Figure 1 also shows an order-of-magnitude difference in the computed and monitored concentrations. This may be because the source term was underestimated, or because there was an additional onsite source. Resuspension of surface contamination is an alternative ^{238}Pu source at Mound.

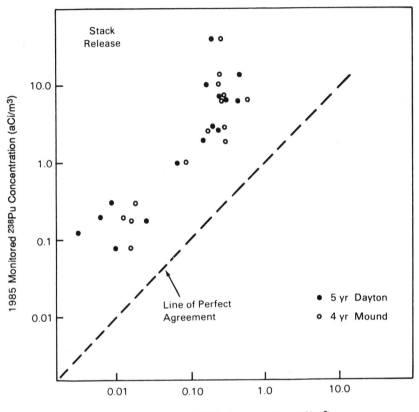

Figure 1. Comparison of modeled and monitored ^{238}Pu concentrations in air for 1985 emissions from U.S. Department of Energy's Mound Facility near Miamisburg, Ohio. Air concentrations were calculated using meteorological data at the Mound Facility (o) and at Dayton, Ohio (●). (1 aCi = 10^{-18} Ci = 3.7 x 10^{-8} radioactive disintegrations per second; from Carfagno and Farmer, 1986.)

This example illustrates the problems in a simple comparison for model verification. Although modeled results reasonably simulate changes in monitored concentrations, monitored and modeled concentrations agree only within an order of magnitude.

CONCLUSIONS

The degree to which a model predicts environmental gradients reflects how well the model simulates the atmospheric processes. Agreement of absolute values with measured and modeled values depends on how well the emission rate is defined. Good agreement in concentration gradients indicates that atmospheric transport and dispersion processes are properly simulated. This agreement is critical where the model is used to predict exposures at locations beyond those where monitoring data are available for verification.

ACKNOWLEDGMENT

Work supported by the U.S. Department of Energy Office of Environmental Audit under Contract DE-AC06-76RLO 1830.

REFERENCES

Carfagno, D. G. and B. M. Farmer. 1986. Environmental Monitoring at Mound: 1985 Report, MLM-3349. Environmental Section of the Administration Department at Monsanto Research Corporation, Miamisburg, OH.

Droppo, J. G., G. Whelan, J. W. Buck, D. L. Strenge, B. L. Hoopes, and M. B. Walter. 1989. Supplemental Mathematical Formulations: The Multimedia Environmental Pollutant Assessment System (MEPAS), PNL-7201. NTIS, Springfield, VA.

Whelan, G., D. L. Strenge, J. G. Droppo, B. L. Steelman, and J. W. Buck. 1987. The Remedial Action Priority System (RAPS): Mathematical Formulations, PNL-6200. NTIS, Springfield, VA.

USE OF COMPUTER MODELS TO DETERMINE ENVIRONMENTAL COMPLIANCE, PREDICT PERFORMANCE, AND ASSESS IMPACTS OF DOE FACILITIES

K. A. Higley and R. A. Geiger*

Pacific Northwest Laboratory, Richland, Washington

Key Words: *models, computer, compliance, performance assessment*

ABSTRACT

Mathematical models are widely used to answer questions that cannot easily be addressed otherwise. Environment-focused computer programs have been developed for various purposes: (1) to predict the long-term performance of repositories, (2) to estimate acute effects from accidental releases of hazardous materials, (3) to demonstrate compliance with federal regulations, and (4) to evaluate effects of environmental releases of hazardous materials. Relying solely on computer programs to provide answers for these four purposes places us in a potentially vulnerable position. Thus, we must ask: What steps should be taken to ensure the accuracy and reasonableness of computer-program-derived assessments? Is there a place for common sense in checking the output of extremely complex models? Should the application determine what effort is necessary to ensure the model is performing as desired? We will suggest criteria for the development, selection, and use of environmental computer models. These criteria will be compared for two situations: (1) using a model to demonstrate compliance with the radionuclide emission standards in 40 CFR Part 61; and (2) using a model as a scientific tool to evaluate effects from environmental releases of radioactive materials. Validation, verification, calibration, and quality assurance will be addressed for specific model applications.

INTRODUCTION

Mathematical models are often used to predict results that cannot easily be measured using current technology. For example, environmental releases of radioactive materials at many U.S. Department of Energy (DOE) facilities have been so low recently that many

---

*Current address: U.S. Department of Energy, Richland, Washington.

radionuclides cannot be measured, once dispersed (Jaquish and Mitchell, 1988). For some radionuclides, it is impossible to distinguish between contributions from site operations and those from worldwide fallout. Consequently, potential offsite doses are frequently estimated, using models that calculate environmental concentrations of radioactive materials from effluent concentrations.

Because of their complexity, these models are frequently encoded as computer programs. In addition to estimating doses from release of radionuclides to the environment, computer programs have been developed to predict long-term performance of high-level waste repositories, to estimate acute effects from accidental releases of hazardous materials, and to demonstrate compliance with federal regulations.

Several authors have reviewed the literature for environmental transport and dose computer codes (e.g., Baker, 1988; Kennedy and Mueller, 1982; Napier et al., 1988). Other sources of information include the Radiation Shielding Information Center at Oak Ridge National Laboratory and the National Energy Software Center at Argonne National Laboratory, which can supply environmental transport and dose-assessment codes (Till and Meyer, 1983).

CURRENT USE OF COMPUTER MODELS

As environmental standards have become more stringent, and levels of environmental contaminants have decreased, we have relied increasingly on computer programs to evaluate impacts. For example, current radionuclide detection limits (DL) for most environmental media (e.g., air, water, foodstuffs) are sufficiently low that an individual exposed to concentrations at DL would receive a dose well below standards (Mills et al., 1988). However, new risk limits, proposed by the U.S. Environmental Protection Agency (EPA) for radionuclide emissions under the Clean Air Act (54 Fed. Reg. 9612-9688) and currently used for guidance under the Comprehensive Environmental Response, Compensation and Liability Act (CERCLA), challenge our ability to directly measure contaminants to determine compliance. For example, annual consumption of 80 kg of beef contaminated with ^{137}Cs to a level equal to the detection limit of 0.02 pCi/g (Jaquish and Mitchell, 1988) equates to a radiation dose of approximately 0.08 mrem effective dose equivalent (DOE, 1988), or about three times the proposed limit of 0.03 mrem (10^{-6} lifetime risk) (Clean Air Act). Adopting these lower dose limits would probably force greater reliance on computer programs to estimate environmental effects.

Regulatory changes have also increased the liability of site owners/ operators if they do not comply with federal or state requirements. In a recent proposed revision to the National Emission Standards for Hazardous Air Pollutants: Radionuclides (EPA, 1989), EPA suggested that the operator's principal executive officer attest, "under penalty of law," to the accuracy of the required annual air emission report.

Legal considerations require completeness, accuracy, and reasonableness in any computer-derived assessment. These factors can be enhanced through proper development, selection, and use of computer programs.

The following criteria should be considered when developing a model and encoding it: (1) determine the objective for the code; (2) select appropriate mathematical models to satisfy the objective; (3) ensure that data requirements of the code can be met; (4) establish a documentation protocol that ensures retention of clear, understandable, and auditable records which document code development, and note which numerical and computing techniques were used in transforming the mathematical models into working computer codes; (5) document any omission of significant environmental pathways, giving reasons and situations for which the code should not be applied; (6) include verification of results, inspection of results, and comparisons with other systems; and (7) have the code peer-reviewed. Validation is a comparison of the model's predictions with reality; commonly it is done against another model that has been accepted. A code is verified if, given the same inputs as the model, it produces the same predictions. If a code is verified and the model on which it is based is validated, then the code *should* make reasonable predictions of reality.

Suggested criteria for selecting a code include: (1) match the code/ model to its application. In most cases, a shielding code should not be used for environmental transport calculations (other than for estimating direct exposure from a plume); (2) know the code's limitations: there may be situations for which it is inappropriate; (3) select a code that is controlled or has auditable versions, including peer-reviewed data/dose factor libraries.

After a code has been selected, consider the following criteria for its application: (1) validate and/or calibrate the code, (2) use a controlled copy, (3) obtain complete documentation for the code. It may be appropriate to compare the selected code/model with other similar codes/models that have been tested (Aaberg and Napier, 1985). Common sense should be used in verifying the acceptability and reasonableness of complex models' output. Preliminary calculations should be used to identify parameters or processes of consequence.

In some instances, use of a computer program may be mandated by law. If so, the user may have few options in its application. However, it is important to ensure that the appropriate version of the code is used, including data libraries and prescribed input parameters. Parameters that can vary (e.g., consumption and occupancy rates) should be reviewed for reasonableness. Lastly, performance of the code(s)/model(s) selected should be compared with that of other codes/models to check for reasonableness of the predictions (e.g., Aaberg and Napier, 1985).

Using a program prescribed by regulation does not guarantee consistency in the resulting assessment. Thus, EPA included the following in its regulation of airborne emissions of radionuclides (EPA, 1973 et seq.):

> "61.93 Emission monitoring and compliance procedures. To determine compliance with the standard, . . . dose equivalents to members of the public shall be calculated using . . . EPA models AIRDOS-EPA and RADRISK, or other procedures, . . . that EPA has determined to be suitable."

Although use of AIRDOS-EPA was prescribed, neither the version of the code nor the data libraries were specified. Thus, it was possible to use "proper" parameters and declare almost any release in compliance. The result has been confusion in applying the code to demonstrate compliance with 40 CFR Part 61 subpart H. Unfortunately, only code/model revisions(s) published in the *Federal Register* can be used to demonstrate compliance. In contrast, DOE requires that doses received by members of the public from radionuclide releases at DOE facilities be estimated using site-specific models or modified versions of accepted models. A dose limit is prescribed, but the mechanism for demonstrating compliance is not. Instead, DOE has specified acceptable dose limits without as low as reasonably achievable considerations and has omitted the unit of dose required (i.e., effective dose equivalent). The result of DOE's leniency in the selection of codes for use by its sites has been a proliferation of dose calculation codes/models but generally more consistent estimates of dose.

CONCLUSION

Criteria should be adopted to ensure that a consistent approach is followed for development, selection, and use of these codes/models and to make the approach technically defensible and auditable.

ACKNOWLEDGMENT

Work supported by the DOE Office of Environmental Audit, U.S. Department of Energy, under Contract DE-AC06-76RLO 1830.

REFERENCES

Aaberg, R. L. and B. A. Napier. 1985. Hanford Dose Overview Program: Comparison of AIRDOS-EPA and Hanford Site Dose Codes, PNL-5633. NTIS, Springfield, VA.

Baker, D. A. 1988. Comments by a Peer Review Panel on the Computerized Radiological Risk Investigation System (CRRIS), ORNL/TM-10879. Oak Ridge National Laboratory, Oak Ridge, TN.

Clean Air Act Code (CAAC) (Undated). Code System for Implementation of Atmospheric Dispersion Assessment Required by the Clean Air Act. RSIC Code Package CCC-476, Oak Ridge National Laboratory, Oak Ridge, TN, and Westinghouse Materials Company of Ohio, Cincinnati, OH. Available at Radiation Shielding Information Center, Oak Ridge National Laboratory, Oak Ridge, TN. (CAAC includes the codes DARTAB, AIRDOS-EPA, PREPAR, PREDA, and RADFMT.)

DOE. 1988. Internal Dose Conversion Factors for Calculation of Dose to the Public, DOE/EH-0071. U.S. Department of Energy, Washington, DC.

EPA. 1973 et seq. National Emission Standards for Hazardous Air Pollutants (NESFlAPs), Title 40, Part 61 (40 CFR 61). U.S. Environmental Protection Agency, Washington, DC.

EPA. 1989. National Emission Standards for Hazardous Air Pollutants; Regulation of Radionuclides - Proposed Rule and Notice of Public Hearing, 54 FR 9612-9688. U.S. Environmental Protection Agency, Washington, DC.

Jaquish, R. E. and P. J. Mitchell. 1988. Environmental Monitoring at Hanford for 1987, PNL-6464. NTIS, Springfield, VA.

Kennedy, W. E., Jr. and M. A. Mueller. 1982. Summary of the Environmental Dose Models Used at DOE Nuclear Sites in 1979, PNL-3916. NTIS, Springfield, VA.

Mills, W. A., D. S. Flack, F. J. Arsenault, and E. F. Conti. 1988. A Compendium of Major U.S. Radiation Protection Standards and Guides: Legal and Technical Facts, ORAU 88/F-111. Oak Ridge Associated Universities, Oak Ridge, TN.

Napier, B. A., R. A. Peloquin, D. L. Strenge, and J. V. Ramsdell. 1988. GENII - The Hanford Environmental Radiation Dosimetry Software System, PNL-6584, Volumes I and II. NTIS, Springfield, VA.

Till, J. E. and H. R. Meyer. 1983. Radiological Assessment: A Textbook on Environmental Dose Analysis, NUREG/CR-3332, ORNL-5968. U.S. Nuclear Regulatory Commission, Washington, DC.

STATISTICAL ANALYSIS OF DATA BELOW THE DETECTION LIMIT: WHAT HAVE WE LEARNED?

D. R. Helsel

U.S. Geological Survey, Reston, Virginia

Key Words: *Statistics, censored data, detection limit, t-test*

ABSTRACT

Environmental data sets often contain values known only to be below one or more limits of detection; such values are often referred to as "less-thans." Traditional statistical analyses, such as computation of means, or parametric tests (e.g., *t*-test), cannot effectively incorporate less-thans. However, less familiar methods that can utilize such data are available. I will discuss methods for estimating summary statistics (mean, standard deviation, median, and interquartile range) for data sets including less-thans. These methods are robust (generally applicable) over a wide range of data distributions and shapes. Limitations of methods, such as substitution of some multiple of the detection limit for less-thans, will also be discussed.

Tests for differences between data sets that include less-thans will be illustrated. Inappropriate methods include deletion of less-thans and fabrication of numerical values for less-thans before testing. Either method may give misleading results for monitoring and/or legal purposes. In contrast, nonparametric tests can validly incorporate data with one detection limit, giving unequivocal results.

INTRODUCTION

As trace substances are increasingly investigated in soil, air, and water, observations with concentrations below the analytical detection limits are more frequently encountered. "Less-than" values present a serious interpretation problem for data analysts. For example, compliance with waste-water discharge regulations is usually judged by comparing to a legal standard the mean of concentrations observed over time. However, sample means cannot be computed from less-than values. Studies of ground-water quality at waste-disposal sites often involve comparisons of data from upgradient and downgradient wells. Usually, *t*-tests are applied. However, the *t*-test requires estimates for means and standard deviations which are impossible to obtain unless numerical values are fabricated to replace less-thans. Results of such tests can vary greatly, depending on the values fabricated. Estimates of summary statistics (e.g., mean, standard deviation, median, and interquartile range) which best represent the entire distribution of data, both below and above the detection limit, are necessary to accurately analyze environmental conditions. Also needed are hypothesis test procedures which provide valid conclusions as to whether differences exist among groups of data. These needs must be met using the only information available: concentrations measured above one or more detection limits, and the frequency of data below those limits.

METHODS FOR ESTIMATING SUMMARY STATISTICS

Methods for estimating summary statistics for data that include less-thans fall in three classes.

Class 1: Simple substitution methods—these substitute a single value, such as one-half the detection limit for each less-than value. Although widely used, these methods have no theoretical basis and may result in poor estimates.

Class 2: Distributional methods—these use an assumed distribution to estimate summary statistics. Data above and below detection limits are assumed to follow a distribution, such as lognormal, and "best" estimates [maximum-likelihood (ML) estimates] for that distribution are computed. Unfortunately, data rarely fit the assumed distribution. Also, ML estimates may be unstable for small (less than 50) data sets that are insufficient to correctly estimate the parameters. Nonetheless, these methods are commonly used in environmental studies, such as air-quality surveillance (Owen and DeRouen, 1981) and soil chemistry (Miesch, 1967).

Class 3: Robust methods—these assume a distributional shape for data below the detection limit. Data above the detection limit are used to fit a distribution; values below the detection limit are estimated using the fitted distribution. These estimates, the number of which is equal to the number of less-thans in the data set, are combined with data above the detection limit before computing summary statistics. Estimated values are not assigned to individual less-thans and are only used collectively to compute summary statistics.

WHICH SUMMARY STATISTICS ARE APPROPRIATE?

Environmental-quality data are usually positively skewed; sometimes, highly skewed. A typical pattern is shown in Figure 1, where most data lie at the lower end, and a few high "outliers" occur. In such cases, the mean and standard deviation, which are strongly affected by the few highest observations, may be quite sensitive to deletion or addition of even one observation, and are therefore poor measures of central value and variability. For positively skewed data, the mean will be exceeded by less than half the values, sometimes by as little as 25% or less. Similarly, the standard deviation will be inflated by outliers, implying larger variability than that which occurs over most of the data set. The mean and standard deviation are useful when considering mass loadings of a constituent. For instance, when computing average sediment concentration at a river cross section, large concentrations at one point in the cross section should increase the overall mean value. However, when one value distorts data summaries, as when summarizing "typical" sediment characteristics found over many streams, the mean and standard deviation are not appropriate measures.

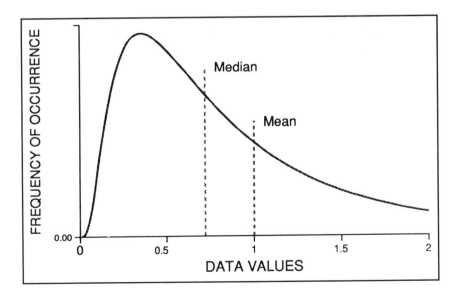

Figure 1. A lognormal distribution, one type of skewed distribution. (See also Table 1.)

Alternative measures of central value and variability for skewed data are percentile parameters such as the median and interquartile range (IQR). The median, by definition, has 50% of the data above it and 50% below. Unlike the mean, it is not affected by a few low or high "outliers." Thus, it is a more stable (or "resistant") estimator for skewed data than is the mean and will be similar to the mean for symmetric (nonskewed) data. The IQR, like the median, is largely unaffected by the lowest or highest values. It is the 75th minus the 25th percentile, and thus is the range of the central 50% of the data. For the normal distribution, the IQR equals 1.35 times the standard deviation. The IQR will often be smaller than the standard deviation and a better estimate of variability for the skewed distributions.

The median and IQR have another advantage: they can be computed even when a substantial part of the data is below detection limits. When less than 50% of the data are below the detection limit, the sample median is known (it is the ith smallest observation, where $i = (n+1)/2$). Similarly, when less than 25% of the data includes less-thans, the sample IQR is known. No fabrication of data values is necessary.

COMPARISONS OF ESTIMATION METHODS

Most papers dealing with the relative performance of methods to estimate summary statistics for less-thans deal with a single detection limit; a few deal with multiple detection limits.

Gleit (1985) compared several methods to estimate means, assuming the data are normally distributed. Simple substitution methods performed poorly. ML produced estimates with large bias and variance for the small ($n = 5$, 10, and 15) sample sizes considered. The method with least error was a robust (Class 3) fill-in technique.

Gilliom and Helsel (1986) found large differences in the ability of different methods to estimate the four summary statistics (mean, standard deviation, median and IQR) for data with a single detection limit. Simple substitution methods (Class 1) performed poorly except when substituting one-half the detection limit to estimate the mean and standard deviation. The ML method for a lognormal distribution (Class 2) gave good estimates of the median and IQR but not of the mean and standard deviation. Theoretical reasons for this phenomenon were described by Cohn (1988). The ML method for a lognormal distribution worked well for percentile statistics even though the data did not always follow a lognormal shape. This is because the data were usually right-skewed, and the lognormal is a flexible distribution providing reasonable approximations to the shape of the data. The lognormal probability plot (Class 3) performed well for all statistics; it was best for estimating mean and standard deviation and second to the ML method for percentile statistics. The probability plotting method was recommended when estimating mean and standard deviation, and the ML procedure was best when estimating median and IQR. Use of these methods rather than simple substitution methods for data with single detection limits would reduce errors in estimates of the four summary statistics by up to 300%, assuming the data were distributed similarly to the water-quality data used here. This assumption appears reasonable given the heavy dependence on lognormal distributions in environmental sciences.

Helsel and Cohn (1988) extended these results to data with multiple detection limits. Both studies showed that when efficient estimation methods are used, the errors in the four summary statistics are essentially the same as if the detection limit had been small and all data had been above the detection limit. Figure 2 shows error rates (root mean squared error) for six estimation methods relative to the error that would occur had all data been above the detection limit (shown as the 1.0 line). Figure 3 shows the same information when the data differ from a lognormal distribution. The simple substitution methods, substitution of zero (ZE), one-half (HA), and one times the detection limit (DL), have more error than does the robust plotting position method (MR). The ML procedures (MM and AM) are excellent for percentiles but are prone to errors when estimating the mean and standard deviation.

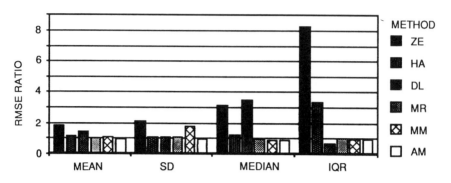

Figure 2. Error rates (root mean squared error, RMSE) of six multiple-detection methods divided by error rates for uncensored data estimates with no less-thans, for data similar to a lognormal distribution (from Helsel and Cohn, 1988). IQR = Interquartile range; ZE = Substitute 0 for less-thans; HA = substitute 1/2 detection limit for less-thans; DL = substitute detection limit for less-thans; MR = plotting position method; MM = maximum likelihood method; AM = adjusted maximum likelihood (Cohn, 1988).

Use of ML methods to estimate percentiles, and the robust plotting position to estimate mean and standard deviation, will decrease errors by up to 400% compared to simple substitution methods for data with multiple detection limits. These methods have no more error for up to 60% less-thans than if the detection limit had been so low that no less-thans were present.

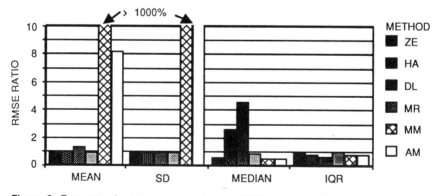

Figure 3. Error rates (root mean squared error, RMSE) of six multiple-detection methods divided by error rates for uncensored data estimates with no less-thans, for data not similar to a lognormal distribution (from Helsel and Cohn, 1988). IQR = Interquartile range; ZE = substitute 0 for less-thans; HA = substitute 1/2 detection limit for less-thans; DL = substitute detection limit for less-thans; MR = plotting position method; MM = maximum likelihood method; AM = adjusted maximum likelihood (Cohn, 1988).

METHODS FOR HYPOTHESIS TESTING

Parametric statistical tests are often used in environmental assessments. These methods assume the data follow some shape, such as the normal distribution. The mean and standard deviation are calculated to perform the statistical analysis. When less-thans are present, values must be fabricated to calculate the mean and standard deviation. Problems caused by fabrication are discussed below. Investigators have also deleted less-than data prior to hypothesis testing. This is the worst procedure, as it causes a large and variable bias in the summary statistics for each group. After deletion, comparisons are made between the upper X% of one group and the upper Y% of another, where X and Y may be very different. Such tests have little or no meaning.

Alternatively, nonparametric tests (Conover, 1980) can be used to rank the data and judge whether the ordering of data points indicates that differences occur, trends exist, etc. No fabrication of values is required; all less-than data are represented by ranks that all have the same value lower than the lowest number above the detection limit. These tests are more powerful than parametric tests when the data are not normally distributed (Helsel and Hirsch, 1987).

To illustrate the differences between parametric and nonparametric approaches for less-than data, two data sets were generated from lognormal distributions having the same variance but with significantly different means at $\alpha = 0.05$ (Helsel, 1987). Sample statistics for the two data sets are shown in Table 1. The means are significantly different by t test (p = 0.04) and by the equivalent nonparametric test, the rank-sum test (p = 0.003) (Table 2). The skewness of these lognormal data sets has reduced the ability of the t test to detect differences in the means, as shown by its higher p-value.

Table 1. Characteristics of two lognormal data groups (A and B).

A		B	A		B
20	No. observations	22	14	No. "less-thans"	5
1.00	Mean	1.32	0.57	Standard deviation	0.39
1.07	75th percentile	1.66	0.65	25th percentile	1.07
0.85	Median	1.25			

Table 2. Tests of significance between groups A and B (from Figure 1).

Hypothesis test results	Test statistic	p
Uncensored data		
t test	-2.13	0.040
Rank-sum test	-2.92	0.003
After imposing artificial detection limit		
t test		
less-thans = 0.0	-2.68	0.011
less-thans = 0.05	-2.28	0.029
less-thans = 1.0	-1.34	0.19
Rank-sum test	-3.07	0.002

Suppose these data represent "true" dissolved arsenic concentrations. A typical detection limit for arsenic is 1 mg/L, therefore all data below 1.0 were set to "less-than 1.0." There were 14 less-than values (70%) in group A, and 5 less-than values (23%) in group B.

First, I fabricate data for less-than values and include these "data" with actual data when performing a *t* test. No *a priori* arguments for substitution of values between 0 and the detection limit are available. Substituting zero for all less-than values, the means are declared significantly different (p = 0.011). However, when the detection limit of 1.0 is substituted, the means are not different (p = 0.19). The conclusion is thus strongly dependent on the value substituted; the method should be considered too arbitrary for use.

I then compute the rank-sum test. The 19 less-than values are considered tied at the lowest value and are therefore all assigned a rank of 10 (the mean of numbers 1-19). The resulting p-value is 0.002, essentially the same as for the original data, and the two groups are declared different. Thus, the nonparametric method makes efficient use of the information in the less-than values, avoids arbitrary assignment of fabricated values, and accurately represents the lack of knowledge below the detection limit.

Although a large number of less-thans will inhibit conclusions about the relative magnitudes of central values, other characteristics can be compared using nonparametric tests. When less-thans exceed 40-50%, the rank-sum test will have little power to detect differences in median values. Instead, a contingency table test may be computed (Conover, 1980). Contingency tables test whether there is a difference in the proportion of data above the detection limit in each group, and can be used when the data are reported only as detected or not detected, or when categorized into three or more groups: below detection, detected but below some health standard, and exceeding standards.

In summary, nonparametric procedures have several advantages over their parametric counterparts when applied to less-than data. These advantages include: (1) the normal distribution required by parametric tests is difficult to validate with less-than data and is not required by nonparametric tests; (2) greater power is achieved for the skewed distributions common to environmental data; (3) comparisons are made between central values such as the median, rather than the mean; (4) data below the detection limit can be used without fabrication of values or bias. Information contained in less-than values is accurately used and does not misrepresent the state of that information.

REFERENCES

Cohn, T. A. 1988. Adjusted Maximum Likelihood Estimation of the Moments of Lognormal Populations from Type I Censored Samples, Open-File Report 88-350. U.S Geological Survey, Reston, VA.

Conover, W. J. 1980. *Practical Nonparametric Statistics, 2nd Edition*. John Wiley, New York.

Gilliom, R. J. and D. R. Helsel. 1986. Estimation of distributional parameters for censored trace-level water- quality data. 1. Estimation Techniques. *Water Resour. Res. 22*:135-146.

Gleit, A. 1985. Estimation for small normal data sets with detection limits. *J. Environ. Sci. Technol. 19*:1201-1206.

Helsel, D. R. 1987. Advantages of nonparametric procedures for analysis of water quality data. *J. Hydrol. Sci. 32*:179-189.

Helsel, D. R. and T. A. Cohn. 1988. Estimation of descriptive statistics for censored water-quality data. *Water Resour. Res. 24*:1997-2004.

Helsel, D. R. and R. M. Hirsch. 1987. Discussion of applicability of the t-test for detecting trends in water quality variables. *Water Resour. Bull. 24*:201-204.

Miesch, A. T. 1967. Methods of Computation for Estimating Geochemical Abundance, Professional Paper 574-B. U.S. Geological Survey, Reston, VA.

Owen, W. J., and T. A.DeRouen. 1981. Estimation of the mean for lognormal data containing zeroes and left-censored values, with applications to the measurement of worker exposure to air contaminants. *Biometrics 36*:707-719.

COMPARISON OF STATISTICAL METHODS FOR ESTIMATING PLUTONIUM INVENTORIES IN SOIL

R. D. McArthur

Desert Research Institute, Las Vegas, Nevada

Key Words: *Spatial sampling, sample designs, kriging, Nevada Test Site (NTS)*

ABSTRACT

Several statistical methods have been used to estimate total plutonium inventory in contaminated surface soil on the Nevada Test Site, including systematic sampling, importance sampling, stratified random sampling, and two forms of kriging. In computer simulation experiments to compare these methods, systematic sampling using regular and preferential grids gave accurate and precise inventory estimates. However, the difficulty in estimating sampling variance from a single sample is a major drawback in field applications. Although importance sampling and stratified random sampling allowed estimation of sampling error, these methods gave less precise results than grid samples and were harder to use. Inventory estimates from kriging were biased, and kriging variances were not representative of true sampling variability. Kriging may not be appropriate where contaminant levels change rapidly over short distances.

INTRODUCTION

Testing of nuclear explosives at the Nevada Test Site (NTS) in the 1950s and 1960s contaminated large amounts of surface soil with plutonium and other radionuclides. Two recent NTS environmental programs, the Nevada Applied Ecology Group and the Radionuclide Inventory and Distribution Program, have attempted to quantify the extent of this contamination. Several different statistical methods were used to estimate the inventory (total amount) of plutonium present at various sites. This paper reviews and compares those methods and offers recommendations for future studies.

Plutonium in NTS surface soil is usually highly localized around the detonation sites (ground zero) of above-ground explosions, with high concentrations near ground zero that decrease rapidly with increasing distance. Because the total contaminated area at a site may cover several square kilometers, the inventory must be estimated from relatively few measurements of plutonium concentrations. How to choose locations for these measurements and how to estimate the

inventory from the resulting data are important statistical considerations in planning an inventory study. The combination of the
measurement plan and estimation method is termed the "sample
design" of the study.

Sample designs described here have been used to estimate plutonium
inventories at one or more contaminated sites on NTS. While the results
appear satisfactory, it is difficult to make definitive statements
concerning how well various designs work without some knowledge
of the "true" inventory. Even when sites were studied independently
by different groups using different sample designs, differences in the
areas surveyed and methods used to measure plutonium concentrations obscured differences due to different statistical techniques.
Because an adequately controlled field experiment to compare sample
designs would be prohibitively expensive, most work reported here
is based on computer simulation.

SIMULATION EXPERIMENTS

Simulation experiments were of the type described by McArthur (1987),
who used 500 replicates of each sample design to verify the results
of earlier experiments with 50 replicates. Some kriging methods were
not compared using the larger sample size because of the high cost.

In each experiment, the probability density function of a bivariate
normal distribution was used to simulate a typical plutonium
distribution around a ground zero. One hundred sample points were
chosen, and the value of the function (representing the plutonium
concentration) at each sample point was computed. The inventory
was then estimated, using one or more methods. The procedure was
repeated 50 or 500 times for each sampling method. The estimates
generated by different sample designs were compared with each other
and with the true inventory, i.e., the known volume under the normal
density function.

INVENTORY ESTIMATION METHODS

Most methods described here are applications of standard ways to
sample a two-dimensional area. The theory underlying these methods
can be found in Cochran (1977). Gilbert (1987) described most of
the methods in the context of environmental monitoring.

Regular Grid

A common arrangement for sampling an area is a regular (usually
square) grid of measurement points. A grid is easily laid out, and data

analysis is simple. The uniform coverage of an area by a grid typically results in smaller sampling variance (the variance resulting from using limited numbers of measurements to estimate the total inventory) than would be obtained by simple random sampling, where each point is chosen independently at random. Data from a grid are also well suited for use in computer contouring programs to produce concentration isopleths. However, a grid is a form of systematic sample, and the sampling variance cannot be estimated from a single grid of measurements unless some assumptions (such as a random order or a linear trend) are made about the spatial distribution (Gilbert, 1987).

Preferential Grid

A regular grid does not use information from previous surveys or historical records about the spatial distribution of contamination within the gridded area. Preferential grids attempt to overcome this problem by using smaller grid spacing where concentrations are believed highest. Simulations have shown that preferential grids give accurate and precise inventory estimates if the grids are positioned independently. However, preferential grids have the same problems with estimating sample variance as regular grids.

Stratified Random Sampling

This is another way the sampling effort can be concentrated where most contamination occurs. Results from an initial survey are used to partition the area into strata such that the variability within strata is small and variability between strata is large. Stratified random sampling was used in the first plutonium inventory studies at the NTS (Gilbert et al., 1975; Gilbert, 1977). In most cases, the resulting estimates had a smaller sampling variance than would have been obtained with simple random sampling, a result that was also obtained in simulations.

Stratified random sampling plans are more difficult to design than grid patterns, and data analysis is not as straightforward. Preliminary data are needed to define the strata to give greater efficiency relative to simple random sampling. In addition, the random nature of selecting measurement locations usually leaves portions of the area unsampled. This may be important if data are used for mapping contaminant distribution as well as estimating the inventory.

Importance Sampling

Like stratified random sampling, importance sampling concentrates the sampling effort in the region where concentrations are highest while preserving the randomness necessary to estimate sampling variance. The probability of a particular location being chosen for measurement is proportional to the concentration at that location. The method requires a considerable amount of prior data and is harder to carry out than stratified random sampling. Simulations suggest that stratified random sampling and importance sampling give about the same sampling variance for a given number of measurements (McArthur, 1987).

Importance sampling was used in studies of four sites in Area 18 at the NTS (McArthur and Mead, 1988). To alleviate uneven coverage resulting from random selection of measurement locations, supplementary measurements were made in unsampled regions. These measurements were not used to estimate the inventory but were included in the data set used to draw concentration isopleths.

Kriging

Originally developed by the mining industry to estimate ore reserves, kriging has been applied in many environmental studies in recent years. Kriging uses the spatial correlation of data and the relative locations of measurements to produce unbiased estimates with minimal variance when assumptions of the kriging model are satisfied. A thorough discussion of kriging is given in Journel and Huijbregts (1978). Only simple kriging, the most elementary form, is considered here.

A problem using simple kriging to estimate plutonium inventories at the NTS is that the key assumption of stationarity (the same average concentration at all locations) is usually not realistic because contamination levels change rapidly in the region near ground zero. Another problem is the difficulty in estimating the spatial correlation structure (variogram), a necessary first step in kriging. The variogram is especially difficult to estimate when the average concentration varies. There is also uncertainty as to whether the kriging variance is an adequate measure of sampling variability. Finally, the amount of computation required for kriging is much greater than that required for the other estimation methods.

Kriging was used to estimate inventories at several ground-zero locations in Yucca Flat at the NTS (McArthur and Kordas, 1983, 1985). In general, the kriging estimates agreed with estimates calculated by other methods (primarily polygons of influence). Gilbert et al. (1985) used lognormal kriging (kriging of log-transformed data) to estimate plutonium inventories at three other ground-zero locations and confirmed the kriging results using poststratification.

McArthur (1987) showed that with data from a locally concentrated contaminant, kriging can give biased estimates of the inventory, and the kriging variance can be essentially unrelated to the sampling variance. To determine to what extent those results were a function of the particular variogram model used, a similar study was conducted using 50 repetitions of a regular grid and two types of preferential grids. Preferential Grid 1 had an inner grid obtained by placing points halfway between the points of the larger outer grid in the region of high concentration. The inner grid of Preferential Grid 2 had greater spacing and was positioned independently of the outer grid. For complete details and the formulas for the weighted means used to calculate inventory estimates, see McArthur (1987).

For the samples generated by all three methods, kriging results were obtained with the spherical variogram model used by McArthur (1987),

$$g(h) = (6.5 \times 10^5) \, [3h/10 - h^3/250],$$

where h is distance between points,

and a Gaussian model,

$$g(h) = (10^6/\pi) \, [1 - \exp(-h^2)],$$

derived from the transitive covariogram (Matheron, 1971) of the bivariate normal density. In addition, two sets of data were analyzed using lognormal kriging (by R.O. Gilbert and D.W. Engel at Battelle, Pacific Northwest Laboratories). The variogram used for lognormal kriging was

$$g(h) = 13 \, [7h^2/a^2 - 35h^3/4a^3 + 7h^5/2a^5 - 3h^7/4a^7],$$

with a = 7.

The mean, range, and variance of each set of 50 estimates and the mean and range of kriging variances are shown in Table 1. All forms of kriging show a moderate bias. The direction of bias depends on the variogram model used. Kriging variances are consistently at least an order of magnitude greater than the variances of inventory estimates, so in this study the kriging variance is not a good estimate of the sampling variance.

Table 1. Results of applying various estimation methods to 50 sets of simulated data collected by three types of sampling plans.

	Inventory estimates			Kriging variance	
	Mean[a]	Range	Variance[b]	Mean	Range
Regular Grid					
Arithmetic mean	100.1	97.5-102.7	2.5	—	—
Kriging- spherical model	95.4	92.3-101.3	5.8	421	276-590
Kriging- Gaussian model	102.7	98.1-106.7	6.5	96	10-221
Lognormal kriging	97.1	92.1-101.1	7.4	—	—
Preferential Grid 1					
Weighted mean	97.4	93.5- 99.3	2.1	—	—
Kriging- spherical model	95.1	83.7-102.5	22.8	545	435-821
Kriging- Gaussian model	102.4	99.2-106.8	5.1	157	29-361
Lognormal kriging	90.1	89.2- 90.5	0.092	—	—
Preferential Grid 2					
Weighted mean	100.0	99.7-100.4	0.020	—	—
Kriging- spherical model	90.7	86.3- 99.6	10.2	523	396-727
Kriging- Gaussian model	103.0	93.7-111.4	16.2	172	43-353

[a]True value = 100.
[b]Variance of the 50 estimates of inventory.

CONCLUSION

Regular or preferential grids are easy to design and give unbiased and relatively precise estimates, but the variance of the estimates cannot readily be calculated from a single sample. Stratified random and importance samples are considerably more difficult to collect but do give an estimate of the variance of the inventory. Kriging is likely to give biased estimates of inventory and meaningless estimates of variance when applied to data with rapidly changing concentrations near ground zero.

ACKNOWLEDGMENTS

The author is grateful to R. O. Gilbert for comments on an earlier draft of this paper. This work was supported by the U.S. Department of Energy under contracts DE-AC08-81NV10162 and DE-AC08-85NV10384.

REFERENCES

Cochran, W. G. 1977. *Sampling Techniques*. Wiley, New York.

Gilbert, R. O. 1977. Revised total amounts of ^{239,240}Pu in surface soil at safety-shot sites, pp. 423-429. In: Transuranics in Desert Ecosystems, NVO-181, M. G. White, P. B. Dunaway, and D. L. Wireman (eds.). U.S. Department of Energy, Las Vegas, NV.

Gilbert, R. O. 1987. *Statistical Methods for Environmental Pollution Monitoring*. Van Nostrand Reinhold, New York.

Gilbert, R. O., L. L. Eberhardt, E. B. Fowler, E. M. Romney, E. H. Essington, and J. E. Kinnear. 1975. Statistical analysis of ^{239,240}Pu and ^{241}Am contamination of soil and vegetation on NAEG study sites, pp. 339-448. In: The Radioecology of Plutonium and Other Transuranics in Desert Environments, NVO-153, M. G. White and P. B. Dunaway (eds.). U.S. Energy Research and Development Administration, Las Vegas, NV.

Gilbert, R. O., J. C. Simpson, D. W. Engel, and R. R. Kinnison. 1985. Estimating isotopic ratios, spatial distribution, and inventory of radionuclides at nuclear sites 201, 219, and 221, pp. 381-429. In: The Dynamics of Transuranics and Other Radionuclides in Natural Environments, NVO-272, W. A. Howard and R. G. Fuller (eds.). U.S. Department of Energy, Las Vegas, NV.

Journel, A. G. and Ch. J. Huijbregts. 1978. *Mining Geostatistics*. Academic Press, London.

Matheron, G. 1971. The theory of regionalized variables and its applications. In: Cahiers du Centre de Morphologie Mathématique, vol. 5. Centre de Géostatistique, Fontainebleau, France.

McArthur, R. D. 1987. An evaluation of sample designs for estimating a locally concentrated pollutant. *Commun. Statistics-Simulation 16*:735-759.

McArthur, R. D. and J. F. Kordas. 1983. Radionuclide Inventory and Distribution Program: The Galileo Area, Publication No. 45035. Water Resources Center, Desert Research Institute, Las Vegas, NV.

McArthur, R. D. and J. F. Kordas. 1985. Nevada Test Site Radionuclide Inventory and Distribution Program: Report #2, Areas 2 and 4, Publication No. 45041. Water Resources Center, Desert Research Institute, Las Vegas, NV.

McArthur, R. D. and S. W. Mead. 1988. Nevada Test Site Radionuclide Inventory and Distribution Program: Report #4, Areas 18 and 20, Publication No. 45063. Water Resources Center, Desert Research Institute, Las Vegas, NV.

REPLICATE MEASUREMENTS IN THE INTERPRETATION OF ENVIRONMENTAL MONITORING

W. S. Liggett

National Institute of Standards and Technology, Gaithersburg, Maryland

Key Words: *Probability density estimation, robust regression, sampling error, measurement error*

ABSTRACT

In simultaneous monitoring at several sites, replicate samples and measurements, when chosen properly, provide a useful and unambiguous basis for data interpretation. Simultaneous monitoring permits calculation of indices of environmental change that are not influenced by weather changes. When the small changes measured by such an index are of interest, comparison of the index with the sampling and measurement error is appropriate. This comparison is made possible by the replicates. The familiar two-way table obtained by sampling a set of locations at several times is also considered. The indices considered are ones that perform well when large errors are more frequent than predicted by the normal distribution. Through the use of replicates, the variation in such indices caused by error alone can be assessed and thus environmental change is determined.

INTRODUCTION

The approach presented is based on a statistical test of whether an index of environmental change is different from zero. The approach requires a monitoring design that provides an index for which this comparison is of interest. In addition, the approach requires replicates that allow assessment of the effect of sampling and measurement error on this index.

The objective of environmental studies considered here is detection of local environmental changes based on measurements at several locations over time. Local changes occur at some but not all monitoring locations. These changes are of interest because their causes, which are local, might be identified and removed. Local changes must be distinguished from differences between monitoring locations that are constant over the study period. Such differences have multiple historical origins that often cannot be untangled. Local changes must be distinguished from variations with time that are the same at all monitoring locations. Such variations are usually caused by weather and other seasonal phenomena.

Consider a commonly used study design. At each point in time, replicate observations are made simultaneously at several locations. Data analysis begins by fitting values for historical differences and global variations. Subtracting these values gives residuals that reflect local environmental changes and sampling and measurement error. Replicates allow characterization of error and provide a way to make statistical judgments about what appears to be a local change. However, there are some problems. For example, some weather-related changes, such as water-quality fluctuations caused by storms, occur very quickly and not simultaneously at all locations. Also, it is difficult to specify a replication procedure that captures all components of the sampling and measurement error. A statistical inference procedure is needed that is valid regardless of the probability density of the error.

NON-NORMAL ERROR

In environmental studies, an objective definition of sampling and measurement error is not easily obtained. Environmental change such as an increase in some contaminant must generally be true of a large mass of soil, water, or air to be of interest. Thus, the value that a measurement represents is the average over some domain (Gilbert, 1987). The error includes sampling variation in this domain, contamination introduced in sampling, sample degradation during transport, variation in subsampling to obtain a quantity appropriate for analysis, fluctuation inherent in wet chemistry before the subsample is analyzed, and variation in the analytical instrument. Any of these sources might occasionally give a large deviation. For example, contamination that can occur in ground-water sampling and sample degradation because of improper preservation procedures is often sporadic, thus producing occasional large deviations. Also, an analytical instrument that requires an exacting procedure for correct operation sometimes produces a large deviation. When all error sources are considered, total elimination of occasional large deviations seems, at best, time-consuming and expensive.

The difficulty in eliminating large deviations is illustrated by the National Institute of Standards and Technology (NIST) experience with the Rocky Flats Soil Standard Reference Material (SRM-4353). This SRM is used for testing the accuracy of measurements for such radionuclides as $^{239+240}$Pu. A 600-kg sample of soil was obtained (Volchok et al., 1980). With this size sample, the difference between the average concentration and true concentration might be ignored in environmental studies. The error arises from subsampling to obtain a quantity of material appropriate for measurement and from measurement itself. The appropriate quantity of material for measurement is between 5 and 20 g. To obtain subsamples, the soil was pulverized so that 2% or less had particle sizes greater than 16 μm in diameter. However, this grinding and mixing were not sufficient to eliminate the material's inhomogeneity (Inn et al., 1984; Liggett et al., 1984). Measurements on several subsamples showed that blended soil has, on average, one hot particle in every 50 g. Hot particles result in subsampling errors that are occasionally large. Subsampling in studying other trace contaminants might have similar tendencies.

Statistical methods discussed here are based on the model

$$y_{jmn} = \mu + \alpha_m + \beta_n + \eta_{mn} + \epsilon_{jmn}, j = 1, \ldots, r_{mn};$$

$$m = 1, \ldots, M; n = 1, \ldots, N.$$

The measurement y_{jmn} is replicate j of the r_{mn} replicate measurements at location m and time n. The background level, historical differences, and global changes are given by μ, α_m, and β_n, respectively. Local environmental changes to be detected are given by η_{mn}. Sampling and measurement errors, given by ϵ_{jmn}, are assumed to be independent and identically distributed. The study must be designed so that sampling and measurement error assumptions hold. First, replicates must reflect all error components mentioned above. Second, any between-batch error components associated with the sequence of measurements must be considered. One unavoidable between-batch component is the variation between sampling times resulting from instrumental drift and recalibration. If all measurements for one value of n are made in a single batch, this component is an indistinguishable part of β_n and can be ignored in inferences about η_{mn}. There is a conflict between the purpose for which replicates are used here and the purpose for which replicates are usually obtained. The purpose here is to assess ϵ_{jmn} so that statistical limits on the size of η_{mn} can be inferred. The usual purpose for replicates is to evaluate laboratory performance, which involves the temptation to suppress variability.

If $r_{mn} \geq 3$ for most (m,n), the density of ϵ_{jmn} can be estimated from replicates without any assumptions about μ, α_m, β_n, or η_{mn} (Liggett, 1989). The strictly positive density estimate seems to be the appropriate alternative (Liggett, 1989). We denote the density of ϵ_{jmn} by p and its estimate by $\hat{p}$. Consider an estimate of η_{mn} that is invariant to changes in μ, α_m, and β_n. Most estimates that might be considered have this property. If p were known, we could make probability statements about this estimate of η_{mn} and test the hypothesis $\eta_{mn} = 0$. Since p is unknown, we substitute $\hat{p}$ and proceed as if p were known. Such an approach is called a bootstrap (Efron and Tibshirani, 1986).

INFERENCE ON RESIDUALS

Detection of local environmental changes requires that the part of the model given by $\mu + \alpha_m + \beta_n$ be estimated and subtracted from the measurements. The resulting residuals $y_{jmn} - \hat{\mu} - \hat{\alpha}_m - \hat{\beta}_n$ can be used for inference on η_{mn}. The choice of an estimator is very important. In many environmental studies, median polish (Tukey, 1977) has been used instead of least-squares decomposition because the least-squares method gives residuals that are almost impossible to interpret when some measurements are outliers. Consider a decomposition closely related to median polish: the one that gives the least (sum of) absolute deviations (LAD), the LAD decomposition (Armstrong and Frome, 1979; Siegel, 1983).

This decomposition is interesting because of its behavior with occasional large error values and isolated large η_{mn} values. Estimates of μ, α_m, and β_n can be obtained from a subset containing $M+N-1$ of the measurements. For these estimates to be unique, the subset must be properly chosen. The values of $\mu + \alpha_m + \beta_n$ from such a subset are called an elemental fit. Since this fit is not affected by measurements not in the subset, a properly chosen elemental fit will not be affected by occasional large ϵ_{jmn} and η_{mn} values, and such large values will not affect other residuals. Interpretation of residuals from such a fit should be feasible (Hawkins et al., 1984; Johnson and Tukey, 1987; Bassett, 1988). The LAD fit (or a LAD fit if the LAD fit is not unique) is an elemental fit that minimizes the sum of absolute deviations, that is, residuals. An alternative choice, the elemental fit that minimizes the median of the absolute residuals, is recommended by Rousseeuw and Leroy (1987) and is an alternative that should be adopted for some regression models.

Advantages of the LAD fit can be specified in terms of the effect of large outliers (Rousseeuw and Leroy, 1987) and in terms of mean square estimation error. Let r_{mn} be constant, and let $M < N$. If the number of arbitrarily large outliers is less than ½ $M r_{mn}$, these outliers have no correspondingly large effect on fit. In contrast, the least-squares fit cannot tolerate any arbitrarily large outliers. Another way to judge fit is in terms of $\Sigma_{m,n} (\hat{\mu} + \hat{\alpha}_m + \hat{\beta}_n - \mu - \alpha_m - \beta_n)^2$. With heavy tailed error, this quantity will be smaller for LAD fit than for least-squares fit.

In practice, interpretation of residuals $y_{jmn} - \hat{\mu} - \hat{\alpha}_m - \hat{\beta}_n$ would begin with graphs of the medians,

$$z_{mn} = \text{median}_j (y_{jmn} - \hat{\mu} - \hat{\alpha}_m - \hat{\beta}_n),$$

versus time (n) for each location (m). Tentative hypotheses about environmental changes would be obtained from the relation between the graphs and other information about the locations being monitored. That is, a large value of $T_1 = \max_m |z_{mN}|$, which indicates a large relative change at the latest sampling time, would undoubtedly attract attention, as would a large value of

$$T_2 = \max_m \left(\sum_{n=N/2+1}^{N} z_{mn} \right) - \min_m \left(\sum_{n=1}^{N/2} z_{mn} \right),$$

which indicates a large difference between the highest location in the most recent half of the data and the lowest location in the first half of the data.

To conclude that an environmental change occurred requires assessment of the probability that error alone caused a value of T_1 or T_2 as large or larger than that observed. If p were known, we could assess this probability by creating many independent realizations of the error and computing the value of the T_1 or T_2 for each. Since we do not know p, we create the error realizations from $\hat{p}$, the density estimate obtained from the replicates. Alternatively, we could obtain this probability for a collection of densities, at least one of which is believed to be like p itself, and base the conclusion on the largest probability. Without replicates, and without any estimate of p, use of a collection of densities might be unacceptably subjective. If an estimate of p were available, other densities close to $\hat{p}$ might be used to guard against the estimation error in $\hat{p}$.

To investigate effects of the estimation error in $\hat{p}$ on the validity of inferences based on T_1 and T_2, I performed an experiment using computer-generated random numbers. In this experiment, $r_{mn} = 3$, M = 3, and N = 8, and the error realizations are given by a standard normal variate divided by a uniform $(0,1)$ variate. The density of this ratio is called the SLASH in the robustness literature. In each independent trial, I computed $\hat{p}$ with a 15-term Hermite function expansion (Liggett, 1989). From $\hat{p}$, I obtained 10% and 5% critical points for T_1 and T_2; I then determined whether T_1 and T_2 computed from original data exceeded these critical points. This experiment gave the following values for the actual significance levels that correspond to intended 10% and 5% levels: 10.1 (1.0) and 6.3 (0.8) for T_1, and 15.3 (2.1) and 10.6 (1.8) for T_2. In parentheses are shown the standard deviations of the values obtained from this computer experiment. For T_1, the differences between the intended and actual significance levels are statistically insignificant. For T_2, the actual levels are higher than intended. This discrepancy is due to the failure of the density estimator to fully portray the very heavy tails of the SLASH density. This problem would disappear for an error density with more moderate tails, that is, an error density with a smaller frequency of unusually large values. More replicates in the study design would give a better estimate of $\hat{p}$ and better critical points.

FURTHER CONSIDERATIONS

If the quantity monitored were to vary over a large range, the first model might be faulty in two ways. First, the causes of global variabilities might lead to larger variations at locations with historically higher levels. Second, the standard deviation of sampling and measurement error might be higher when the true value is higher. In some situations, $\mu + \alpha_m + \beta_n$ should be replaced by a multiplicative model, and the standard deviation of error should be taken to be proportional to the true value being measured. In this case, the analysis described above should be applied to the logarithms of measurements. However, in most cases, a more general replacement for $\mu + \alpha_m + \beta_n$ and a more general dependence of the standard deviation on the true quantity must be considered.

Because measurements are expensive, a sequential procedure in which replicates are obtained when needed is attractive. Unfortunately, returning to a previous sampling time is impossible. Thus, the study should start with adequate replicates and provide for reduction in the number of replicates if possible. Having adequate replicates at the outset allows the causes of large errors to be found, and might indicate inadequacies in the way replicates reflect total error. Also, adequate replicates provide the error characterization needed for inference on local changes that occur early in the study.

REFERENCES

Armstrong, R. D. and E. L. Frome. 1979. Least-absolute-value estimators for one-way and two-way tables. *Nav. Res. Logist. Q. 26*:79-96.

Bassett, G. W. 1988. A p-subset property of L_1 and regression quantile estimates. *Comput. Stat. Data Anal. 6*:297-304.

Efron, B. and R. Tibshirani. 1986. Bootstrap methods for standard errors, confidence intervals, and other measures of statistical accuracy. *Statist. Sci. 1*:54-77.

Gilbert, R. O. 1987. *Statistical Methods for Environmental Pollution Monitoring.* Van Nostrand Reinhold, New York.

Hawkins, D. M., D. Bradu, and G. V. Kass. 1984. Location of several outliers in multiple-regression data using elemental sets. *Technometrics 26*:197-208.

Inn, K.G.W., W. S. Liggett, and J. M. R. Hutchinson. 1984. The National Bureau of Standards Rocky Flats soil standard reference material. *Nucl. Instrum. Meth. Phys. Res. 223*:443-450.

Johnson, E. G. and J. W. Tukey. 1987. Graphical exploratory analysis of variance illustrated on a splitting of the Johnson and Tsao data, pp. 171-244. In: Design, Data and Analysis by Some Friends of Cuthbert Daniel. John Wiley and Sons, New York.

Liggett, W. 1989. Estimation of an asymmetrical density from several small samples. *Biometrika 76*:13-21.

Liggett, W. S., K.G.W. Inn, and J.M.R. Hutchinson. 1984. Statistical assessment of subsampling procedures. *Environ. Int. 10*:143-151.

Rousseeuw, P. J. and A. M. Leroy. 1987. *Robust Regression and Outlier Detection.* John Wiley and Sons, New York.

Siegel, A. F. 1983. Low median and least absolute residual analysis of two-way tables. *J. Am. Stat. Assoc. 78*:371-374.

Tukey, J. W. 1977. *Exploratory Data Analysis.* Addison-Wesley, Reading, MA.

Volchok, H. L., M. Feiner, K.G.W. Inn, and J. F. McInroy. 1980. Development of some natural matrix standards-progress report. *Environ. Int. 3*:395-398.

DEVELOPMENT OF A HYBRID QUALITY ASSURANCE PLAN FOR RESOURCE CONSERVATION AND RECOVERY ACT (RCRA) GROUND-WATER MONITORING PROJECTS

R. R. LaBarge and D. R. Dahl

Pacific Northwest Laboratory, Richland, Washington

Key Words: *QA Plan, environmental, NQA-1-1986, QAMS-005/80*

ABSTRACT

Quality assurance (QA) programs attempt to enhance the traceability, reproducibility, and legal defensibility of project results and assure clients and regulators that work is performed according to established guidelines. Pacific Northwest Laboratory's (PNL) QA program is based on the nationally recognized American National Standards Institute/American Society of Mechanical Engineers Standard NQA-1-1986. Because NQA-1-1986 was developed for the design, construction, and operation of nuclear facilities, we had to adapt and supplement our program with elements from QA programs developed by the U.S. Environmental Protection Agency. To provide documentation and traceability of all work related to Resource Conservation and Recovery Act ground-water monitoring and to ensure that reproducible results are attained, PNL's hybrid QA plans address activities from initial planning through well installation, and from sample collection and transportation through sample analysis and data evaluation.

INTRODUCTION

Quality assurance (QA) enhances the traceability, reproducibility, and legal defensibility of project results and assures clients and regulators that work is performed according to established guidelines. Growing emphasis on environmental issues at U.S. Department of Energy (DOE) nuclear facilities requires that individual projects address both nuclear and environmental QA criteria. Pacific Northwest Laboratory's (PNL) QA program is based on the national quality assurance consensus standard NQA-1-1986 (ANSI/ASME, 1986). This standard is the basis for developing Resource Conservation and Recovery Act (RCRA, 1976) ground-water monitoring QA plans.

Although nuclear and environmental QA programs have much in common, some items addressed by the former are not addressed by the latter. Especially important is the fact that both programs require the development of a prework planning document (QA plan) that describes specific methods, equipment, and/or management systems for controlling project activities.

DISCUSSION

The DOE Richland Operations Office Order 5700.1A (DOE, 1983) requires contractors to develop, implement, and monitor QA programs based on ANSI/ASME Standard NQA-1-1986. This standard describes a model QA program intended for the design, construction, and operation of nuclear power plants. Thus, considerable emphasis is placed on design reviews, personnel training and qualification, procurement control, records control, and inspection. To comply with NQA-1-1986, a QA program must address certain basic requirements (Table 1), as applicable.

Table 1. Typical Hybrid QA Plan Table of Contents.

	Table of Contents	Requirement Source[a]
1	Title Page with Provision for Approval Signatures	Q
2	Table of Contents	Q
3	Project Description	Q/N (2)[b]
4	Project Organization and Responsibility	Q/N (1)
5	QA Objectives for Measurement Data in Terms of Precision, Accuracy, Representativeness, Completeness, and Comparability	Q
6	Sampling Procedures	Q/N (9) (11)
7	Sample Custody	Q/N(8, 13)
8	Calibration Procedures and Frequency	Q/N (12)
9	Analytical Procedures	Q/N (9) (11)
10	Data Reduction, Validation, and Reporting	Q/N (11)
11	Internal Quality Control Checks and Frequency	Q
12	Performance and System Audits	Q/N (18)
13	Preventive Maintenance Procedures and Schedules	Q/N (12)
14	Specific Routine Procedures to be Used to Assess Data Precision, Accuracy, Representativeness, Completeness, and Comparability (PARCC) of Specific Measurement Parameters Involved	Q
15	Corrective Action	Q/N (16)
16	Quality Assurance Reports to Management	Q
17	QA Records	N (17)
18	Procurement Control	N (4, 7)
19	Staff Training	N (2)
20	Software Control	N (3)
21	Nonconformances and Deficiencies	N (15, 16)
22	Document Control	Q[c]/N (6)
23	Monitoring New Installations	N (5, 9, 10)

[a]N = required by NQA-1-1986.
 Q = required by QAMS-005/08.
[b]Number in parentheses refers to the section in NQA-1-1986 where item is found.
[c]QAMS discusses document control for QA project plans only, not for technical procedures and other documentation that accompany each project.

To develop a comprehensive environmental QA program for RCRA ground-water monitoring at Hanford, we adapted the NQA-1-1986 program, and supplemented it with elements from QAMS-005/80, a QA program developed by the U.S. Environmental Protection Agency (EPA, 1983). The EPA QA program contains QA or quality control (QC) elements essential to gathering traceable, reproducible, and legally defensible environmental data.

Because EPA administers and monitors the RCRA program (EPA, 1976), laboratory analyses of soil, surface water, and ground water in support of RCRA activities must comply with EPA's solid-waste test methods (EPA, 1982). Chapter 1 of the EPA's Test Methods for Evaluating Solid Waste Manual (SW-846; EPA, 1982) requires organizations to prepare, implement, and utilize a QA plan prepared by Quality Assurance Management Staff in accordance with QAMS-005/80 (EPA, 1983). All facets of PNL's RCRA ground-water monitoring projects at Hanford are controlled by hybrid QA plans designed to address these essential elements (Table 1). However, QAMS-005/80 does not address all subject areas covered by NQA-1-1986, nor does it provide project management and the client with the degree of control required to ensure the defensibility and traceability of project results. For instance, software control, procurement control, and staff training are not covered in QAMS.

Our hybrid QA plan satisfies the format and content requirements of QAMS-005/80 as well as the content requirements of NQA-1-1986. It also provides QA controls for a program or project (in this case, RCRA) whose results must be traceable, reproducible, and legally defensible.

Because QAMS-005/80 requires a specific format, and NQA-1-1986 does not, we selected the QAMS-005/08 format for our QA plan. In addition, we have combined some sections to eliminate redundancy.

Table 1 shows the table of contents from a typical RCRA ground-water monitoring project hybrid QA plan. Items identified with an "N" are required by NQA-1-1986; those identified with a "Q" are required by QAMS-005/80. We have added items 17 through 22, which, we believe, are inadequately addressed by QAMS-005/80.

Our RCRA QA plans are similar in format and content, they are project- and task-specific, and are used as working documents. That is, they are designed for use in the office or in the field.

Our hybrid QA plan format has a couple of distinct advantages: (1) the standard format addresses all requirements of NQA-1-1986 and QAMS-005/80; (2) the format can easily be expanded to include items not required by NQA-1-1986 or QAMS-005/80.

CONCLUSION

We know of no prescriptive, "off-the-shelf" QA program that addresses all essential elements necessary for collecting and evaluating ground-water samples. To provide comprehensive QA plans, we have combined applicable portions of several nationally recognized QA programs to meet the QA and QC needs of RCRA ground-water monitoring activities. To provide documentation and traceability and to ensure that reproducible results are attained, the hybrid QA plans address efforts from initial planning through well installation, and from sample collection and transportation through sample analysis and data evaluation. Development and use of these hybrid QA plans provide compliance with applicable directives in a concise, user-friendly format that can be easily expanded and updated.

ACKNOWLEDGMENT

Work supported by the U.S. Department of Energy (DOE) under Contract DE-AC06-76RLO 1830 and by the U.S. Environmental Protection Agency under a Related Services Agreement with DOE, Interagency Agreement DW930094-1.

REFERENCES

ANSI/ASME. 1986. Quality Assurance Program Requirements for Nuclear Facilities, ANSI/ASME NQA-1-1986. American National Standards Institute/American Society of Mechanical Engineers, New York.

DOE. 1983. Quality Assurance, DOE-RL Order 5700.1A. U.S. Department of Energy, Richland Operations Office, Richland, WA.

EPA. 1976. 42 USC 6901 et seq., as amended.

EPA. 1982. Test Methods for Evaluating Solid Waste, SW-846. Office of Solid Waste and Emergency Response, U.S. Environmental Protection Agency, Washington, DC.

EPA. 1983. Interim Guidelines and Specifications for Preparing Quality Assurance Project Plans, QAMS-005/80. U.S. Environmental Protection Agency, Washington, DC.

ENVIRONMENTAL DATA QUALIFICATION SYSTEM

O. V. Hester and M. R. Groh

Idaho National Engineering Laboratory, EG&G Idaho, Idaho Falls, Idaho

Key Words: *Environmental, chemical, qualification, data base*

ABSTRACT

The Integrated Environmental Data Management System (IEDMS) is a personal-computer-based system that can support environmental investigations from design stage through termination of the study. The system integrates information such as that from the sampling and analysis plan, field data, and analytical results. Automated features include sampling guidance forms, bar-coded sample labels and tags, field and analytical forms production, sample tracking, checks for the completeness and technical compliance of the data, completeness reports (the amount of valid data obtained compared to the amount that was planned), and results and quality control (QC) data reporting. The IEDMS supports a systematic and comprehensive quality assessment of the U.S. Environmental Protection Agency's Contract Laboratory Program (CLP) chemical analyses data. One product is a unique, tabular presentation of the data that contains complete results and QC data from CLP forms in the same chronology as the analyses.

INTRODUCTION

The Integrated Environmental Data Management System (IEDMS) was developed at EG&G Idaho, in support of the U.S. Department of Energy (DOE) Environmental Survey. The IEDMS was designed to support Sampling and Analysis (S&A) activities from development of an S&A Plan through final reporting of analytical results. The IEDMS capabilities are greatest in the areas of qualifying and reporting analytical data. This refers, in particular, to the U.S. Environmental Protection Agency (EPA) level IV chemical analysis data generated under Contract Laboratory Program (CLP) protocols (EPA, 1987a,b).

The IEDMS was developed with three major objectives: (1) ensure rapid and error-free data transfer from point of collection through several levels of verification and validation to use in reports; (2) establish a defensible and known level of data quality; (3) provide a management system for long-term data archival and retrieval.

DATABASE ENVIRONMENT

The IEDMS is a networked IBM personal-computer-based system developed using dBASE III PLUS software. All software (e.g., data entry, quality assessment routines, verification and validation software, and applications programs) are either dBASE III PLUS or Clipper compiled dBASE III PLUS programs. To ensure use of the most current versions and to maintain a documentation trail of all file modifications, all programs and data bases are maintained under POLYTRON Version Control Software (POLYTRON, 1985). The system can accommodate multiple users. Data integrity is maintained through daily archival of all data on a Write Once Read Many optical disk. Because of the relational structure of the data base and because the data are stored as flat files, reconstruction of the data into its original input format or variations thereof is a straightforward process.

IEDMS CAPABILITIES

The IEDMS supports S&A activities throughout an environmental investigation. Data originating in the S&A Plan, from the field, and from analytical reports are captured by the IEDMS, primarily via electronic data entry screens that simulate the forms on which the data are supplied. All data can be integrated through the relational structure of the data bases. The flow process for capturing data with the IEDMS is shown in Figure 1. Automated features of the IEDMS include: sampling guidance forms, bar-coded sample labels and tags, field and analytical forms production, sample tracking, analytical data qualification, completeness reports, and results and quality control (QC) data reporting. We will focus our discussion on IEDMS capabilities for qualification and reporting of chemical analyses data.

DATA PACKAGE

We must understand the make-up of a chemical analysis data set to assess data quality. Chemical analyses data are supplied to the IEDMS by an analytical laboratory. The data deliverable may contain one or multiple data packages. Chemical data are entered into the IEDMS in discrete units called data packages. Each CLP data package includes a set of analytical results and associated QC data for a set of samples that were analyzed as one (analytical) batch. A data package typically includes a case narrative, chain-of-custody (COC) forms, a raw data set (e.g., ion chromatograms), and a set of EPA standardized forms on which results and associated QC data are reported.

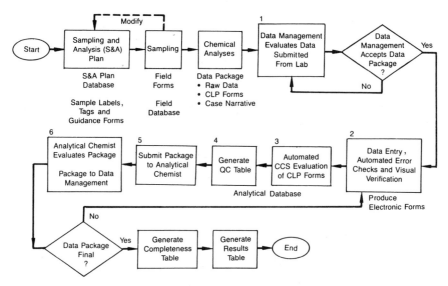

Figure 1. Integrated Environmental Data Management System (IEDMS) data flow process.

The complete data package (data set on standardized forms) is captured electronically by the IEDMS. Analytical results for each individual sample are recorded on a standard CLP form, designated Form 1. Additional forms summarize QC data, including calibration standard response factors, duplicates, matrix and surrogate spike recoveries, and method blanks.

DATA FLOW/QUALIFICATION PROCESS

Steps in the IEDMS data flow process that apply to qualification and reporting of analytical data are shown in Figure 1. After receipt of a data package, its adequacy for entry in the IEDMS is evaluated. Data are then entered manually via programs that use electronic images of analytical data forms, complemented by automated error checks of calculated values (Step 2, Figure 1). During this step, data management staff attempt to resolve errors. The entry clerk visually verifies the data by comparing the original forms with the electronically produced forms.

Data are then comprehensively checked for conformance to the analytical protocol specified in the Statement of Work (SOW) under which the samples were analyzed. Data are processed through an automated version of the EPA Contract Compliance Screening (CCS) procedures (Step 3, Figure 1; EPA, 1987a,b), which checks for completeness and technical compliance. A hard copy of any deficiencies is produced, and the deficiencies are resolved if possible.

After processing through Step 3 (Figure 1), data are stored electronically, a preliminary quality assessment is made, and initial verification and validation of the data are made. All data (results and QC) are also presented in a concise, easily readable table (QC table, Step 4). To enhance the table's usefulness as a visual tool to reconstruct and assess the analysis process, the information is chronologically consistent with the order in which the analysis was performed; sample specific results and QC information are reported in the same column. Figure 2 is a sample page from a QC table for volatile organics.

In Step 4 of the data qualification process, the data package is transferred from data management to an analytical chemist. This data transfer is highlighted for two reasons. First, the analytical chemist's review is performed by an individual totally independent of both the data management group and the laboratory that performed the analysis. This independent review is standard for quality control practices. Secondly, the analytical chemist's review intentionally overlaps with the data management review. This designed redundancy helps to ensure comprehensiveness and consistency in the data qualification process.

The entire data package is reviewed by an analytical chemist, who continues the data quality assessment (Step 5, Figure 1) and resolves deficiencies identified in the error file and CCS listing. Efficiency and focus of the chemist's evaluation are enhanced by the information supplied by data management staff. The error file provides a set of deficiencies requiring resolution. The CCS output serves as a fine "filter" by identifying areas of noncompliance and incompleteness with respect to the analytical SOW. Thus, the chemist can immediately address areas where known deficiencies have been identified. For example, the CCS output shows whether a continuing calibration was performed within the required time interval. Additionally, the automated process standardizes the numerous CCS checks, and ensures that the complete set of checks is made on each data package.

AREA / LOCATION / TYPE OF LOCATION / SAMPLE NUMBER (ENVIR PROB) / MEDIA / UNITS	QC INITIAL CALIBRATN VSTD050 09/10/87 RRF	%RSD	QC CONTINUING CALIBRATN VSTD050 11/13/87 RRF50	%D	QC METHOD BLANK VBLKH13EA WATER ug/L	TRIP BLANK DM64110XA WATER ug/L	TRIP BLANK QC MA DM68111XA WATER ug/L	MG15 M-13/G-17 EFFLUENT DM10002XA(13) SURFACE WATER ug/L	OH17 O-15/H-19 EFFLUENT DM10003XA(13) SURFACE WATER ug/L
SPCC Chloromethane	0.42	4.3	6.00	1000	10 U	10 U	10 U	10 U	10 U
Bromomethane	0.69	3.5	0.52	24.9	10 U	10 U	10 U	10 U	10 U
CCC Vinyl Chloride	0.72	5.1	0.59	17.3	10 U	10 U	10 U	10 U	10 U
Chloroethane	0.52	5.2	0.43	17.8	10 U	10 U	10 U	10 U	10 U
Methylene Chloride	1.30	11.8	1.17	9.9	14	5 U	5 U	5 U	5 U
Acetone	0.48	11.2	0.36	23.2	10 U	10 U	10 U	42	10 U
Carbon Disulfide	2.15	25.4	2.15	0.1	5 U	5 U	5 U	5 U	5 U
CCC 1,1-Dichloroethene	1.30	4.8	1.21	6.8	5 U	5 U	5 U	5 U	5 U
SPCC 1,1-Dichloroethane	2.38	3.4	2.17	8.8	5 U	5 U	5 U	5 U	5 U
1,2-Dichloroethene_(total)	1.42	5.4	1.26	10.9	5 U	5 U	5 U	5 U	5 U
CCC Chloroform	2.94	4.0	3.05	3.9	5 U	4 J	4 J	29	5 U
1,2-Dichloroethane	2.24	5.2	2.27	0.9	5 U	5 U	5 U	5 U	5 U
2-Butanone	0.04	15.8	0.02	34.0	10 U	10 U	10 U	10 U	10 U
1,1,1-Trichloroethane	0.59	6.4	0.62	5.5	5 U	5 U	5 U	5 U	5 U
Carbon Tetrachloride	0.74	3.6	0.74	0.4	5 U	5 U	5 U	5 U	5 U
Vinyl Acetate	0.64	1.5	0.53	18.1	10 U	10 U	10 U	10 U	10 U
Bromodichloromethane	0.68	4.4	0.65	5.2	5 U	5 U	5 U	12 J	5 U
CCC 1,2-Dichloropropane	0.31	6.5	0.23	23.6	5 U	5 U	5 U	5 U	5 U
cis-1,3-Dichloropropene	0.59	3.8	0.31	26.3	5 U	5 U	5 U	5 U	5 U
Trichloroethene	0.52	6.6	0.41	22.1	5 U	5 U	5 U	5 U	5 U
Toluene-d8	1.03	1.0	0.98	4.7					
Bromofluorobenzene	1.01	1.5	0.96	5.4					
1,2-Dichloroethane-d4	1.80	2.9	1.75	2.9					
Surrogate 1(TOL) %Recovery					101	104	97	98	106
Surrogate 2(BFB) %Recovery					101	104	99	100	100
Surrogate 3(DCE) %Recovery					103	107	111	114	106
Method Blank Run (Y/N) Tunes Out of Criteria Minutes Past 12-Hour Tune					YES	YES	YES	YES	YES
Internal Standard Area(BCM)					529495	472659	423217	419359	425481
Internal Standard Area(DFB)					2387618	2023165	1845646	1842944	1800947
Internal Standard Area(CBZ)					2022893	1772792	1559310	1562654	1471847
BCM Return Time Shift									
DFB Return Time Shift									
CBZ Return Time Shift									
Dilution Factor					1.000	1.000	1.000	1.000	1.000
Percent Moisture									
Field/Shipping Time						6d	5d	5d	4d
Analytical (Allowed) Hold Time						7(10)d	7(10)d	3(10)d	3(10)d
Total (Allowed) Hold Time						13(14)d	12(14)d	8(14)d	7(14)d
ELEVated/DECReased CRQL									

MIN RRF AND RRF50 FOR SPCC = 0.300 (0.250 FOR BROMOFORM).
MAX %RSD = 30.0% AND MAX %D = 25.0% FOR CCC.

Figure 2. Sample volatile organic QC data, SDG Number DM64501XA, for instrument gas chromatography/mass spectrometry-E.

Concurrently, the chemist reviews raw data for internal consistencies, assesses whether analyses were performed according to specifications (e.g., whether or not QC criteria were met), and checks that data on the reporting forms are consistent with raw data. Each inquiry provides additional input for the final quality assessment and reports on the ultimate limitations and qualifications of the data.

After the chemist's evaluation, modified data forms are returned to data management staff. Required changes to the data base, dated and initialed by the chemist, maintain traceability for modifications. Steps 2-6 are then repeated until the data quality assessment is complete: the point at which the remaining data package deficiencies cannot be resolved. Data qualifications and limitations statements and completeness and results tables are then prepared.

Only after the process described above is complete are the data interpreted and findings and conclusions reported. This helps minimize the chance for erroneous, premature, or costly conclusions being made from the data.

The IEDMS will be modified as needed to support changes in EPA's CLP analytical SOW. If and when the different analytical laboratories adopt a standardized format for the data deliverable, electronic transfer and entry of the analytical data will be pursued. Electronic data transfer already exists with EG&G's analytical lab for inorganic ICP analysis and is being developed for other analysis types. The IEDMS is concurrently being expanded to support an EG&G Idaho, Inc., Appendix IX Analytical SOW that is currently in draft form.

ACKNOWLEDGMENTS

This work was supported by U.S. Department of Energy Contract No. DE-AC07-76IDO1570 with EG&G. The entire staff of the Data Applications Section, Statistics and Reliability Engineering Groups provided support to this effort.

REFERENCES

EPA. 1987a. Contract Laboratory Program - Statement of Work for Organic Analysis No. 10/86, Revision 8/87. U.S. Environmental Protection Agency, Washington, DC.

EPA. 1987b. Contract Laboratory Program, Statement of Work for Inorganic Analysis No. 787, Revision 12/87. U.S. Environmental Protection Agency, Washington, DC.

POLYTRON. 1985. The POLYTRON Version Control System.® POLYTRON Corp., Beaverton, OR.

AN INTEGRATED COMPUTER-BASED SYSTEM TO FACILITATE ENVIRONMENTAL MONITORING, ASSESSMENT, AND RESTORATION

P. J. Cowley and J. C. Brown

Pacific Northwest Laboratory, Richland, Washington

Key Words: *Data base, environmental information system, geographic information system (GIS), computer graphics*

ABSTRACT

The extensive scientific and technical data gathered during environmental monitoring, assessment, and restoration make effective application of a computer-based information system essential. An integrated computer system is being applied at the U.S. Department of Energy's Hanford Site to manage data gathered during site characterization and environmental monitoring and to facilitate analysis and assessment. The Hanford Environmental Information System can significantly enhance our ability to manage, retrieve, and display data. Integrating a data base, a geographic information system (that allows data display on a map), and support graphics allows the user to generate spatially related visualizations and to extract data. The user can quickly obtain a complete data picture and easily transfer data to other software environments for further analysis and assessment. We will describe the approach used to design and develop the system, how it was integrated, lessons learned through its development, how it is being used, how it can aid in meeting regulatory requirements, and natural extensions of the system to support environmental restoration.

INTRODUCTION

Extensive site characterization and environmental monitoring have been conducted on the 560-mi² U.S. Department of Energy's Hanford Site in southeastern Washington for decades. The site is divided into 78 operable units* with over 1500 active or inactive waste sites. At each operable unit, air, sediment, soil gas, biotic, and surface- and ground-water samples may be analyzed for numerous contaminants. Managing the data to facilitate environmental monitoring, assessment, and restoration is a significant challenge. An automated system was

---

*A collection of waste sites that are in close proximity to one another and are expected to require similar remediation techniques.

needed to support the more than 125 billion data characters to be accumulated and to access existing data; new capabilities were required to view and analyze data.

The Hanford Environmental Information System (HEIS) is more than a data base. Although the data base forms the heart of the system, HEIS also includes a geographic information system (GIS), support graphics, user-friendly access software, database query and report generation software, networking, data and system security, documentation, and user support. The system is intended to meet the needs of the operational user, who is responsible for scheduling, data collection, data processing, and quality assurance, and the scientist who will use the system for environmental monitoring, assessment, and restoration planning. The HEIS data base is available to the entire user community to promote effective data sharing.

Creating a large and complex information system such as the HEIS requires an interdisciplinary team of computer scientists, hydrologists, geologists, and environmental scientists. The team must be committed to design and planning and have sufficient financing, time, and management support.

Prototyping permits the iterative clarification of user requirements and has been used to provide additional knowledge to design and implement the final production system before large amounts of data are entered into it. We are also using computer-aided software engineering (CASE) tools. The current HEIS data model and its documentation consume several million characters of disk storage, making it too complex to track manually.

HEIS DATA BASE

The HEIS uses the ORACLE™ (Oracle Corporation, Belmont, CA) data base management system (DBMS) to store, manipulate, and retrieve data. The HEIS data base is being designed and implemented so that it is easy to use and understand, and provides flexibility and security. It integrates several existing data bases and subject areas not accommodated in previous data bases (Figure 1).

"Entity-relationship" modeling is used to create models of each data subject area. Within each subject area, data are partitioned into entities. An "entity" is a place, thing, event, or concept about which information is recorded (for example, a site, well, facility, sample, or analytical result). These entities, implemented as "tables" in the data base, are related in different ways and for different reasons, indicated by named "relationship" lines among entities (Figure 2). A "relationship" defines the role of one entity with respect to another. (There can be one-to-one [1-1] and one-to-many [1-m] relationships.) Figure 2 is an entity-relationship diagram showing primary entities of interest for vadose zone and geologic data.

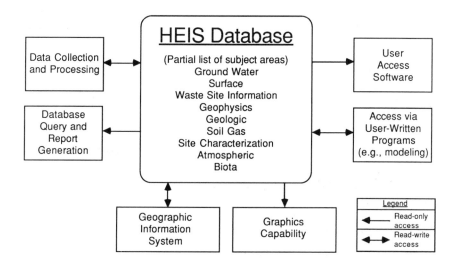

Figure 1. Software components of the Hanford Environmental Information System.

The current HEIS entity-relationship model includes 140 entities, 161 relationships, and 913 attributes (fields). The HEIS model is managed with the KnowledgeWare CASE tool (KnowledgeWare™, Atlanta, GA).

While several Hanford data bases contain information on the same topic, data from one do not always agree with data from another. Extracting similar data from two data bases could result in two different answers. By integrating data from different data bases into the HEIS, we can provide consistent data to all users. When necessary changes are identified and made, all will have access to the changes.

ORACLE provides data protection from system failure and prevents unauthorized data access. ORACLE provides capabilities for backing-up and restoring the data base (in case of system failure) and for logging entries to a journal file to recover "lost" data that have not been "committed" to the data base.

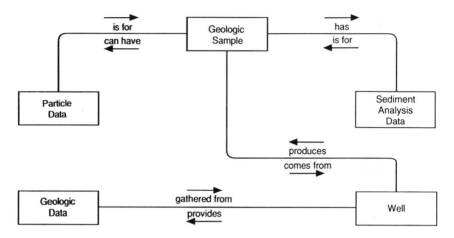

Figure 2. Entity-Relationships for geologic data in the Hanford Environmental Information System.

The DBMS provides protection against accidental or malicious alteration or destruction of the data at several levels: data base, table, record, field, view, project, and account. It also provides "read" and "write" access protection at different levels.

At a large site, such as Hanford, it is imperative to have unique identifiers for all items (for example, two wells cannot have the same identifier). Synonyms and homonyms for data, which exist because data bases were created by different groups or organizations, make communication of information between data bases and integration of those data bases difficult. Thus, we formed a Data Administration Board subcommittee, consisting of individuals representing different programs and contractors. Recommendations of the subcommittee are being formalized, and written policies and guidelines are being developed. Standard names, abbreviations, and naming conventions are being adopted for use in all environmental restoration work at Hanford.

The HEIS can help meet regulatory requirements and prepare for potential litigation by providing data access and traceability. The HEIS data base can automatically generate reports and tables required by regulatory agencies. The database contains directory information for supporting documentation and keeps traceability data, such as when samples were taken and analyzed, who performed the analysis, which analytical method was used, and evaluations of data quality.

GIS AND SUPPORT GRAPHICS

The GIS is an important component of the HEIS because most aspects of the system are related to a location on a map. GIS can be thought of as a "smart map" that allows the user to start with a base map, then selects from a series of overlays to develop a customized, computer-generated map. The HEIS base map includes roads, trails, railroads, water bodies, and administrative boundaries. We are developing overlays of Hanford's 1500 waste sites, ground-water monitoring wells, geologic boreholes, soil gas sampling locations, geophysical survey lines, and facilities.

The GIS user can "zoom" in and out, generate contours, change colors and symbols, query the data base, and display results on the map. The GIS will also be able to create map overlays for analysis and remediation modeling. Because drawing a map involves extensive processing and output to a screen, GIS software is ideally suited to an engineering workstation, where processing power is close to the user and is dedicated to either a single user or small group of users.

Users often want to display data graphically in two and three dimensions. The HEIS supports a graphics capability that is integrated with data selection and extraction software. (Autodesk, Inc., Sausalito, CA), a computer-aided design package, is used to generate lithology and well construction diagrams. Through its AutoLISP programming language, AutoCAD can automatically generate well diagrams from data extracted from the data base.

HEIS COMPUTING ENVIRONMENT

We are using a Sequent S27™ UNIX-based multiprocessor computer (Sequent Computer Systems, Inc., Beaverton, OR) and ORACLE for the central HEIS data base. One advantage of this computer is its expandability: more processors, memory, and disk storage can be added as more data, functions, and processing capabilities are required.

While the data base is centralized, other components of the system are distributed over the Hanford Site (Figure 3). The HEIS is available through an extensive computer network that allows many terminals, personal computers, engineering workstations, minicomputers, and mainframes to communicate. Distributed processing with networking allows the user to take advantage of the appropriate computing environment for the work performed. For example, inexpensive terminals can be used for data entry and data processing. Those doing GIS and graphics work can use high-powered engineering workstations to retrieve the most current data from the ORACLE data base. Those doing data analysis can use their favorite software and hardware to access the data base remotely or download data sets for stand-alone processing.

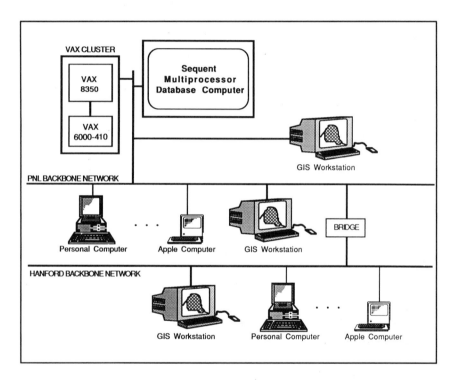

Figure 3. Hardware and networking configuration for the Hanford Environmental Information System. PNL = Pacific Northwest Laboratory; GIS = geographic information system.

This type of computing environment provides great flexibility. System integration allows the distributed components to work together in a manner that is transparent to the user. For example, the GIS requires access to the central data base. Rather than going through a process of data extraction and downloading, the GIS allows the user to access the data base directly through the network. The HEIS provides forms-based data entry, menu-driven user access software, data browsing facilities, *ad hoc* querying, and a multiwindowing computing environment on the engineering workstation. User support is provided through documentation, on-line help, training, and consultation.

LESSONS LEARNED

The HEIS is currently oriented toward environmental monitoring and assessment; it is not intended to meet computer requirements for project management, cost accounting, milestone or health-effects tracking. However, plans are underway to meet these other needs. Our experience has shown that flexibility is essential. The system must evolve as functions, data requirements, software, and hardware evolve, and we must keep pace with technological advances. The current computing environment makes expansion possible, and we expect to expand and update the system to meet user needs as environmental restoration activities continue.

Implementation of an automated information system such as the HEIS is expensive. However, environmental restoration data are important in remediation decisions. For a site as large and complex as Hanford, an effective integrated information system to support environmental monitoring, assessment, and restoration is essential.

ACKNOWLEDGMENT

Work supported by the U.S. Department of Energy under Contract DE-AC06-76RLO 1830.

POSTERS

RESULTS FROM THE 1988 QUALITY ASSURANCE TASK FORCE HANFORD INTERCOMPARISON PROGRAM

J. L. Erickson,[1] R. D. Hildebrand,[1] G. L. Toombs,[2] C. J. Card,[3] L. Josephson,[4] N. Buske,[4] R. L. Dirkes,[5] R. E. Jaquish,[5] J. Leitch,[6] R. F. Brich,[7] and M. W. Tiernan[7]

[1]State of Washington Department of Social & Health Services, Olympia, Washington

[2]Oregon State Department of Human Resources, Portland, Oregon

[3]Washington Public Power Supply System, Richland, Washington

[4]Hanford Education Action League (represented by Search Technical Services), Davenport, Washington

[5]Pacific Northwest Laboratory, Richland, Washington

[6]U.S. Environmental Protection Agency, Seattle, Washington

[7]U.S. Department of Energy, Richland, Washington

Key Words: *Environmental monitoring, quality assurance, data analysis, intercomparison program*

ABSTRACT

Cooperative environmental sampling along the Columbia River at Hanford was conducted in September 1988. Sample collections included river sediment and water from the river and selected shoreline springs. Participants included the states of Washington and Oregon, the Washington Public Power Supply System, the Hanford Education Action League (represented by Search Technical Services), the U.S. Environmental Protection Agency, and the U.S. Department of Energy (represented by Pacific Northwest Laboratory). We present the sampling and analysis protocols and data analysis.

INTRODUCTION

The cooperative program described here is sponsored by the Environmental Radiation Quality Assurance Task Force of the Pacific Northwest to allow intercomparison of environmental radiation monitoring data and enhance program capabilities. Participants include the states of Washington and Oregon, the Washington Public Power Supply System, the Hanford Education Action League (represented by Search Technical Services), the U.S. Environmental

277

Protection Agency, and the U.S. Department of Energy (represented by Pacific Northwest Laboratory). The program encourages communication among these organizations, minimizing program overlap and achieving economical use of resources.

METHODS

Samples of water from Columbia River shoreline springs and river water and sediment were collected and analyzed (gross alpha and beta, gamma scan, tritium, $^{89/90}$Sr). Spring samples were collected when water level was low and when flow was approximately 38,000 cfs. Samples at each site were thoroughly mixed and split among the participants. Surface water was collected in a bottle and mixed and split in a similar manner.

Sediment samples were collected from several locations, using a shovel or "clamshell" dredge. The Washington State Environmental Radiation Laboratory dried, homogenized, and split the samples before sending them to participants for analysis.

Analysis protocols required an initial filtration of water samples through a 0.45-μm filter before analysis for gross alpha and beta, $^{80/90}$Sr, tritium, and gamma scan. Additional analyses using alpha spectrometry for total plutonium, total uranium, ^{226,228}Ra, and ^{230,232}Th were required for sediment and water samples when gross alpha levels exceeded 5 pCi/L.

Data analysis procedures were those prescribed by the American Society for Testing and Materials (ASTM, 1976). Standard values for expected laboratory precision were those used by the U.S. Environmental Protection Agency (EPA, 1978). EPA established these values by evaluating data from program participants over several years. The value for total uranium in sediment was that from the Environmental Measurements Laboratory Quality Assessment Program (Jaquish and Kinnison, 1984); EPA did not include standard values for this analysis.

A range analysis was performed on each group of data if results were reported by at least two laboratories and were not reported as "less than." Where one result was different from the others, an outlier analysis was performed, using ASTM method E178-80 (ASTM, 1976). Data were excluded if calculations indicated they would occur by chance less than 1% of the time. The normalized range, calculated from the mean range, control limit, and standard error of the range, measures data dispersion and allows comparison of present performance with expected performance.

Results for samples from shoreline springs are shown in Tables 1 and 2. Where normalized range exceeds three standard deviations (upper control limit), participants evaluate sampling and analytical procedures to identify possible causes.

Table 1. Analysis of 1988 shoreline sediment sampling data (units: pCi/g [dry]).

Location	Analysis	Number of Results	Mean Activity	Expected Laboratory Precision	Range of Results	Mean Range	Std Error of the Range	Normalized Range
100F	^{40}K	5	13.60	0.7	2.7	1.58	0.59	2.9
Slough	^{60}Co	5	0.06	0.005	0.03	0.01	0.004	5.3[b]
	^{137}Cs	6	0.23	0.01	0.13	0.03	0.01	12.6[b]
	^{152}Eu	2	0.14	0.005	0.05	0.11	0.008	1.4
	^{226}Ra	5	0.76	0.11	0.38	0.26	0.010	2.2
	U-Total	2	1.37	0.14[a]	0.06	0.16	0.12	0.4
	P-Total	3	0.0021	0.0002	0.0017	0.0004	0.0002	7.5[b]
McNary	^{40}K	5	14.3	0.7	3.5	1.66	0.6	4.1[b]
Dam	^{60}Co	5	0.27	0.01	0.07	0.03	0.01	4.3[b]
	^{137}Cs	4	0.05	0.005	0.05	0.01	0.004	10.0[b]
	^{152}Eu	6	0.77	0.04	0.11	0.10	0.03	1.4
	^{226}Ra	6	0.53	0.03	0.30	0.07	0.02	11.3[b]
	U-Total	5	0.88	0.13	0.39	0.31	0.1	1.8
	P-Total	3	2.30	0.23*	0.14	0.39	0.2	0.4
		3	0.0094	0.001	0.0011	0.002	0.0008	0.7

[a]Expected laboratory precision from environmental measurements laboratory data; (Jaquish and Kinnison, 1984). No EPA data available.
[b]Exceeds the upper control limit of three standard deviations.

Results generally showed good agreement among participants. This annual sampling and laboratory intercomparison activity have encouraged communications and promoted cooperation among various organizations involved in environmental radiation monitoring at Hanford. It has also improved public confidence in these programs.

Table 2. Analysis of 1988 seep sampling data analysis (units: pCi/L).

Location	Analysis	Number of Results	Mean Activity	Expected Laboratory Precision	Range of Results	Mean Range	Std Error of the Range	Normalized Range
N8T	Gross Alpha	2	1.3	5	1.4	5.6	4.2	0.2
Well	Gross Beta	4	16,800	840	5,200	1729.6	739.1	5.7[b]
	^{3}H	4	102,000	10,200	123,100	21,002	8,974.9	12.4[b]
(-1 Outlier)		3	72,900	7,290	10,900	12,342	6,479.5	0.9
	^{90}Sr	4	7,750	390	1,820	803	343.2	4.0[b]
	^{60}Co	5	50	5	12.9	11.6	4.3	1.3
	^{106}Ru	2	11	5	5	5.6	4.3	0.9
	^{125}Sb	4	38	5	13.7	10.3	4.4	1.8
Spring	Gross Alpha	2	0.3	5	0.17	5.6	4.3	0.0
Rm9.3	Gross Beta	4	52	5	32	10.3	4.4	5.9[b]
	^{3}H	4	112,000	11,200	15,000	23,060	9,854.9	0.6
	^{90}Sr	2	0.26	a				
	^{60}Co	5	35	5	11	11.6	4.3	0.9
	^{106}Ru	3	12	5	6	8.5	4.4	0.7
Ferry	Gross Alpha	2	0.36	5	0.27	5.6	4.3	0.1
Ldg	Gross Beta	4	9.2	5	28	10.3	4.4	5.0[b]
	^{3}H	2	-24	a				
	^{90}Sr	2	3.7	1.5	7	1.7	1.3	5.1[b]
	^{60}Co	2	0.08	a				
Spring	Gross Alpha	3	3.3	5	2.8	8.5	4.4	0.3
Rm28.2	Gross Beta	4	80	5	140	10.3	4.4	30.5[b]
	^{3}H	4	140,000	14,000	23,000	28,826	12,318.3	0.8
	^{90}Sr	2	0.2	a				
	^{60}Co	3	4.2	a				
	^{137}Cs	2	-0.1	a				
Spring	Gross Alpha	3	10	5	9	8.5	4.4	1.1
Rm42.2	Gross Beta	4	16	5	16	10.3	4.4	2.3
	^{3}H	3	200	280	140	474	248.9	0.3
	^{90}Sr	3	60	3	180	5.1	2.7	65.8[b]
(-1 Outlier)		2	0.7	a				
	^{137}Cs	2	0.2	a				
	U-Total	2	9.9	6	0.46	6.8	5.1	0.1

[a]No expected laboratory precision values available.
[b]Exceeds the upper control limit of three standard deviations.

REFERENCES

ASTM. 1976. Manual on Presentation of Data and Control Chart Analysis, STP 15D. American Society for Testing and Materials, Lancaster, PA.

EPA. 1978. Environmental Radioactivity Laboratory Intercomparison Studies Program 1978-1979, EPA-600/4-78-032. U.S. Environmental Protection Agency, Las Vegas, NV.

Jaquish, R. E and R. R. Kinnison. 1984. U.S. Department of Energy Quality Assessment Program Data Evaluation Report, PNL-5059. Pacific Northwest Laboratory, Richland, WA.

LAND RECLAMATION AT THE BASALT WASTE ISOLATION PROJECT

C. A. Brandt and W. H. Rickard, Jr.

Pacific Northwest Laboratory, Richland, Washington

Key Words: *Reclamation, native plants*

ABSTRACT

Between 1976 and 1987, the U.S. Department of Energy (DOE) conducted extensive studies to evaluate Hanford as a potential site for a commercial nuclear waste repository (Basalt Waste Isolation Project). In October, 1987, all repository activities at Hanford except reclamation were terminated. DOE made the commitment to restore areas disturbed by repository studies, as nearly as practicable, to original conditions. Lands previously denuded of plants are being planted with native grasses and shrubs. The objective is to stabilize soil against wind and water erosion and to restore habitat suitable for native wildlife.

INTRODUCTION

The U.S. Department of Energy's Hanford Site occupies 1400 km² of semiarid land in southeastern Washington. Between 1976 and 1987, portions of the site were intensively studied as a possible location for a high-level radioactive-waste geological repository (Basalt Waste Isolation Project). In December, 1987, all repository-related activities except land reclamation were stopped. Land reclamation was initiated to establish a cover of native plants to resist wind and water erosion of soil and to provide habitat suitable for native wildlife.

During the years of study, land was bared of vegetation at numerous boreholes, an Exploratory Shaft Facility (ESF), and a Near Surface Test Facility (NSTF) at the western end of Gable Mountain (Figure 1). At NSTF, three adits were mined into the north face of Gable Mountain. Following site closure, the adits were backfilled and sealed. The surrounding land was recontoured to approximate the original slope shape and steepness and covered with a thin layer of imported soil. Artificial outcrops of native stones were arranged to simulate the appearance of the surrounding area. Because the ESF and boreholes were on level or gently sloping land, vegetation around each borehole was scraped away, and the bare area was covered with a layer of pit-run gravel. Following site closure, the gravel was removed to the level of the native soil.

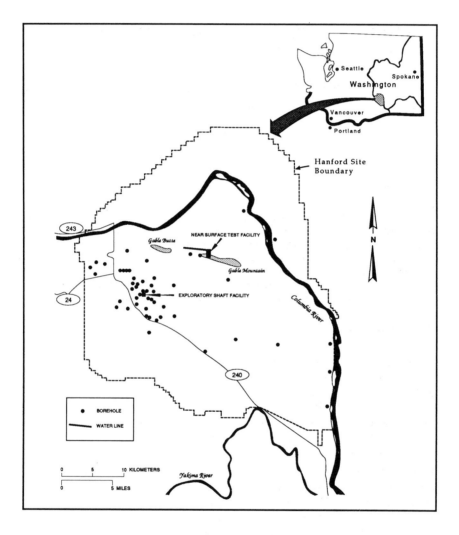

Figure 1. Distribution of boreholes and Near Surface Test Facility on Gable Mountain, U.S. Department of Energy's Hanford Site, southeastern Washington.

RECLAMATION

We visited the reclamation sites to determine species composition and relative abundance of native plants on nearby relatively undisturbed ground. Each reclamation area was assigned to one of five major native plant habitat types: big sagebrush/Sandberg bluegrass, spiny hopsage/ Sandberg bluegrass, stiff sage/Sandberg bluegrass, bitterbrush/needle and thread grass, big sagebrush/bluebunch wheatgrass. Stiff sage/ Sandberg bluegrass is restricted to stony soil on Gable Mountain; the other habitat-types are widespread on silt loam or sandy loam soils.

Sandberg bluegrass, the most widely distributed grass, occurred in 21 of 23 study plots, and canopy cover ranged between 3 and 82%. The amount of cover varied with habitat type and land use history prior to 1943, when much of the land was grazed by cattle and sheep. Decades of overgrazing encouraged the spread of alien cheatgrass at the expense of weakened native grasses (Daubenmire, 1970). However, even after 45 yr without livestock grazing, native grasses on the Hanford Site have been slow to recolonize areas dominated by cheatgrass (Rickard and Vaughan, 1988).

In 1988, Sandberg bluegrass, needle and thread grass, Indian ricegrass, and bottlebrush squirreltail were selected to seed the prepared borehole sites and the ESF. Seed beds were prepared by disking and tacking chopped wheat straw into the surface to help hold the soil against wind erosion until the plants became established. Seeding was done in the autumn, using a furrowing drill.

Big sagebrush was hand-planted as tubelings on three of the borehole sites in February and March, 1989. Mortality within the first 6 months was between 3.5% and 57%. Non-native weedy annuals, especially cheatgrass and Russian thistle, invaded the borehole sites and competed with the planted grasses for space, water, and nutrients. Thus, on future reclamation sites, weeds should be suppressed by applications of selective herbicides to assist in establishing native species.

ACKNOWLEDGMENT

This work was supported by the U.S. Department of Energy under Contract DE-AC06-76RLO 1830.

REFERENCES

Daubenmire, R. 1970. Steppe vegetation of Washington. *Wash. Agric. Expt. Sta. Tech. Bull.* 62.

Rickard, W. H. and B. E. Vaughan. 1988. Plant community characteristics and responses, pp. 109-179. In: Shrub Steppe Balance and Change in a Semi-Arid Ecosystem, W. H. Rickard et al. (eds.). Elsevier, Amsterdam.

ESTIMATED EXPOSURES FROM A POSTULATED ACCIDENT, USING PROPELLER AND SUPERSONIC WIND DATA

S. J. Hu,[1] H. Katagiri,[2] and H. Kobayashi[2]

[1]School of Physics, Universiti Sains Malaysia, Penang, Malaysia

[2]Tokai Research Establishment, Japan Atomic Energy Research Institute, Tokai, Japan

Key Words: *Adult thyroid exposure dose, whole-body gamma exposure, postulated accident, wind data*

ABSTRACT

The propeller anemometer widely used in environmental wind monitoring does not yield accurate readings at low wind speed. Diffusion of radioactive materials released to the atmosphere depends on wind speed and direction, and atmospheric stability. Therefore, low wind speeds and directions must be accurately measured using a supersonic anemometer, which determines wind speeds as low as 0.01 m/sec.

INTRODUCTION

The objective of our analysis is to compare adult thyroid exposure doses and external whole-body gamma-ray exposures for a postulated accident with a 1-hr effective release time, calculated using supersonic and propeller wind data obtained over a period of 1 yr in the Japan Atomic Energy Research Institute (JAERI), Tokai.

METHODS

A standard Gaussian plume equation was used to calculate air concentration. The atmospheric stability was classified by the Pasquill-Maede method. For radiation dose calculation, we used the maximum x/Q and D/Q values of 97% of annual cumulative frequency from 16 downwind directions.

Estimates of adult thyroid exposure were sufficiently accurate when based on the contributions of individual iodine nuclides without considering their decay, and when using the supersonic wind data without modifying the assumed mean wind speed for calm conditions.

For external whole-body gamma-ray exposure, accurate and realistic estimates should be based on the contributions of individual radionuclides with their decay considered, using supersonic wind data for atmospheric dispersion analysis.

For wind speed ≤ 1 m/sec, readings obtained with a propeller anemometer were 0.5 m/sec less than those obtained with the supersonic anemometer. The average air concentrations and ground-level gamma exposure rates resulting from routine releases from a nuclear facility are therefore overestimated when calculated using wind data obtained with a propeller anemometer. Low wind speeds during calm periods affect average air concentrations and calculated gamma exposure rates. If the number of calm periods is high, low wind speeds and the appropriate directions should be used to analyze radionuclide dispersion (Hu et al., 1989).

RESULTS

Estimated dose to adult thyroids that allow for decay of iodine in nuclear facility effluents (^{131}I, [132]I, [133]I, [134]I and [135]I) were obtained using both a propeller anemometer and a supersonic anemometer at wind speeds of < 0.5 m/sec and < 0.1 m/sec (calm conditions) (Table 1). Dose factors for iodine were taken from ICRP (1979). The source terms for iodine, xenon, and krypton were obtained from the inventory of the JAERI Nuclear Fuel Cycle Safety Engineering Research Facility.

Table 1. Adult thyroid gamma doses (mrem) from release of iodine in nuclear facility effluents, with and without decay considered. Data calculated using both propeller and supersonic anemometers.

Iodine	Using Propeller Anemometer	Supersonic Anemometer (wind speed < 0.5 m/s)	Supersonic Anemometer (wind speed < 0.1 m/s)
Decay considered	20.35	19.01	18.99
Decay not considered	21.43	20.17	19.84

External whole-body gamma exposures resulting from release of xenon and krypton in nuclear plant effluents (allowing for decay of the nuclides) and exposure to rare gases, calculated from the two wind data sets, are given in Table 2. Isotopes considered were ^{131m}Xe, ^{133}Xe, ^{133m}Xe, ^{135}Xe, ^{135m}Xe, ^{137}Xe, ^{138}Xe, ^{139}Xe, ^{85m}Kr, ^{85}Kr, ^{87}Kr, ^{88}Kr, ^{89}Kr, and ^{90}Kr.

Table 2. External whole-body gamma dose (mrem) from release of xenon, krypton, and rare gases in nuclear facility effluents. Data calculated using both propeller and supersonic anemometers.

Anemometer Type	Xe	Kr	Total (Xe + Kr)	Rare Gases
Propeller	6.36	6.81	13.17	25.86
Supersonic (wind speed < 0.5 m/s)	5.74	6.01	11.75	23.51

Estimated adult thyroid doses were slightly higher (7%) using the propeller anemometer wind data. Decay of the individual radionuclide and changing the assumed mean wind speed for calm conditions to 0.1 m/sec had little effect on estimated doses (partly because we chose to use the maximum 97% value of x/Q). Thus, estimates of adult thyroid exposure for a postulated accident are sufficiently accurate without considering radionuclide decay or changing the assumed mean wind speed during calm periods.

External whole-body gamma exposure estimated from wind data obtained with a propeller anemometer was also higher (~11%) than from data obtained using a supersonic anemometer. Estimated external whole-body gamma exposure from rare gases was twice that calculated when the decay of xenon and krypton were considered. Therefore, to estimate a more accurate and realistic external whole-body gamma exposure for a postulated accident, decay of individual nuclides should be considered, and wind data for dispersion analysis should be obtained using a supersonic anemometer.

REFERENCE

Hu, S.J., H. Katagiri, and H. Kobayashi. 1989. JAERI-M 89-041 Report, Analysis of the Wind Data and Estimation of the Resultant Doses from the Supersonic Anemometer. Japanese Atomic Energy Research Institute, Tokai, Japan.

ICRP. (1979). Limits for Intakes of Radionuclides by Workers, Publication 30. International Commission on Radiation Protection, Washington, DC.

MONITORING RADIONUCLIDES IN MARINE ORGANISMS

T. Ishii, M. Matsuba, M. Kurosawa, and T. Koyanagi

National Institute of Radiological Sciences, Ibaraki, Japan

Key Words: *ICP-MS, high mass elements, marine organisms, branchial heart*

ABSTRACT

Concentration of stable elements corresponding to important radionuclides was determined by inductively coupled plasma atomic emission spectrometry (ICP-AES) and inductively coupled plasma mass spectrometry (ICP-MS) for various marine organisms to find indicator organisms for environmental monitoring. Both analytical techniques indicated linearity over a range of concentrations covering 2-4 orders of magnitude. Detection limits of elements by ICP-MS were 10 or 100 times higher than those of ICP-AES, although the precision and accuracy of ICP-MS was slightly inferior to that of ICP-AES. For quantitative analysis of elements with medium mass numbers (chromium, manganese, iron, nickel, copper, zinc, etc.), matrix interferences in ICP-MS were caused mainly by overlaps of spectra from coexisting elements in biological samples. The presence of background ions from atmosphere, water, and argon plasma interfered with determination of some isotopes. Most elements of high mass number could not be determined by ICP-AES because of its poor detection limits, whereas ICP-MS indicated high sensitivity and low background for elements of interest. We used ICP-MS analysis to determine the specific accumulation of certain elements in organs or tissues of 30 marine organisms.

INTRODUCTION

Bioaccumulation of high concentrations of certain elements is considered a useful indicator for monitoring radionuclides in the marine environment. To find effective indicator organisms, we are analyzing for stable elements corresponding to radionuclides in various marine organisms by means of atomic absorption spectrometry, neutron activation analysis, inductively coupled plasma atomic emission spectroscopy, and particle-induced x-ray emission.

METHOD

We evaluated the use of inductively coupled plasma mass spectro-metry (ICP-MS system VG Elemental PlasmaQuad PQ2 system; VG

Elemental, England) for determining the high mass elements (140-240 amu). The apparatus showed multielement detection capability (more than 50 elements), low detection limits (10-100 ppt), wide dynamic ranges (six orders of magnitude), good precision (relative standard deviation = 1-2%), satisfactory accuracy, and the ability to directly determine isotopes.

RESULTS

Figure 1 shows the mass spectrum of rare earth elements in the branchial heart of an octopus *(Octopus vulgaris)*. Ion peaks, e.g., those for lanthanum, cerium, and praseodymium, were clearly visible. By studying other marine species we found that the branchial heart of cephalopods specifically accumulates rare earth elements. The highest concentration of cerium was in the branchial heart of *O. vulgaris* and ranged from 160 to 900 ng/g wet wt (430-4200 ng/g dry wt). Because the concentration of uranium in Japanese coastal sea water was 3-4 ng/ml (Table 1), the concentration factor for uranium in the branchial heart was calculated to be 10^3; the radioactivity of ^{238}U in that tissue was as high as 62 mBq/g. Table 1 also shows uranium concentrations in other marine organisms.

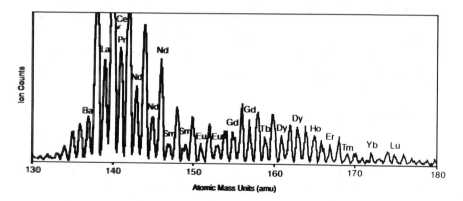

Figure 1. Mass spectra of rare earth elements obtained by inductively coupled plasma mass spectrometry (ICP-MS) for the branchial heart of *Octopus vulgaris;* amu = atomic mass units.

DISCUSSION

The branchial heart of cephalopods also accumulates other elements, for example, cobalt (Ueda et al., 1979), as well as the actinide elements

(Guary et al., 1981). Thus, we believe this organism is an important indicator of marine pollution by radionuclides.

Table 1. Concentrations of ^{238}U in marine organisms and in Japanese coastal sea water.

Species	Organ or Tissue	Concentrations (ng/g wet wt)	Concentrations (μBq/g wet wt)
Fish			
Paralichthys olivaceus	Muscle	0.32	4.0
Lateolabrax japonicus	Muscle	0.25	3.1
Molluscs			
Octopus vulgaris	Arm muscle	0.25	3.1
	Liver	85	1050
	Branchial heart	5000	62000
Mytilus edulis	Soft part	16	200
Algae			
Hizikia fusiforme	Whole body	500[a]	6200[a]
Ulva pertusa	Whole body	10[a]	120[a]
Sea water		3-4 ng/ml	36-48 μBq/ml

[a]Uranium concentrations in algae expressed as dry weight.

REFERENCES

Ueda, T., M. Nakahara, T. Ishii, Y. Suzuki, and H. Suzuki. 1979. Amounts of trace elements in marine cephalopods. *Nihon Hoshasen Eikyo Gakkai (J. Radiat. Res.)* *20*:338-342.

Guary, J. C., J. J. W. Higgo, R. D. Cherry, and M. Heyraud. 1981. High concentrations of transuranics and natural radioactive elements in the branchial hearts of the cephalopod *Octopus vulgaris*. *Mar. Ecol. Prog. Ser.* *4*:123-126.

CHANGES IN HANFORD ENVIRONMENTAL MONITORING, 1957-1988

R. E. Jaquish

Pacific Northwest Laboratory, Richland, Washington

Key Words: *Environmental, Hanford, monitoring, sampling*

ABSTRACT

Environmental monitoring has been conducted at Hanford since 1944. Before 1957, monitoring efforts concentrated on field measurements and were not directed toward dose assessment. Since 1957, efforts have included estimates of potential radiation exposure to the public as well as field measurements and sample analyses. Changes in the number and types of operating facilities over the years have changed the quantity and types of radioactive effluents released to the environment and, therefore, the potential radiation exposure of the public. The highest radiation doses occurred between 1957 and 1970; the maximum was reported in 1963. Although radiation doses decreased from the early 1970s to the present, the monitoring effort has generally increased. The most significant changes were in sampling locations, radionuclides measured, and the variety of samples collected.

INTRODUCTION

This paper reviews the Hanford environmental monitoring program over the period 1957 to 1989 (Andersen, 1959; Jaquish and Bryce, 1989) and describes changes in the program relative to changes in operations and radiation dose to the public.

AIR MONITORING

Although site operations and radiation dose to the maximally exposed individual declined, the number of air monitoring stations increased from 13 to 29. In 1957, there were 13 offsite stations, four in communities within 10 km of the Hanford Site, two were about 50 km from the Site, and seven were 100 to 1000 km from the Site. The latter included stations as far away as Klamath Falls, Oregon, and Boise, Idaho, which were needed to evaluate the contribution of fallout from the Nevada Test Site. By 1965, the farthest station was in Pendleton, Oregon, about 100 km from Hanford. By 1988, the distribution of stations reflected a pattern of concentric rings around the Site: 14 along the site perimeter, 9 in nearby communities, and 6 in communities up to 80 km away.

In 1957, air samples were routinely monitored for gross beta activity and for [131]I. Since then, the number of air analyses has increased as new methods, such as gamma spectroscopy, became available and as interest in low levels of specific radionuclides intensified. With the restart of the Plutonium-Uranium Extraction (PUREX) plant in 1983, special sampling and analytical procedures were initiated to monitor ^{85}Kr, ^{14}C, ^{3}H, and ^{129}I. Sample sizes and analytical techniques were also modified to measure ambient levels of ^{90}Sr, ^{137}Cs, ^{239,240}Pu, and uranium in the environment.

WATER, FISH, WATERFOWL, AND VEGETATION

As the eight original Hanford Site reactors were shut down, the Columbia River became a less significant contributor to radiation dose. The number of surface-water monitoring stations has remained relatively constant, while their locations and the radionuclides of interest have changed. In 1965, the Columbia River was monitored from Hanford to Bonneville Dam, 300 km away, primarily for short-lived radionuclides (^{24}Na, ^{32}P, ^{131}I, and ^{239}Np). In 1988, radionuclides of interest included ^{3}H, ^{90}Sr, ^{129}I, ^{239,240}Pu, and uranium.

In 1965, more than 1000 fish (11 species) were collected from the Columbia River between Priest Rapids and McNary dams and analyzed. In contrast, only 20 fish (2 species) were collected in 1988. Likewise, in 1965, nine species of ducks, geese, and coots were collected and analyzed, compared with one species in 1988.

In 1959, vegetation was collected from the Idaho border, near Spokane, to as far south as Portland, Oregon. In 1988, farm products were collected closer to the site, background stations were located approximately 80 km from the site, and the number of samples increased.

SUMMARY

The overall level of monitoring at Hanford increased from 1957 to 1988. Program content has changed to reflect changing conditions and concerns. In 1988, more emphasis was on air monitoring and less on water, fish, and waterfowl monitoring. Current efforts focus on areas close to Hanford because most effluents cannot be detected beyond the site perimeter.

ACKNOWLEDGMENT

Work supported by the U.S. Department of Energy under Contract DE-AC06-76RLO 1830.

REFERENCES

Andersen, B. V. 1959. Hanford Environmental Monitoring Annual Report 1958, HW-61676. Hanford Atomic Products Operation, Richland, WA.

Jaquish, R. E. and R. W. Bryce. 1989. Hanford Site Environmental Report for Calendar Year 1988, PNL-6825. NTIS, Springfield, VA.

CONCENTRATION OF TECHNETIUM BY MARINE ORGANISMS

T. Koyanagi, Y. Suzuki, R. Nakamura, and M. Nakahara

National Institute of Radiological Sciences, Ibaraki, Japan

Key Words: *Concentration factor, technetium, marine organisms, indicator organisms*

ABSTRACT

Accumulation and excretion of technetium by marine organisms were observed in radioisotope tracer experiments to determine concentration factors for estimating radiation dose to humans from radioactive pollution of marine environments. Marine fish, crustaceans, mollusks, echinoderms, and seaweeds were reared in sea water labeled with ^{95m}Tc to observe uptake from sea water. These organisms were then transferred into unlabeled sea water for depuration experiments. Concentration factors were calculated from uptake and excretion rates. Also considered was the contribution of food-chain transfer of technetium, observed by administering labeled seaweeds to mollusks or echinoderms. Low accumulations were shown by fish, crustaceans, pelecypods and cephalopods, whereas high concentration factors were observed in gastropods and seaweeds. Species specificity or specific accumulation in special organs or tissues was not evident except in seaweed, where the difference was clearly species-associated. Relatively high rates of technetium retention were observed in the organisms administered labeled seaweed. The higher concentrations observed in gastropods, compared to those in pelecypods, were thought to result from different feeding habits. The adaptability of some species as indicator organisms for monitoring ^{99}Tc in sea water was recognized, but the contribution of technetium to radiation dose was considered insignificant.

BACKGROUND

Marine organisms were observed; concentration factors of technetium were determined, and their use as indicator organisms for monitoring ^{99}Tc in the environment was examined. Technetium-99 is introduced to the marine environment by radioactive fallout from nuclear weapons tests, effluents from nuclear facilities, and from disposal of medical waste. Although the biological and geochemical behavior of technetium in some marine environments was reviewed (Beasley and Lorz, 1986), there are few such data for Japan (Hirano et al., 1989). Concentration factors for technetium recommended by the International Atomic Energy Agency (IAEA, 1985) are 3×10^1 for fish and 1×10^3 for crustaceans, mollusks, and macroalgae, but large fluctuations are also shown for each species. We previously reported high accumulation of manganese by a species of marine bivalves *(Cyclosunetta menstrualis)* (Ishii et al., 1986). Thus, we studied the bioconcentration of technetium to identify indicator organisms.

METHODS

A marine fish *(Chrysophrys major)*; a crab *(Ovalips punctatus)*; shellfish *(Meretrix lamarckii, Gomphina melanaegis, Cyclosunetta menstrualis, Haliotis discus)*; an octopus *(Octopus vulgaris)*; a sea urchin *(Strongylocentrotus nudus)*; and green, brown, and red algae were reared in sea water labeled with [95m]Tc. The organisms were then transferred to unlabeled sea water for loss experiments. Radioactivity of whole body or organs was measured to calculate concentration factors and to examine the distribution of technetium in the organisms. In addition, radiolabeled algae were fed to sea urchins and abalone to observe technetium accumulation in food chains.

RESULTS

Fish, crab, bivalves, and octopus had low accumulations of technetium; gastropods and algae had high concentration factors. Species specificity was not evident in technetium accumulation or excretion by bivalves (Figure 1) but was clear in algae (Figure 2). Five species of brown algae showed concentration factors ranging from 900 to 35,000, while those of green and red algae were from 1 to 4. Relatively high retention rates were observed in the feeding experiments, suggesting significant food-chain transfer of technetium. The brown alga, *Sargassum*, was the best indicator organism for monitoring ^{99}Tc because of its high concentration factor and ubiquitous distribution.

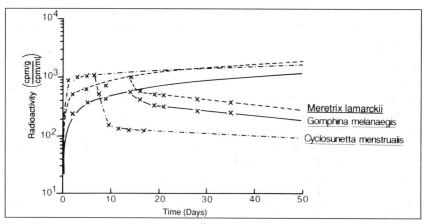

Figure 1. Accumulation and excretion of [95m]Tc by mollusks; cpm/g = counts per minute per gram.

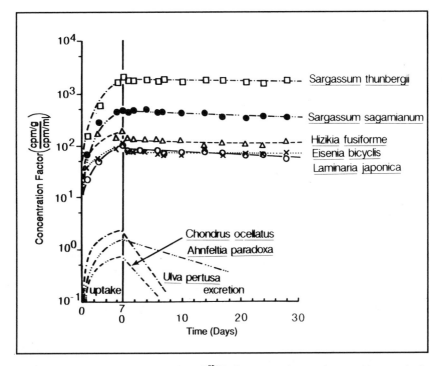

Figure 2. Accumulation and excretion of ^{95m}Tc by seaweeds; cpm/g = counts per minute per gram.

REFERENCES

Beasley, T. M. and H. V. Lorz. 1986. A review of the biological and geochemical behavior of technetium in the marine environment. *J. Environ. Radioact.* 3:1-22.

Hirano, S., M. Matsuba, and H. Kamada. 1989. The determination of ^{99}Tc in marine algae. *Radioisotopes* 38:186-189.

IAEA. 1985. Sediment kds and Concentration Factors for Radionuclides in the Marine Environment, Technical Report Series No. 247. International Atomic Energy Agency, Vienna.

Ishii, T., K. Ikuta, T. Otake, M. Hara, M. Ishikawa, and T. Koyanagi. 1986. High accumulation of elements in the kidney of the marine bivalve *Cyclosunetta menstrualis. Bull. Jpn. Soc. Sci. Fish. 52*:147-154.

ASSESSMENT OF MONITORING PROCEDURES FOR AIRBORNE PLUTONIUM PARTICLES IN THE WORKPLACE

G. Langer

EG&G, Rocky Flats Plant, Golden, Colorado

Key Words: *Air tracer, contamination, dispersion, plutonium*

ABSTRACT

Recent U.S. Department of Energy regulations require upgrades of fixed airheads and selective air monitors (SAAM) to verify that the lowest possible radiation exposures are achieved. Airheads establish the level of routine worker exposure, and SAAM gives an alarm if confinement fails. Monitoring effectiveness was systematically determined to provide input on worker protection decisions. Airflow patterns were studied in the workplace with an air tracer system that simulated glove-box leaks. The aerosol tracer was tracked by laser particle counters in real time in the 0.5- to 5- and >5-μm-diameter ranges. Flow in the entire room and in specific areas was compared to the response of fixed airhead samplers and SAAM. Particle inhomogeneity near fixed airhead samplers limited the usefulness of exposure estimates. Increasing the number of airheads did not effectively improve estimation of worker exposure. For critical work, lapel samplers provide effective exposure data based on tracer tests. Tracer tests showed that the SAAM alarm nearest a simulated leak may not go off first. The SAAM should be located at each exhaust to assure room coverage. A portable SAAM is recommended for unusual operations such as box modifications. The SAAM should be located near a local air flow in combination with a tracer particle counter.

INTRODUCTION

Airflow patterns were studied in a plutonium manufacturing room at the U.S. Department of Energy (DOE) Rocky Flats Plant (Golden, Colorado) to verify that both exposure assessment and confinement failure procedures were in compliance with recent DOE orders. Because the established smoke candle procedure for air tracing does not provide quantitative data, a new tracer procedure was developed.

METHODS

The tracer aerosol was produced by atomizing a corn syrup solution. In the test, dry particles in the 0.1- to 15-μm range simulated potential plutonium particle leaks at an airflow rate of 5.4 x 10^8 particles (ptcls)/

303

min. The aerosol was visible only at the point of release and had no adverse impact on the environment. Tests were conducted during normal work conditions. The tracer, detected with laser particle counters (LPC) in the 0.5- to 5- and >5-μm ranges, had to be at above-background aerosol levels. I placed eight LPC at room exhausts, which are continuous alpha-monitoring (CAM) sites. Supply air entered through upward-pointing diffusers near the ceiling. The tracer was released from floor, glove-port, and glove-box-top levels.

Figure 1 shows glove boxes, LPC locations, tracer release sites, and tracer concentrations for two tests that illustrate the dispersion extremes. In the figure, the two upper numbers are tracer concentrations (ptcls/L) or dispersion factors (DF) for the 0.5- to 5- and >5-μm ranges, normalized to correspond to a release (leak) of 1.0 x 10^6 ptcls/min in each range. The pair of numbers on the left are for a release from Site 2, those on the right from Site 5. The lower numbers indicate, for the two size ranges, the time (min) for the particles to reach a given LPC.

RESULTS

There were no well-defined flow patterns from release points to the nearest exhausts. Instead, turbulent eddies throughout the room mixed the tracer upward and laterally (i.e., supply air inlets were decoupled from the exhausts). Vertical tracer distribution was relatively uniform. The tracer showed only limited dispersion from Site 5, an open area, where most tracer flowed to a nearby wall exhaust.

The 0.5- to 5-μm particles were relatively evenly distributed throughout the room from Site 2 and most other sites, ranging in concentration from 13 to 100 ptcls/L. The >5-μm particles showed wider spread and relatively lower concentrations (1 to 42 ptcls/L), indicative of removal by deposition. The time for first detection of a release varied from only 1 to 6 min and 1.3 to 12 min for 0.5- to 5- and >5-μm particles, respectively. The release spread rapidly in all directions.

Quantitative airflow characterization is desirable for good practice. Established air tracer procedures must be improved; for example, particle deposition should be considered. For some releases, particles >5 μm did not reach several LPC; such leaks would not be detected unless collected by surface wipes. Established procedures do not quantify how fast contaminants reach various CAM. As we have shown, this speed is not usually a function of distance. Although the effect of worker activity on contaminant dispersal is significant, it is not defined by smoke candles, the usual monitoring procedure. Such data merely establish when personal samplers should be used.

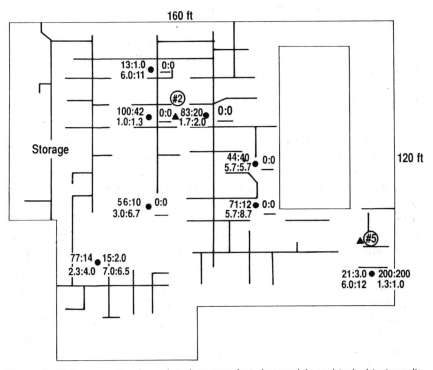

Figure 1. Air tracer system in a plutonium manufacturing module and typical test results at high air flow. Solid lines indicate glove box outline. ●, Laser particle counter; ▲, tracer release site. Dispersion factor (DF) = number particles/L found from tracer release of 10^6 particles/min in 0.5- to 5- and >5-μm particle size range. Time (T) = number minutes elapsed until tracer was detected for 0.5- to 5- and >5-μm particle size range. Example of test results (#2 site in figure): $DF_{0.5}$: $DF_{>5}$ 13:1.0); $T_{0.5}$: $T_{>5}$ (6.0:11). Test results at site #5 in figure: $DF_{0.5}$: $DF_{>5}$ (21:3.0); $T_{0.5}$: $T_{>5}$ (6.0:12).

Optimization of room air change (AC) rate is also required by the new DOE orders for maximum worker safety. The new air tracer procedure provides quantitative data on contaminant spread, concentration, and rate of dispersal. In the room depicted in Figure 1, increasing air flow from 2.9 to 5.1 AC/hr increased the average tracer particle concentration by a factor of two. Because of dilution, a twofold decrease would be expected for the higher flow. In contrast, particle deposition at the higher AC rate decreased by a factor of four. However, at lower flow, stagnation was evident in some glove-box bays.

In the room shown, flow patterns remained stable. Repeated tests showed that after 6 months, no statistically significant changes took place for time to first response to tracer release, time to reach equilibrium concentration, and equilibrium concentration. Clearance of the tracer was not reproducible, perhaps because particles originated from many points rather than from one point, as in the original release.

CONCLUSIONS

To verify that worker exposure is properly measured and that leaks are detected, the number and locations of airhead samplers should be evaluated. Measurements must be related to breathing zone exposure. Particle deposition can bias airhead data. In our tests, tracer concentrations from a simulated leak fluctuated widely at the source; but only a short distance away, turbulent mixing caused lower but more uniform particle concentrations. For exposure/inventory measurements, one airhead for every 30 ft of glove-box frontage seems adequate. Personal samplers are recommended for critical operations.

Optimal location of CAM for early warning was studied with 18 releases that simulated leaks at different sites. Only one release site elicited a response at all LPC. Overall, 30% of the LPC did not respond, but these were not always the same devices. All exhausts should have a CAM for maximum safety, because locations of leaks cannot be detected from the response patterns of LPC.

DEVELOPING DATA QUALITY OBJECTIVES FOR MEASURED AND DERIVED HYDROGEOLOGIC PARAMETERS

D. R. Dahl, S. P. Luttrell, J. V. Borghese, R. Schalla, and D. J. Bates

Pacific Northwest Laboratory, Richland, Washington

Key Words: *Data Quality Objective (DQO), Quality Assurance (QA), aquifer, transmissivity*

ABSTRACT

Data quality objectives (DQO), or acceptable levels of uncertainty, should be established for hydrogeologic parameters to guide selection of data collection techniques that cost-effectively meet data needs. The hydrogeologic parameters "transmissivity" (T) and "storativity" (S), typically derived from measurements made during aquifer tests, are used in designing and estimating costs for remedial action alternatives. The DQO for T and S should be established based on the project objectives and hydrogeologic setting.

Before DQO for T and S can be established, their relationship to uncertainties in the measured values used to calculate them (i.e., discharge rate, water level, time, and distance between wells) must be understood. This is essential to determine whether a given set of DQO for T and S are viable, given limitations in measurement techniques employed during aquifer testing. We are evaluating the sensitivity of T and S to these uncertainties (measurement errors). Preliminary results indicate that T is more sensitive to these uncertainties than S and that the greatest effect occurs when uncertainty in water-level measurements increase. Higher T values are more sensitive to uncertainties in the measured values than lower T values. Variations in measured values for water level and time have little effect on S.

INTRODUCTION

Data quality objectives (DQO) are qualitative and quantitative statements concerning the required quality of data used as the basis for, or to support, decisions (EPA, 1987). DQO, established during project planning, are typically expressed in terms of precision, accuracy, representativeness, completeness, and comparability (PARCC). DQO aid in the selection of appropriate data collection techniques to cost-effectively meet data needs.

U.S. Environmental Protection Agency (EPA) policy is that DQO be established for all monitoring and measurement projects (EPA, 1983).

Historically, EPA guidance has focused on DQO for chemical parameters; development of DQO for other information needs has not been specified. We discuss here the factors to consider in defining DQO needs for hydrogeologic parameters determined by aquifer testing and how these objectives are affected by uncertainty in measured values. We will focus on objectives for accuracy.

DQO FOR HYDROGEOLOGIC PARAMETERS

Pumping tests are conducted primarily to determine an aquifer's transmissivity (T) and storativity (S) properties. Knowledge of the distribution of these properties is needed to select and design appropriate remedial alternatives for contaminated ground water. The acceptable levels of uncertainty (DQO) of these hydrogeologic parameters may vary, depending on the intended use of the data. Before DQO for T and S can be established, their relationship to uncertainties in the measured values used to calculate them (i.e., discharge rate, water level, time, and distance between wells) must be understood. Sources of uncertainty in measured values include inaccurate measurement devices, lack of care in making measurements, mechanical problems in test equipment, and poor well design or construction (e.g., cascading water, insufficient well development).

The effect of uncertainty in measured values on estimating T and S was evaluated for a pumping well, assuming an ideal aquifer. A high T of 100,000 ft²/day and a low T of 500 ft²/day were assumed for uncertainty analysis. Using the Cooper-Jacob method (Cooper and Jacob, 1946) and an assumed discharge rate (Q), a hypothetical data set was generated for the assumed T values. The accuracy objectives used for drawdown were ±0.04 and ±0.2 ft, and for time and discharge, ±5 sec and ±10%, respectively. These values were then altered on the hypothetical data set, using the extremes of the accuracy DQO. Slopes of the data lines were adjusted to yield the greatest change. The slope was determined graphically for each case, and the resulting T was determined. The greatest uncertainties in T estimates occurred using the data set generated assuming high T. An uncertainty in the drawdown of ±0.2 ft resulted in the calculated T ranging from 38% less to 460% greater than the assumed value. The addition of a 10% uncertainty in discharge rate resulted in a range from 44% less to 517% greater than the assumed T. An uncertainty of ±0.04 ft in drawdown, coupled with a 10% uncertainty in the discharge rate, resulted in values from 21% less to 36% greater than the assumed

T. Less apparent variations were noted using the data set generated assuming low T. The most extreme condition occurred with an uncertainty of ±0.20 ft in drawdown and ±10% in discharge rate; results indicated a range from 22% less to 25% greater than the assumed T.

DISCUSSION

These findings indicate the importance of establishing DQO for field measurements before planning and conducting aquifer tests, especially when high-quality hydrogeologic parameters are necessary as, for instance, when designing remedial systems. A calculated T that is 460% greater than the true value, as noted in one case, would likely result in improper design of the system, excessive costs, and/or ineffective remediation. Understanding the relationship between uncertainties in measured values and the hydrogeologic parameters calculated from them is essential.

ACKNOWLEDGMENT

This research was supported by the U.S. Department of Energy under contract DE-AC06-76RLO 1830.

REFERENCES

Cooper, H. H. Jr. and C. E. Jacob. 1946. A generalized graphical method for evaluating formation constants and summarizing well-field history. *Am. Geophys. Union Trans.* 27:526-534.

EPA. 1983. Interim Guidelines and Specifications for Preparing Quality Assurance Project Plans, EPA-600/4-83-004 (QAMS-OO5/8O). U.S. Environmental Protection Agency, Washington, DC.

EPA. 1987. Data Quality Objectives For Remedial Response Activities, Development Process, OSWER 9355.0-7B. U.S. Environmental Protection Agency, Washington, DC.

CONTROL OF SOIL COLUMN DISCHARGES AT THE HANFORD SITE

D. E. McKenney and D. L. Flyckt

Westinghouse Hanford Company, Richland, Washington

Key Words: *Effluents, soil column, discharges, releases*

ABSTRACT

For the past 45 yr, Hanford has used the ion exchange capabilities of soils to dispose of low-level aqueous waste streams. Those that are discharged to the soil column include effluents with very low contamination. Examples of such effluent streams include steam condensates, process cooling waters, and process condensates (evaporator overhead). Currently, 33 waste streams are discharged to the soil column. In 1987, the U.S. Department of Energy issued a plan and schedule to discontinue soil column disposal at Hanford. We will discuss the progress to date in attaining this objective.

INTRODUCTION

When the soil column discharge program began at Hanford, the U.S. Department of Energy (DOE) required that discharge of liquid-waste streams to soil to treat and retain suspended or dissolved radionuclides be discontinued at the earliest date practicable in favor of waste-water treatment and minimization. This policy was implemented through DOE orders, based on relevant federal and state environmental regulations (DOE, 1984). In March, 1987, DOE's Richland Operations Office issued a plan and schedule (DOE, 1987) to discontinue disposal of contaminated liquids into the soil column at Hanford. This plan reflected ongoing work and provided additional direction and coordination. Significant progress has been made toward implementing the plan.

IMPLEMENTATION

Implementation of the plan will be in phases. Thirty-three effluent streams have been selected for priority, based on factors such as radionuclide concentration, waste characteristics, reportable quantities of waste constituents, and life of potential disposal facilities. Phase I streams (19 identified) will have treatment and disposal systems in place prior to 1995. Phase II streams (14 identified) will be addressed as funding and scheduling allow.

METHODS

Evaluations of the best available technologies (BAT) that are economically achievable have been conducted for many contaminated streams. The BAT determination includes four methods for technology evaluation and two methods for determining cost effectiveness. Primary treatment, consisting of a combination of standard unit operations, such as filtration, ion exchange and reverse osmosis, will follow.

Primary treatment will result in a secondary waste stream (spent resins, filtered solids, etc.) and a treated effluent stream. The secondary waste stream will be processed for disposal in the Waste Receiving and Processing Facility. The treated effluent stream (Phases I and II) will be handled by a Treated Effluent Disposal System, consisting of a retention basin, with capabilities for sampling, analysis, and standby treatment. Effluents that meet discharge limits will either be disposed to the river via a National Pollution Discharge Elimination System Permit or to the soil, consistently with state requirements.

ACKNOWLEDGMENT

Work supported by the U.S. Department of Energy under Contract DE-AC06-87RL10930.

REFERENCES

DOE. 1984. Radioactive Waste Management, DOE Order 5820.2. U.S. Department of Energy, Washington, DC.

DOE. 1987. Plan and Schedule to Discontinue Disposal of Contaminated Liquids into the Soil Column at the Hanford Site. U.S. Department of Energy, Richland, WA.

QUALITY ASSURANCE TASK FORCE, AN INTERAGENCY COOPERATIVE APPROACH TO ASSESS QUALITY OF ENVIRONMENTAL DATA

L. Melby Albin, R. R. Mooney, J. L. Erickson, and A. W. Conklin

State of Washington Department of Health, Olympia, Washington

Key Words: *Quality assurance, environmental radiation data, QATF, public health*

ABSTRACT

In 1985, the Washington State Legislature charged the Department of Social and Health Services' Office of Radiation Protection with reviewing, evaluating and improving environmental monitoring programs within the state. Special emphasis was placed on the Hanford Site in Richland. Government and private organizations involved in monitoring radiation effects on the environment were asked to advise and support the State of Washington. Together, these organizations formed the Environmental Radiation Quality Assurance Task Force for the Pacific Northwest.

Data on radiation levels are collected by the various organizations and compared. If findings are not consistent, the Task Force investigates and makes recommendations for long-term solutions. Thus, a system of checks and balances is created, enhancing the credibility of the various monitoring programs. Efficiency in use of resources is increased because overlap and duplication by different monitoring agencies are minimized.

INTRODUCTION

In 1985, the Washington State Legislature authorized the Department of Health (DOH, formerly Social and Health Services) to organize and chair a task force to ensure that environmental radiation data are of the best quality, and to evaluate and improve environmental radiation monitoring programs within the state. Through this regional task force, DOH aims to achieve economical use of resources and encourage input from all interested parties on questions or concerns about environmental radiation monitoring, and to enhance and maintain the credibility of results obtained by all monitoring organizations. Government and private organizations that monitor radiation effects on the environment were asked to advise and support DOH in its duties. Together, these groups formed the Environmental Radiation Quality Assurance Task Force (QATF) of the Pacific

Northwest. Current members include: Washington State Department of Health (chair); Oregon State Health Division; U.S. Department of Energy; Battelle, Pacific Northwest Laboratories; Washington Public Power Supply System; Advanced Nuclear Fuels Corporation; US Ecology Incorporated; U.S. Nuclear Regulatory Commission; U.S. Environmental Protection Agency; Portland General Electric Company; Washington State Public Health Association; Nez Perce Tribe; Confederated Tribes of the Umatilla Indian Reservation; and the Yakima Indian Nation.

Goals established were: to ensure that data collected are accurate and adequate; to coordinate sampling, analyses, and reporting among monitoring programs; and to communicate information to professionals and the public.

One accomplishment of the task force was to sponsor an independent review of regional monitoring programs (DSHS, 1987); the review identified the primary strengths and weaknesses of the programs. Future reviews are planned to evaluate the programs in further detail.

The QATF also established an ongoing data intercomparison project, in which samples are collected, split, and then analyzed by QATF members and a public interest group representative. If results are not consistent, the Task Force evaluates the problem and makes recommendations for long-term solutions.

Through the QATF, efficiency is increased because overlap and duplication by the various monitoring agencies are minimized. This cooperative system of checks and balances improves communication among members and results in enhanced public credibility of environmental radiation monitoring programs in the Pacific Northwest.

REFERENCE

DSHS. 1987. Review of Pacific Northwest Environmental Radiation Monitoring Programs Around Hanford. Environmental Radiation Review Panel, Department of Social and Health Services, State of Washington, Olympia, WA.

ENVIRONMENTAL CHARACTERIZATION TO ASSESS POTENTIAL IMPACTS OF THERMAL DISCHARGE TO THE COLUMBIA RIVER

D. A. Neitzel,[1] D. D. Dauble,[1] T. L. Page,[1] and E. M. Greager[2]

[1]Pacific Northwest Laboratory, Richland, Washington

[2]Westinghouse Hanford Company, Richland, Washington

Key Words: *Thermal impacts, Columbia River, assessment model*

ABSTRACT

Laboratory and field studies were conducted to assess the potential impact of the N-Reactor thermal plume on fish from the Hanford Reach of the Columbia River. Discharge water temperatures were measured over a range of river flows and reactor operating conditions. Data were mathematically modeled to define spatial and thermal characteristics of the plume. Four species of Columbia River fish were exposed to thermal conditions expected in the plume. Exposed fish were subjected to predators and disease organisms to test for secondary effects from thermal stress. Spatial and temporal distribution of anadromous fish in the river near N-Reactor were also evaluated to define location relative to the plume. Potential thermal exposures were insufficient to kill or injure fish during operation of N-Reactor. These studies demonstrate that characterization of hydrological conditions and thermal tolerance can adequately assess potential impacts of a thermal discharge to fish.

INTRODUCTION

We characterized thermal tolerance of selected Columbia River fish in relation to N-Reactor discharge on the Hanford Site (Ecker et al., 1983a,b). Resulting data were used by the U.S. Environmental Protection Agency and the Washington State Department of Ecology to establish thermal discharge limits for an operational permit. The scope of these studies was based, in part, on consultation with state and federal regulatory and management agencies.

METHODS

Thermal tolerance data needed to assess potential impacts of N-Reactor discharge were developed in five steps: (1) plume size and temperature were measured; (2) plume measurements were used to calibrate a

315

hydrologic model; (3) modeling data were used to develop time/ temperature exposures expected in the plume; (4) fish were subjected to thermal exposures and tested for direct and indirect mortalities from increasing temperatures; and (5) the longest and warmest time/ temperature exposures in which all test fish survived were compared with time/temperature exposures expected in the plume.

We tested four species of fish: chinook salmon *(Oncorhynchus tshawytscha)*, coho salmon *(O. kisutch)*, steelhead *(O. mykiss,* formerly *Salmo gairdneri)*, and northern squawfish *(Ptychocheilus oregonesis)*. Fish were placed in a glass aquarium plumbed to receive and discharge water at temperatures that mimicked plume temperatures. Surviving fish were either placed in troughs for 96-hr postexposure observation or were evaluated for potential susceptibility to other environmental stresses. Fish that survived a thermal exposure were subjected to predators (Coutant, 1973) or disease organisms (Poston et al., 1982). Predators were 3- to 4-yr-old rainbow trout *(O. mykiss)*. Disease organisms were *Flexibacter columnaris* or *Yersinia ruckeri*.

Two comparisons were made between test and control groups to determine the time/temperature exposures at which effects might occur: (1) percent survival in thermal tolerance and predation tests, and (2) the time to infection or death in disease tests.

RESULTS

Thermal conditions permitted by the current National Pollutant Discharge Elimination System permit do not cause direct or indirect fish mortalities. To define thermal tolerance, fish were exposed to discharge conditions that could occur only at greater discharge temperatures than currently permitted.

Juvenile chinook salmon in river water at 18°C and 10°C and juvenile coho salmon, steelhead, and northern squawfish in river water at 10°C showed 100% survival in tests simulating river flow as low as 1020 m³/sec. The initial test temperature in the simulated plume was 33°C, which is about three times the elevation in temperature expected to occur below the outfall. Other river flows up to 5000 m³/sec were also tested and helped define conditions where 100% of test fish survive.

COMPARISONS BETWEEN SURVIVAL CURVES AND EXPECTED DISCHARGE TEMPERATURES

The time/temperature exposure at which 100% of test fish survived was compared with the time/temperature exposure expected to occur in the N-Reactor plume during dual-purpose mode of operation. The initial temperature that test fish were exposed to was 33°C, which is greater than the lethal temperature reported for the test species (Brett, 1952; Kerr, 1953; Coutant, 1972). However, this temperature is not lethal when the heated water is dissipated by water at ambient temperature. The laboratory simulations demonstrate that the temperature dissipation downstream of the outfall reduces the temperature to sublethal levels. The rate of dissipation is dependent on river discharge; as river discharge increases, exposure duration decreases.

Chinook salmon, steelhead trout, and northern squawfish were subjected to predators after exposure to sublethal thermal conditions. Survivors of thermal exposures were eaten at the same rate as controls.

Chinook salmon were exposed to *F. columnaris* and *Y. ruckeri* (separate tests). Steelhead trout, coho salmon, and northern squawfish were exposed to *Y. ruckeri*. Rates of infection and numbers of deaths in thermally treated groups did not differ from those of controls.

ASSESSMENT OF POTENTIAL IMPACTS

Thermal exposures at which fish died were three to eight times greater than those expected in the plume. We compared thermal data generated from laboratory simulations and thermal exposures expected in the plume. We can predict that no direct mortalities will result from fish passage through the plume. Also, thermally exposed fish did not experience greater mortality from predation or disease than did controls. These studies demonstrate that characterization of hydrological conditions and thermal tolerance can adequately assess potential impacts of a thermal discharge to fish.

ACKNOWLEDGMENT

This work was supported by the U.S. Department of Energy under Contract DE-AC06-76RLO 1830.

REFERENCES

Brett, J. R. 1952. Temperature tolerance in young Pacific salmon, *genus Oncorhynchus. J. Fish. Res. Bd. Can.* 9:265-323.

Coutant, C. C. 1972. Biological aspects of thermal pollution II. Scientific basis for water temperature standards at power plants. *CRC Crit. Rev. Environ. Control* 3:1-24.

Coutant, C. C. 1973. Effect of thermal shock on vulnerability of juvenile salmonids to predation. *J. Fish. Res. Bd. Can. 30*:965-973.

Ecker, R. M., R. G. Parkhurst, F. L. Thompson, and G. Whelan. 1983a. N Reactor Thermal Plume Characterization During Pu-Only Mode of Operation, UNI-2618. Prepared by Pacific Northwest Laboratory for UNC Nuclear Industries, Inc., Richland, WA.

Ecker, R. M., W. H. Walters, and F. L. Thompson. 1983b. N Reactor Thermal Plume Characterization During Dual-Purpose Mode of Operation, UNI-2620. Prepared by Pacific Northwest Laboratory for UNC Nuclear Industries, Inc., Richland, WA.

Kerr, J. E. 1953. Studies on Fish Preservation at the Contra Costa Steam Plant of the PGE Company, Fish Bulletin No. 92. California Department of Fish and Game, Sacramento, CA.

Poston, T. M., T. L. Page, and R. W. Hanf, Jr. 1982. Effects of suspended volcanic ash on susceptibility to fish disease, pp. 64-81. In: Proceedings of the 14th Dredging Seminar, TAMU-SG-83-103. Texas A&M University, College Station, TX.

DEVELOPMENT AND ASSESSMENT OF CLOSURE TECHNOLOGY FOR LIQUID-WASTE DISPOSAL SITES

S. J. Phillips, J. F. Relyea, R. R. Seitz, and J. W. Cammann

Westinghouse Hanford Company, Richland, Washington

Key Words: *Site closure, geotechnical engineering, model assessment, waste isolation*

ABSTRACT

Discharge of low-level liquid wastes into soils was practiced previously at the Hanford Site. Technologies for long-term confinement of subsurface contaminants are needed. Additionally, methods are needed to assess the effectiveness of confinement technologies in remediating potentially diverse environmental conditions. Recently developed site remediation systems and assessment methods for *in situ* stabilization and isolation of radioactive and other contaminants within and below low-level liquid-waste disposal structures are summarized.

INTRODUCTION

Failure to treat low-level liquid-waste disposal structures may result in unacceptable radiological and industrial risks. These structures typically include large void-volume subsurface vaults, aggregate drainage layers, distribution systems, piping, auxiliary vessels, and diversion systems. If left untreated, they may structurally fail from decomposition, differential settlement, or catastrophic subsidence. Treatment may involve void fill and eliminating or reducing chemical mobility of contaminants within and below the structures. Untreated sites may release contaminants directly or indirectly to the environment through ground water, atmospheric, biological, and direct radiation pathways.

Development of stabilization and isolation technologies is augmented by assessment of baseline and post-treatment conditions for low-level waste-disposal structures. Performance is assessed by conceptual and numerical simulation modeling of hypothetical disposal structures relative to type and quantity of contaminants and related physico-chemical conditions.

TREATMENT SYSTEM AND ASSESSMENT

Geotechnical Waste Treatment System

Subsurface liquid-waste disposal structures may be treated *in situ*, with resulting long-term physical stabilization and chemical isolation of contaminants, using a dynamic consolidation and slurry injection system (Phillips and Relyea, 1987; Phillips and Hinschberger, 1989). The system (Figure 1) induces liquefaction, compacts waste, and injects disposal structures with single or hybrid slurry materials. The system transfers 1×10^5 W of energy at a frequency of 30 Hz from grade to depth and simultaneously injects grout at a maximum rate of 2.6 $\times 10^{-3}$ m$^3 \cdot$ s^{-1} and pressure of 2.2×10^6 Pa.

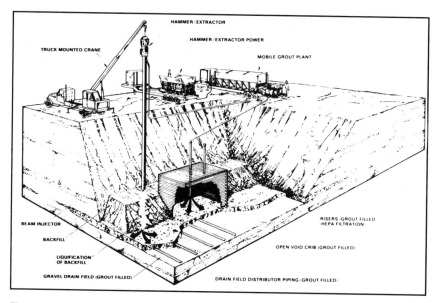

Figure 1. Dynamic consolidation and slurry injection system for liquid-waste disposal site.

Assessment Simulation Modeling

Effectiveness of dynamic consolidation and slurry injection is assessed, and treatment methods are evaluated, by numerical simulation modeling, using PORFLO-3 (Runchal and Sagar, 1989). The code simulates fluid flow and contaminant transport through variably saturated media and untreated and treated liquid-waste disposal structures. The code simulates a hypothetical crib represented in axisymmetric cylindrical coordinates. Simulation is conducted by: (1) setting the upper boundary fluid flux corresponding to an evenly distributed annual precipitation rate; (2) setting the lower boundary at a matrix potential of zero, corresponding to the water elevation in a saturated unconfined aquifer; and (3) eliminating lateral flux through vertical boundaries of the model domain. Two domains were considered: an untreated, open void with underlying contaminated geologic media, and a particulate, slurry-filled, open void with polymer-injected contaminated geologic media. Fluid retention, flux, and geochemical properties of the pretreatment domain were modified to simulate the treated domain.

RESULTS

Figure 2 shows results from computer simulations, in terms of a dimensionless cumulative flux of contaminant into the water table. Flux is nondimensionalized by dividing calculated flux by the maximum flux predicted for either treated or untreated systems. Figure 2A compares treated and untreated systems for a distribution coefficient of $K_d = 10$. Flux from the treated system is about three times less than that from the untreated system at 100 yr. Initially, the untreated system appears to perform better than the treated system. This is likely a short-term anomaly resulting from assumptions regarding moisture content of the injected polymer and slurry. Figure 2B shows the effect of changes in the K_d assumed for materials. A 10-fold increase in K_d results in a three orders-of-magnitude decrease in flux at 100 yr.

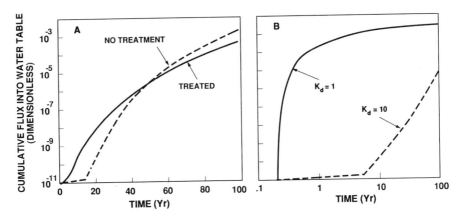

Figure 2. Sample results from computer simulations of liquid waste dynamic consolidation and slurry injection. A, treated versus untreated system; $K_d = 10$; B, effect of 10-fold increase in K_d.

REFERENCES

Phillips, S. J. and J. F. Relyea. 1987. Low-level liquid waste site disposal site remediation: Technology development at the Hanford Site, pp. 12-24. In: Proceedings of the Ninth Annual Low-Level Waste Management Conference, September 14-17, 1987, Denver, CO. CONF-8708, NTIS, Springfield, VA.

Phillips, S. J. and S. T. Hinschberger. Concurrent in situ treatment and disposal of low-level radioactive waste: Technology development. In: Proceedings of the International Radioactive Waste Management Conference, May 2-6, 1989, Brighton, England. Thomas Telford Ltd., London. (in press).

Runchal, A. K. and B. Sagar. 1989. PORFLO-3: A Mathematical Model for Fluid Flow, Heat, and Mass Transport in Variably Saturated Geologic Media, Report No. WHC-EP-0041. Westinghouse Hanford Company, Richland, WA.

TEMPORAL VARIATIONS IN ATMOSPHERIC DISPERSION AT HANFORD

J. V. Ramsdell and K. W. Burk

Pacific Northwest Laboratory, Richland, Washington

Key Words: *Atmospheric dispersion, annual variability, seasonal variability, diurnal variability*

ABSTRACT

Climatological data are frequently used to estimate atmospheric dispersion factors for historical periods and for future releases for which adequate meteorological data are unavailable. This practice routinely leads to questions concerning the representativeness of data used. The work described here was performed to provide a basis for answering these questions at the U.S. Department of Energy's Hanford Site in eastern Washington.

Atmospheric transport and diffusion near Hanford have been examined using a Lagrangian puff dispersion model and hourly meteorological data from the Hanford Meteorological Station and a network of 24 surface wind stations for a 5-yr period. Average normalized monthly concentrations were computed at 2.5-km intervals on a 31 by 31 grid from January 1983 through 1987, assuming an elevated release in the 200-East Area. Monthly average concentrations were used to determine 5-yr mean pattern and monthly mean patterns and the interannual variability about each pattern. Intra-annual and diurnal variations in dispersion factors are examined for six locations near Hanford.

INTRODUCTION

Atmospheric dispersion estimates in environmental impact statements and environmental monitoring studies are generally based on climatological summaries (joint frequency distributions) that mask systematic temporal variations in the dispersion process. Five years of hourly meteorological data were analyzed to characterize the year-to-year variability in atmospheric dispersion from the 200-E Area at Hanford and to show systematic seasonal and diurnal variations in dispersion. We present methods of displaying these temporal variations. Methods include mapping mean dispersion factors (X/Q') and their standard deviations, plotting dispersion factors as a function of calendar month, and plotting dispersion factors as a function of time of day and month.

DISPERSION FACTOR MAPS

Maps of mean dispersion factors primarily show effects of prevailing winds. Often, this is the only dispersion information given in environmental statements and monitoring reports. Year-to-year variability is generally neglected, even when the analysis is based on data for many years. Year-to-year variability, as well as average patterns, can be shown on maps if annual dispersion is estimated and interannual standard deviations of dispersion estimates are computed. At Hanford, the standard deviations of the annual dispersion estimates are about one-tenth order of magnitude from near the release point to more than 40 km to the southeast. They increase slowly toward the northeast and north, and reach about one-fifth order of magnitude at 30 km. To the west and southwest the increase is more rapid, with the standard deviation reaching one-half order of magnitude at 30 km.

Maps can also show seasonal changes and interannual variation in dispersion factors as a function of time of year. Monthly mean dispersion factor patterns at Hanford are similar to annual mean patterns, with larger dispersion factors in winter and smaller values in summer. The seasonal variation in dispersion factors is about one-half order of magnitude.

Although intake patterns of interannual variability of monthly average dispersion factors in winter resemble the pattern of variability of annual dispersion factors, magnitudes of the standard deviations in winter are larger (generally, greater than one-fifth order of magnitude). From southwest through north, standard deviations increase to more than one-half order of magnitude within 20 km. In contrast, there is no well-defined pattern of variation for monthly average dispersion factors in summer, when they are generally about one-quarter order of magnitude in all directions to a distance of 40 km.

INTRA-ANNUAL VARIATIONS AT SELECTED LOCATIONS

Monthly average dispersion factors were evaluated for six locations about 40 km from the release point. Three locations east and southeast of the release point have similar annual-average dispersion factors. However, the seasonal variation of dispersion factors at the easterly location (lowest in the winter and increasing to a summer maximum) is different from that at other locations (winter maxima and summer minima). The range between winter and summer values for these three locations is about half an order of magnitude.

Annual-average dispersion factors at the other three locations, which are northeast and southwest of Hanford, are one and two orders of magnitude less than they are to the east and southeast. The differences in dispersion factors are mainly caused by greater intermittency: In some months, plumes from 200-E Area do not reach these locations, thus intermittency also increases the range of seasonal variations in the dispersion factor and in the standard deviation of interannual variation of monthly averages at these locations.

Atmospheric dispersion is a function of time of day. The effects of time of day on dispersion factors at the locations described above are indicated by dispersion factors computed for a continuous release and for releases limited to graveyard, day, and swing shifts. To the east and southeast, dispersion factors were generally greater for releases during swing shift and least for day-shift releases. Differences between shifts were small in winter and generally exceeded an order of magnitude in summer. To the southwest and northeast, shift-to-shift differences in dispersion factors were smaller. In a few instances, dispersion factors for day-shift releases were larger than corresponding dispersion factors for releases on other shifts. In these areas, dispersion factors were affected more by specific weather patterns, when they occurred, than by diurnal variations in atmospheric conditions.

Analysis of atmospheric dispersion using hourly data shows temporal variations not seen in dispersion factors based on climatological data summaries. Significance of the variability must be determined in the context of specific applications.

ACKNOWLEDGMENT

The work reported here was funded as a part of the Hanford Environmental Dose Reconstruction Project.

EFFECTIVE SAMPLE LABELING

J. T. Rieger and R. W. Bryce

Pacific Northwest Laboratory, Richland, Washington

Key Words: *Ground-water sampling, sample document, sample labeling*

ABSTRACT

Ground-water samples collected for hazardous-waste and radiological monitoring have come under strict regulatory and quality assurance requirements as a result of laws such as the Resource Conservation and Recovery Act. To comply with these laws, the labeling system used to identify environmental samples had to be upgraded to ensure proper handling and to protect collection personnel from exposure to sample contaminants and sample preservatives. The sample label now used at the Pacific Northwest Laboratory is a complete sample document. In the event other paperwork on a labeled sample were lost, the necessary information could be found on the label.

BACKGROUND

Ground-water samples collected by Pacific Northwest Laboratory for hazardous-waste and radiological monitoring have come under strict regulatory and quality assurance requirements as a result of laws such as the Resource Conservation and Recovery Act. Before these laws were in effect, sample collection consisted mainly of filling a single plastic bottle that was then submitted for limited analysis; this was a relatively simple system. To comply with new laws, the labeling system had to be upgraded to ensure proper handling and to protect sampling personnel from exposure to ground-water contaminants and sample preservatives.

METHODS

Labels are printed monthly, using a computer data base that contains the following information: sample identification, date and time of collection, pump and bottle type, sample size, and special handling requirements. There is also space on the label for the sample collector to sign and date the sample. Special handling requirements are indicated by codes and/or colored dots that can be easily recognized by field personnel.

327

A typical sample label is shown in Figure 1. Items identified on the label (e.g., size and type of bottle, type of preservative) aid in sample preparation. Identification of sample location, pump type, filtering requirements, and analysis laboratory aid field personnel in proper sample collection and delivery. Analysis codes and handling requirements also provide important

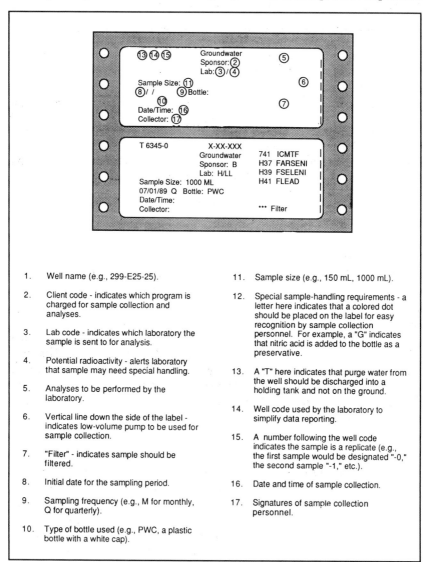

1. Well name (e.g., 299-E25-25).

2. Client code - indicates which program is charged for sample collection and analyses.

3. Lab code - indicates which laboratory the sample is sent to for analysis.

4. Potential radioactivity - alerts laboratory that sample may need special handling.

5. Analyses to be performed by the laboratory.

6. Vertical line down the side of the label - indicates low-volume pump to be used for sample collection.

7. "Filter" - indicates sample should be filtered.

8. Initial date for the sampling period.

9. Sampling frequency (e.g., M for monthly, Q for quarterly).

10. Type of bottle used (e.g., PWC, a plastic bottle with a white cap).

11. Sample size (e.g., 150 mL, 1000 mL).

12. Special sample-handling requirements - a letter here indicates that a colored dot should be placed on the label for easy recognition by sample collection personnel. For example, a "G" indicates that nitric acid is added to the bottle as a preservative.

13. A "T" here indicates that purge water from the well should be discharged into a holding tank and not on the ground.

14. Well code used by the laboratory to simplify data reporting.

15. A number following the well code indicates the sample is a replicate (e.g., the first sample would be designated "-0," the second sample "-1," etc.).

16. Date and time of sample collection.

17. Signatures of sample collection personnel.

Figure 1. Typical ground-water sample label.

information to laboratory personnel. Collection date, time, and signature of sample collector are vital for sample identification and quality assurance. The sample label is a complete sample document. In the event other paperwork on a labeled sample were lost, the necessary information could be found on the label.

FUTURE PLANS

Improvements are being made to the sample control system to produce chain-of-custody and field record forms from the same data base used to produce the labels. This will reduce the time required to prepare forms and minimize errors created when the forms are filled out by hand. Other enhancements being considered include adding bar codes to labels to enable close tracking of samples during collection and analysis and to speed sample processing.

ACKNOWLEDGMENT

Work supported by the U.S. Department of Energy under Contract DE-AC06-76RLO 1830.

DOSE ASSESSMENT AND ENVIRONMENTAL MONITORING TO DEMONSTRATE COMPLIANCE WITH THE U.S. ENVIRONMENTAL PROTECTION AGENCY'S ENVIRONMENTAL RADIATION STANDARDS FOR NUCLEAR FUEL CYCLE FACILITIES

E. Y. Shum and D. M. Sollenberger

U.S. Nuclear Regulatory Commission, Washington, DC

Key Words: *Dose assessment, nuclear facilities*

ABSTRACT

The U.S. Environmental Protection Agency issued regulations in 1977 setting forth environmental radiation protection standards for uranium fuel cycle facilities. The regulations require that radioactivity in planned effluent releases from uranium fuel cycle facilities (radon and its daughters excepted) be limited so that no member of the public receives an annual dose equivalent of more than 25 mrem to the whole body, 75 mrem to the thyroid, or 25 mrem to any other organ. The Nuclear Regulatory Commission (NRC) is responsible for assuring that licensees' uranium fuel cycle facilities meet these requirements.

Since issuing environmental radiation protection standards, NRC developed a method for radiological assessment to demonstrate compliance with standards covering uranium mills, UF_6 conversion, and fuel fabrication facilities. Generally, this includes models for atmospheric transport, pathway analysis, and dose assessment. For certain unique facilities, the models may not be adequate to demonstrate compliance without using a supplemental environmental monitoring program, i.e., actual measurement of radionuclide concentration, particle size distribution, and solubility of particulates in air. We will discuss the dose assessment models; their inadequacies to demonstrate compliance for certain unique facilities; and the ways environmental monitoring can be used to provide reasonable assurance that standards are met. Design criteria for a cost-effective monitoring program will be discussed.

INTRODUCTION

On January 13, 1977, the U.S. Environmental Protection Agency (EPA) issued regulations (EPA, 1977) on environmental radiation standards for uranium fuel cycle facilities. The regulations specify that radioactivity in planned effluent releases (radon and its daughters excepted) from the uranium fuel cycle be limited so that no member of the public receives an annual dose equivalent of more than 25 mrem to the whole body, 75 mrem to the thyroid, or 25 mrem to any other organs. The Nuclear Regulatory Commission (NRC) is responsible for assuring that uranium fuel cycle facilities licensed by the Commission meet these requirements. The following describes NRC's experience in enforcing the standards covering uranium milling, UF_6 conversion, and fuel fabrication facilities.

DEMONSTRATING COMPLIANCE WITH ENVIRONMENTAL RADIATION STANDARDS

To demonstrate compliance with EPA's standards, NRC conducted a radiological assessment on each facility, using effluent release data as source terms. The radiological assessment included pathway analysis, consisting of (1) pathway identification, (2) pathway modeling, and (3) dose calculation. Annual maximum doses to the nearest resident were calculated using (1) measured effluent (air and liquid) released rates; (2) Regulatory Guide 1.111 for atmospheric dispersion calculation (NRC, 1977); (3) Regulatory Guide 1.109 for modeling pathways and dose calculation (NRC, 1976), except that for the inhalation pathway, dose conversion factors were generated using International Commission on Radiological Protection (ICRP) Publication-30 methods (ICRP, 1979); (4) Regulatory Guide 3.51 for estimating radiation doses to man from airborne radioactive material resulting from uranium milling operation (NRC, 1982a); and (5) NUREG-0859 for environmental radiation protection standards for uranium recovery facilities (NRC, 1982b). The NRC's assessment showed that air was the critical pathway for radiation dose to man.

For certain facilities, these models may not be adequate to demonstrate compliance without a supplemental environmental monitoring program. Requirements for specific monitoring include (1) continuous air sampling at receptor locations and analysis of composite air samples for radionuclides; (2) measurement of uranium solubility in air particulates collected near receptors; and (3) measurement of air particle size distribution. Details on environmental monitoring for uranium mills are given in Regulatory Guide 4.14 (NRC, 1980).

CONCLUSION

In enforcing EPA's environmental radiation standards for uranium fuel cycle facilities, NRC learned that generic models may not adequately demonstrate compliance in some facilities. Rather sophisticated measurements and analyses must sometimes be made to accurately estimate dose. At present, all facilities are generally in compliance with the standards.

REFERENCES

EPA. 1977. Environmental Radiation Protection Standards for Uranium Fuel Cycle Facilities, CFR Title 40, Part 190. U.S. Environmental Protection Agency, Washington, DC.

ICRP. 1979. Limits for Intakes of Radionuclides by Workers, Publication 30. International Commission on Radiological Protection. Pergamon Press, New York.

NRC. 1976. Calculation of Annual Doses to Man from Routine Releases of Reactor Effluents for the Purpose of Evaluating Compliance with 10 CFR Part 50, Appendix I, Regulatory Guide 1.109. U.S. Nuclear Regulatory Commission, Washington, DC.

NRC. 1977. Methods for Estimating Atmospheric Transport and Dispersion of Gaseous Effluents in Routine Releases from Light-Water-Cooled Reactors, Regulatory Guide 1.111. U.S. Nuclear Regulatory Commission, Washington, DC.

NRC. 1980. Radiological/Effluent and Environmental Monitoring at Uranium Mills, Regulatory Guide 4.14. U.S. Nuclear Regulatory Commission, Washington, DC.

NRC. 1982a. Calculational Models for Estimating Radiation Doses to Man from Airborne Radioactive Material Resulting from Uranium Milling Operation, Regulatory Guide 3.51. U.S. Nuclear Regulatory Commission, Washington, DC.

NRC. 1982b. Compliance Determination Procedures for Environmental Radiation Protection Standards for Uranium Recovery Facilities, NUREG-0859 40 CFR Part 190. U.S. Nuclear Regulatory Commission, Washington, DC.

CHEMICAL EXPOSURE EVALUATION IN THE MULTIMEDIA ENVIRONMENTAL POLLUTANT ASSESSMENT SYSTEM (MEPAS)

D. L. Strenge and J. W. Buck

Pacific Northwest Laboratory, Richland, Washington

Key Words: *Health impacts, MEPAS, population exposure, individual exposure*

ABSTRACT

The Multimedia Environmental Pollutant Assessment System (MEPAS) has been used by the U.S. Department of Energy (DOE) to evaluate the relative importance of remedial actions at several DOE facilities. We reviewed the MEPAS analyses to assess the value of the health-impact indicators available in MEPAS for chemical exposures. Health-impact indicators were compared for population and individual exposures and for the primary transport and exposure pathways involved. Transport pathways include ground water, surface water, and the atmosphere. Potential exposure pathways to offsite individuals include inhalation of atmospheric pollutants; ingestion of water, farm products, and aquatic foods; and inadvertent ingestion resulting from dermal contact with pollutants. Individual and population health-impact indicators in MEPAS provide valuable information when evaluating the need for remedial actions of chemical waste sites.

INTRODUCTION

The Multimedia Environmental Pollutant Assessment System (MEPAS) was developed at the Pacific Northwest Laboratory (PNL) to prioritize environmental problems based on potential public-health impacts. MEPAS methods and formulations, including description of transport and exposure pathways, are described in Whelan et al. (1986, 1987).

In its 1988 Environmental Survey, the U.S. Department of Energy's (DOE) Office of Environment, Safety, and Health used the MEPAS program to evaluate the relative importance of potential environmental problems at 16 defense production facilities containing hazardous materials across the United States (DOE, 1988). The survey analyses included several hundred "cases" associated with the facilities; each case represented one potential environmental problem, one transport mode (ground water, surface water, or atmosphere), and one pollutant. MEPAS ranked the cases to prioritize the facilities for remediation.

ANALYSIS

Researchers at PNL evaluated the two ranking methods used by MEPAS: the Hazard Potential Index (HPI) and the Maximum Individual Exposure Index (MII). Although the two methods are used to rank the same cases, they treat populations and exposure pathways differently. The HPI estimates total exposure of all populations from all pathways; the MII ranking is based on highest individual exposure from each pathway. This distinction is important because most exposure regulations are based on potential exposure to individuals, while total risk assessments usually estimate total health effects in populations. To evaluate the two methods, all cases were ranked twice (once for each method) and compared.

RESULTS AND CONCLUSIONS

Both ranking methods generated similar results (Figure 1); that is, cases with the greatest potential health impacts are indicated as the lowest numbers on the figure. The Pearson correlation coefficient for the two methods is 0.9147. Thus both methods can be expected to give similar rankings when applied to a large number of sites with a variety of characteristics. Specific exceptions may occur when significantly large or small populations are involved.

ACKNOWLEDGMENT

Work supported by the U.S. Department of Energy Office of Environmental Audit.

REFERENCES

DOE. 1988. Environmental Survey Preliminary Summary Report of the Defense Production Facilities, DOE/EH-0072. U.S. Department of Energy, Environment, Safety, and Health, Office of Environmental Audit, Washington, DC.

Whelan, G., B. L. Steelman, D. L. Strenge, and J. G. Droppo. 1986. Overview of the Remedial Action Priority System (RAPS), pp. 191-227. In: Pollutants in a Multimedia Environment, Y. Cohen (ed). Plenum Press, New York.

Whelan, G., D. L. Strenge, J. G. Droppo Jr., B. L. Steelman, and J. W. Buck. 1987. The Remedial Action Priority System (RAPS): Mathematical Formulations, DOE/RL/87-09, PNL-6200. Pacific Northwest Laboratory, Richland, WA.

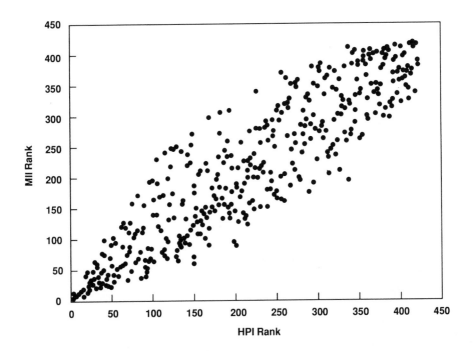

Figure 1. Comparison of MEPAS-generated rankings for facilities containing hazardous materials. Ranking methods were based on population (Hazard Potential Index, HPI) and individual (Maximum Individual Exposure Index, MII) exposures. The lower the number, the greater the potential for impacting public health.

AUTHOR INDEX